Michael Payne

The Most Respectable Place in the Territory

Everyday Life
in Hudson's Bay Company Service
York Factory, 1788 to 1870

Studies in Archaeology
Architecture and History

National Historic Parks and Sites
Canadian Parks Service
Environment Canada

Available in Canada through authorized bookstore agents and other bookstores, or by mail from the Canadian Government Publishing Centre, Supply and Services Canada, Hull, Quebec, Canada K1A 0S9

Published under the authority
of the Minister of the Environment,
Ottawa, 1989.

Editing and design: Jean Brathwaite

Parks publishes the results of its research in archaeology, architecture, and history. A list of publications is available from Research Publications, Canadian Parks Service, Environment Canada, 1600 Liverpool Court, Ottawa, Ontario K1A 0H3.

Canadian Cataloguing in Publication Data

Payne, Michael, 1951–

Everyday life in Hudson's Bay Company service at York Factory, 1788 to 1870

(Studies in archaeology, architecture, and history, ISSN 0821–1027)
Issued also in French under title: La vie quotidienne au service de la Baie d'Hudson à York Factory.
Includes bibliographical references.
ISBN 0–660–12940–X
DSS cat. no. R61–2/9–43E

1. York Factory (Man.) — History.
2. Fur trade — Social aspects — Manitoba — York Factory.
3. Hudson's Bay Company — History.
4. Fur traders — Northwest, Canadian — History.
5. Frontier and pioneer life — Northwest, Canadian.
6. Fur Trade — Northwest, Canadian — History.
7. York Factory (Man.) — Social conditions.
I.   Canada. National Historic Parks and Sites.
II. Title. III. Series.

FC3207.P39 1988   C88–097030–8   971.27'01
F1060.P39 1988

Cover: York Factory in the 1850s.
Provincial Archives of Manitoba, Rupert's Land Collection, No. 13, detail.

Contents

Acknowledgments

Many individuals and institutions aided in the research and writing of this study. Special thanks are owed to the governor and committee of the Hudson's Bay Company for permission to consult and quote material from the Hudson's Bay Company Archives. The staffs of the National Archives of Canada, National Library of Canada, Provincial Archives of Manitoba, Provincial Library of Manitoba, Hudson's Bay House, and Hudson's Bay Company Archives have been unfailingly helpful and a pleasure to work with over the years. Professors Jennifer Brown and S.R. Mealing kindly consented to read this study in manuscript form and offered valuable suggestions for its improvement. Friends and colleagues who commented on an earlier version of the work, and Jean Brathwaite who edited it, all contributed to the final product. As did Deborah and Christopher in their own ways.

Despite the best efforts of editors, readers, archivists, and librarians, no study is ever perfect and this is no exception. Errors of fact or interpretation are the author's alone.

Introduction

Throughout most of the 18th and 19th centuries the North-West, a huge expanse of land stretching from what is now northwestern Ontario to the Rocky Mountains and from the 49th parallel to the Barren Grounds of the present Northwest Territories, was fur trade country. As one author has noted, "every phase of life" in this region was "dominated by the fur trade." It was "the only enterprise in the country and all of the activities of every white man, as well as most of the Indians, [were] directly or indirectly concerned with it."[1] Fur trade companies built hundreds of posts throughout the region, but none were so important for so long as York Factory.

When the Hudson's Bay Company finally closed York Factory in June 1957 it marked the end of 275 years of trading in the area. In recognition of this enormous contribution to the history of Canada the factory was declared a national historic site in 1960. In 1968 the Hudson's Bay Company transferred ownership of its property at York to the federal government. Unfortunately this magnificent historic site is too isolated to be accessible to all but a handful of visitors, and this study is intended to bring a part of its history to those who will never be able to see York Factory for themselves.

The Canadian Parks Service, as part of its responsibilities for the site, has either commissioned or produced itself many historical, anthropological, and archaeological studies of the site and its former inhabitants. Many subjects not touched upon in the following paper have appeared in other Parks publications or in the many scholarly and popular histories of the fur trade. A short list of suggestions for further reading following this study

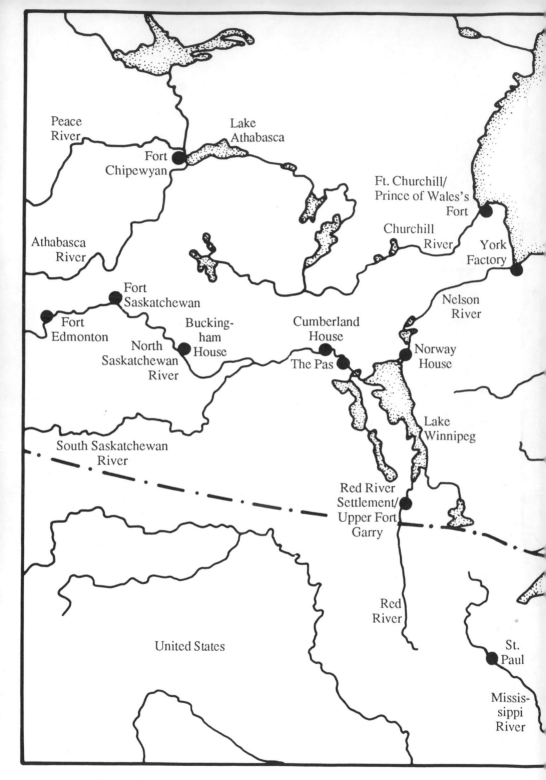

1 Major posts and settlements in the North-West, 1788-1870.
Map by D. Elrick and D. Kappler.

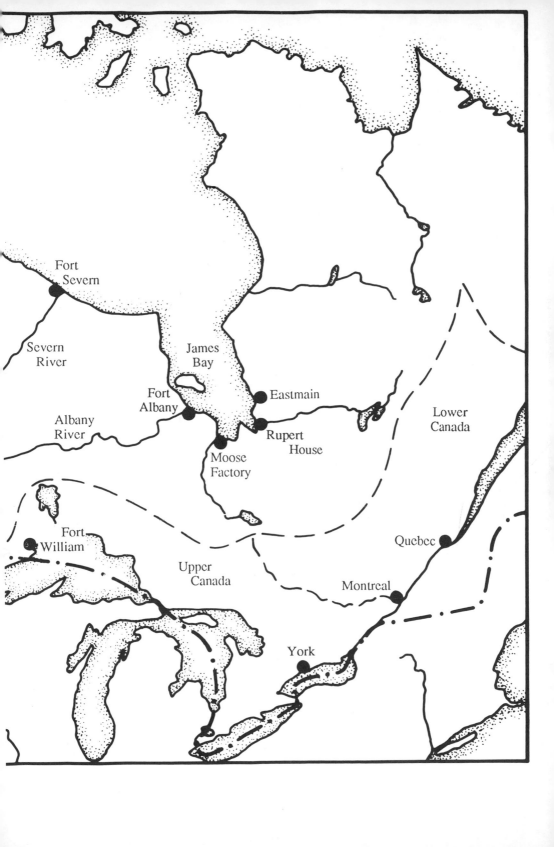

Fort
Severn

Severn
River

James
Bay

Fort
Albany

Eastmain

Albany
River

Rupert
House

Moose
Factory

Lower
Canada

Fort
William

Upper
Canada

Quebec

Montreal

York

outlines sources of information on matters either not discussed or described only briefly in these pages.

York Factory is one of the best-documented communities in Canadian history. The Hudson's Bay Company demanded that its officers stationed overseas report in detail on the operations of its posts, and the collection of post journals, correspondence, account books, servants' ledgers, inventories, and other materials in the Hudson's Bay Company Archives provides researchers with an embarrassment of riches. It is possible to reconstruct many features of life in the post with great accuracy, but unfortunately not all subjects or residents of the community were documented equally well. Historical records, however voluminous, are never perfect and York Factory's records are no exception.

The company was primarily interested in the activities of its employees, and the officers who kept these records were more inclined to describe their own activities and thoughts than those of other residents. As a result, what is known about company men varies in many respects in inverse proportion to their numbers. Much more is known about officers in charge of York Factory than about junior officers, who in turn are discussed in post records more frequently than the tradesmen and labourers who made up the bulk of company employees at York. Fur trade history is often accused of having an elitist bias, but unfortunately so do the records. Recognizing this fact, I have attempted in this study to ensure that the lives of company servants are not ignored, but on some subjects post records are simply mute.

Although the wives and children of company employees formed an important part of the York Factory community, available records do not discuss their activities in much detail. Fortunately, two studies detail the role of women in the fur trade and the significance of family structures and kinship ties: Sylvia Van Kirk, *"Many Tender Ties": Women in Fur-Trade Society in Western Canada, 1670-1870*, and Jennifer Brown, *Strangers in Blood: Fur Trade Company Families in Indian Country*. Both include information on the wives and children of the men posted to York Factory though they do not focus specifically on that community. The native population of York Factory and vicinity is difficult to document, and a full treatment of the Homeguard Cree at York Factory, their relations with the company, and their roles in the York Factory community has not as yet been attempted.

This study, which originated as a research report for Parks as part of the interpretative program for the site, is concerned primarily with a description of some of the main features of life at York Factory during the time it held a central position in the Hudson's Bay Company's fur trade operations. The study concentrates on the period between 1788, when the present factory was first occupied, and 1870, when York's central position in the fur trade was clearly in decline. The chapters that follow on social structure and social relations; work; recreation and leisure; accidents, disease, and medical care; education and religion; and the standard of living represent subjects York residents themselves often raised in post journals, correspondence, and personal papers and reminiscences. They were matters of deep and persistent concern to company employees at York Factory and thus seem central to any attempt to understand and describe the everyday life of their community.

(The research report that this book is based upon appeared as "A Social History of York Factory, 1788-1870," in the Canadian Parks Service's Microfiche Report Series, No. 110 [Ottawa, 1984]. It includes information that for reasons of brevity does not appear in this book. A number of appendices including a study of smallpox and burial practices at York and detailed personnel records are available for other researchers in the microfiche report.)

The quotations used in this study are reproduced in as close a manner as possible to the originals. Phonetic and idiosyncratic spelling and unusual punctuation may on occasion create problems of comprehension for modern readers; however, most may be read with no great difficulty if one remembers that spelling was often phonetic and the comma, dash, and period were frequently used interchangeably. An attempt has been made to keep editorial interjections in quotations to a minimum on the grounds that the history of a community ought to be recounted as much as possible in the words of its residents.

A Short History of York Factory to 1870

York Factory is located on a low, swampy peninsula of land lying between the mouths of the Hayes and Nelson rivers on the western shore of Hudson Bay. The area is part of the Hudson Bay Lowland region of Canada, a vast saucer-shaped basin of land that surrounds much of Hudson and James bays. The climate is cold and wet, and the area is marked by marshes, ponds, and very little dry ground. Little is known about the original native inhabitants of the region, and some scholars speculate that they only visited it seasonally to hunt migrating waterfowl and mammals prior to the establishment of fur trade posts on the shores of Hudson Bay in the late 17th century.[1] Early European explorers of Hudson and James bays found evidence of the presence of native people in the region, but only Henry Hudson's expedition of 1611 actually encountered Indians, probably Cree, on the James Bay coast.[2]

These explorers did not find what they were looking for in Hudson Bay — a northern sea passage to Asia — but they had inadvertently stumbled on another potential source of trade. The drainage basins of Hudson and James bays included some of the richest fur lands in North America and an indigenous population skilled in hunting and eager to exchange furs for European goods. The French fur traders Groseilliers and Radisson first recognized the enormous trade potential of the area that could be tapped by building a series of posts at the mouths of the major rivers that flowed through the Hudson Bay Lowland region. The great economic advantage of coastal trading posts was that they could be supplied by ships without incurring the heavy expense of transporting goods and furs along inland waterways.

Radisson and Groseilliers, after failing to interest French and American colonial investors in their scheme, turned to English investors, who took up the idea. A trading expedition was mounted and in 1668 the first fur trade post was built on James Bay near the mouth of the Rupert River. From this small and tentative beginning the Hudson's Bay Company was founded in 1670 after returns from the Rupert River venture indicated Radisson and Groseilliers' plan held great potential.

Initially the Hudson's Bay Company concentrated on establishing posts in the James Bay area, but in 1682 it turned its attention to trade prospects on western Hudson Bay. Nor was it alone in its interest. That year three groups of traders from France, New England, and England all established posts in the area of the Hayes and Nelson rivers. The French venture was led by Radisson, who had switched his allegiance to the Compagnie du Nord, the French counterpart of the Hudson's Bay Company. Radisson, with more guile than attention to legal niceties, captured the posts of his rivals in 1683. His New England rivals abandoned the game, but the Hudson's Bay Company proved to be a more dogged and effective competitor. The company rebuilt its post on the Nelson River and through a combination of diplomatic and legal pressure on Radisson and the Compagnie du Nord, secured indemnification for their losses. Radisson switched his allegiance again and returned in 1684 to the Nelson River area as an employee of the Hudson's Bay Company.

To strengthen its claim to the region the company moved its main post in the area to a site on the north bank of the Hayes River, naming the post York Fort after the duke of York, then governor of the company and soon to be King James II.[3] The French temporarily abandoned their efforts to maintain a post on the Hayes in 1685, but not before they had inadvertently helped to establish a trade in the area that was largely to profit their English rivals. In 1682 Radisson and in 1683 Radisson's nephew, Jean-Baptiste Chouart, had travelled inland some distance along the Hayes River to inform the Cree of that area of the French presence on the bay. The speed with which this news spread among the tribes of the interior was remarkable.

By 1684, groups of Indians, both Cree and Assiniboine, were making the long trip down to the bay.[4] Some travelled as long as 15 to 20 days to reach York Fort — a considerable investment of time and energy considering that the return journey against the current of the Hayes would have taken much longer. One can only marvel at how quickly these Indians integrated a lengthy trading voyage into the seasonal pattern of their lives.

Between 1685 and 1714 York Fort changed hands several times. Captured by the French in 1694, it was retaken by the Hudson's Bay Company in 1696. In 1697 the brilliant French commander Pierre Le Moyne d'Iberville in his ship the *Pelican* sank the much larger and more heavily armed HMS *Hampshire* off the mouth of the Nelson River, and York changed hands again. The French renamed it Fort Bourbon and remained there until 1714.[5]

York was returned to the Hudson's Bay Company in one of the terms of the Treaty of Utrecht in 1713, and on 5 September 1714 James Knight, the new governor of the post, retook possession from the French. York Factory quickly became the single most important trading post in the Hudson's Bay Company's territories. The first year trade at York amounted to only about 4000 made beaver, the unit of measure employed by the company. (The value of all goods and furs traded by the company was expressed in terms of made beaver — the value of a single prime beaver skin in good condition). As early as the 1720s the trade at York was larger than at any other post, and by the 1730s trade was two to three times greater than that of York's closest competitors in the company's service, Fort Albany and Prince of Wales's Fort. Trade returns at York, however, peaked around 1730 at about 40 000 made beaver a year and then began to decline slowly.[6]

The main reason for this decline was increased competition from inland posts established by Canadian traders operating out of Montreal. Still the Hudson's Bay Company remained content to leave the collection and transport of furs down to its bayside posts to Indian middlemen. Although it sent some individuals inland to winter with Indian bands in the 1750s and 1760s, the company made no attempt to set up inland posts, apparently on the assumption that the costs of such a policy would far outweigh any increase in trade volume.

Following the fall of New France and the transfer of Quebec to British possession in 1763, this view became more difficult to support. New merchants, many of them Scots and Americans, assumed control of a revived and expanded fur trade from Montreal. The company's new rivals were much more aggressive competitors, and fur returns at York suffered badly. In the late 1760s they averaged about 26 000 made beaver a year, but in 1775 this total had dropped to 10 000 made beaver — the lowest level of trade at York in over 50 years.[7] The old policy Joseph Robson, a former employee and a critic of the company, had characterized as a long sleep on the shores of a frozen sea had to be abandoned.[8]

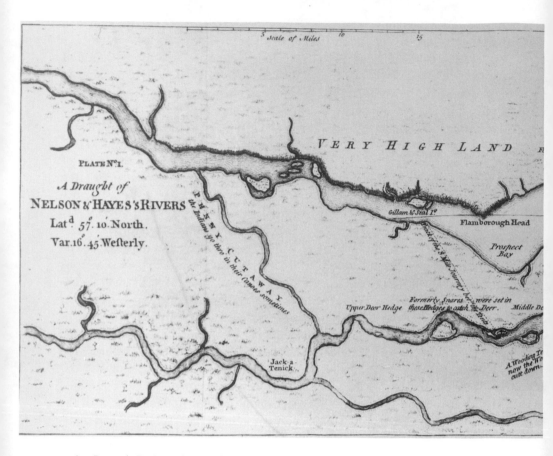

2 Joseph Robson's 1740s map shows the location of York Factory
40 years before the post was moved a short distance upriver.
Hudson's Bay Company Archives, Provincial Archives of Manitoba.

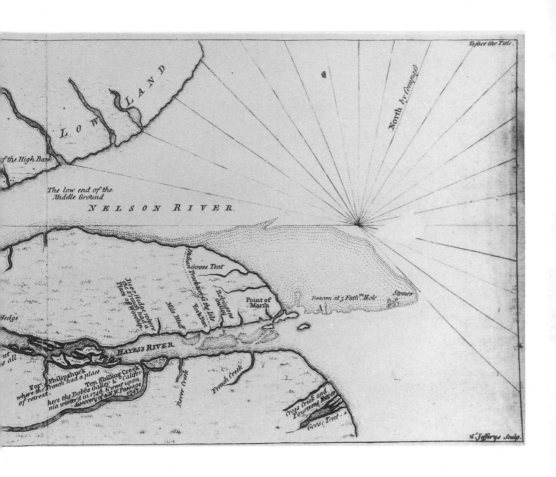

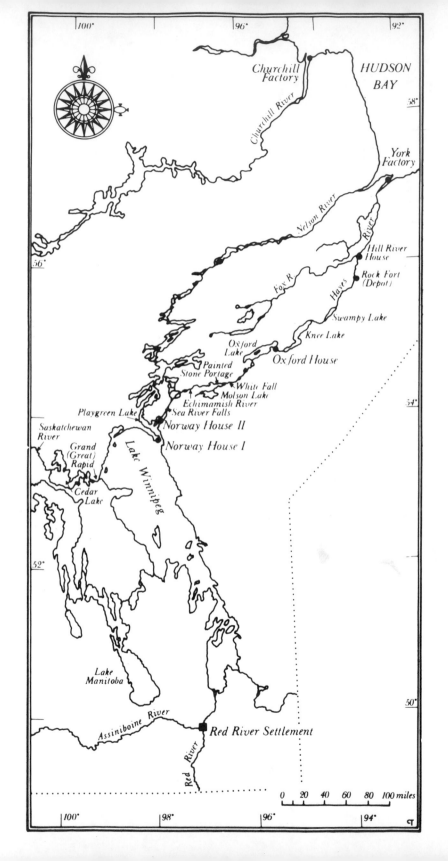

100° 96° 92°

Churchill
Factory

HUDSON
BAY

Churchill River

58°

Nelson River

York
Factory

56°

River

Hill River
House

Fox R.

Hayes

Rock Fort
(Depot)

Swampy Lake

Knee Lake

Oxford
Lake

Oxford House

54°

Painted
Stone Portage

White Fall
Molson Lake
Echimamish River

Playgreen Lake

Sea River Falls

Norway House II

Saskatchewan
River

Lake Winnipeg

Norway House I

Grand
(Great)
Rapid

Cedar
Lake

52°

Lake
Manitoba

50°

Assiniboine River

Red River

Red River Settlement

0   20   40   60   80   100 miles

100° 98° 96° 94°

CT

In 1774 the company built its first inland post in the North-West, Cumberland House, on Pine Island Lake near the North Saskatchewan River. Thereafter the company attempted to match its rivals post for post throughout the interior. The establishment of inland posts forced major adjustments on the Hudson's Bay Company, and the status of the old bayside posts changed considerably.[9] As trading posts they lost most of their former significance. By the late 1780s the fur trade at York Factory was almost entirely local. The flotillas of canoes bringing Saulteaux, Assiniboine, and Woods and Swampy Cree down from the interior to trade were no more, and only a small trade with a few bands of Homeguard Indians — as the Cree living in the vicinity of York were called — remained.

At most bayside posts diminished trade meant declining importance, but York Factory's strategic location meant it soon acquired new and very important functions. As early as 1682 Radisson had realized that the Hayes and not the Nelson River was the key to the fur trade in the North-West. While the Nelson River was a much larger river and drained much more territory, its current and the volume of water it carried made it both dangerous and daunting as a canoe route. The Indians of the interior much preferred to use the Hayes River as a way down to the bay, and the company soon found it was the best route inland as well. After some trial and error it learned that most inland posts could best be supplied from York Factory using a route that travelled up the Hayes River to the Fox River. After that several routes inland were possible, but the main route travelled through Swampy, Knee, and Oxford lakes to the Echimamish River, which in turn flowed into the headwaters of the Nelson River flowing out of Lake Winnipeg. This route became known as the York Factory "main line," and it would serve as the main trunk route for the Hudson's Bay Company until the late 1850s.

The new conditions in the fur trade in the late 18th century required considerable adjustments at York Factory that were complicated by two disasters. In 1782 a French naval expedition under the command of the comte de Lapérouse attacked and destroyed both Prince of Wales's Fort and

3 The York "mainline" — the route from York Factory to the interior.
Map by Caroline Trottier, by permission of *The Beaver* magazine.

York Factory in one of the lesser-known actions of the American War of Independence. Both posts were rebuilt in 1783, but in 1788 York was badly damaged by flooding and the company decided to rebuild York on a new, higher site about 7.5 kilometres from Hudson Bay, only a short distance upstream from the old site on the north bank of the Hayes.

The changed functions of York Factory were clearly represented in the buildings constructed at the new site. York was increasingly a warehouse and transhipment post with considerable administrative responsibilities. It also became the main centre in the North-West for the manufacture of locally produced trade goods and supplies like barrels, iron and tinware, and even the boats that were introduced in the 1790s to replace canoes on inland waterways. The main building at York was a large two-storey bastioned structure, part warehouse and part dwelling. Because of the shape of its interior courtyard, this building was known as the "Old Octagon." Around the Old Octagon a series of smaller outbuildings were arranged roughly in a square. These buildings included workshops, storerooms, supply sheds, dwellings, cook and mess rooms, a powder magazine, and a distillery. In addition, gardens and a small pasture formed part of the factory complex. Aside from a stockade that surrounded most of these buildings, York Factory looked less like the usual picture of a fur trade post than like the small village settlement it had in effect become.[10]

The period between 1790 and 1821 was nonetheless a troubled time in the fur trade and at York Factory. Competition was fierce and all too often violent. Alcohol was increasingly used and abused as a trade good. Production at York's distillery mirrors the growing importance of alcohol in the trade. When the factory was first built by Joseph Colen, the officer in charge of York between 1786 and 1798, an average year saw 1300 to 1600 gallons of high-proof spirits distilled there. By 1815 this total had grown to 3300 gallons of distilled rum, and by 1821 over 6000 gallons of high-proof spirits were distilled at York Factory alone.[11]

At York labour unrest was common, particularly over the issue of substituting York boats for canoes for shipping trade goods and furs. Scurvy was much more frequently reported than in the years before 1790 and after 1821 because the post population had increased without finding reliable new sources of fresh provisions. Conflict between the officers in charge of York and their nominal superiors in charge of inland posts often hindered the smooth operation of the factory. Finally, the growth of the company's system of inland posts and the establishment of the Red River Settlement by Lord Selkirk, a Scottish philanthropist, in 1812 strained the capacity of warehouse and storage facilities at York, not to mention the ability of company employees to transport goods and people inland.

The company responded to these problems in several ways including a significant overhaul of its administrative, salary, and provisioning systems embodied in the "retrenching scheme" of Andrew Wedderburn Colvile, Lord Selkirk's brother-in-law and a member of the Hudson's Bay Company's London committee. Colvile's reorganization of the company succeeded in ending six' years of no dividends for company investors in 1815, and from then until 1821, dividends of four per cent per annum were paid. The company was at least solvent and better able to compete with the North West Company.

The North West Company, on the other hand, faced serious problems. The company's wintering partners and their Montreal agents were at odds over finances and policy. The partnership agreement that governed the company was due to expire in 1821. The crux of the Nor'Westers' problem, however, was the high costs and considerable difficulties caused by their transport route from their posts in the North-West to Montreal. The economic advantages of the Hudson's Bay Company's shorter and cheaper route to its posts through Hudson Bay and York Factory could not be overcome despite the energy and entrepreneurial skills of the Nor'Westers.

Rather than renewing its partnership agreement in 1821, the North West Company merged its operations with those of the Hudson's Bay Company after some judicious prompting from the British Colonial Office. The new firm was really a coalition of interests, but it continued to operate under the name and charter of the Hudson's Bay Company. The North West Company's depot and transhipment centre, Fort William, saw most of its functions transferred to York Factory, which became in effect the capital of the fur trade in western Canada.

The result was a new burst of construction at York culminating in the building of the "Depot" warehouse between 1830 and 1838 to replace the Old Octagon.[12] The depot building, which still stands at the site, was the largest single structure built by the Hudson's Bay Company in North America until the 20th century. It provided nearly 18 000 square feet, or 1675 square metres, of warehouse space, yet even so, other warehouse and storage buildings had to be built at York to handle the volume of goods and furs that passed through the post.

With the replacement of the Old Octagon the last real vestiges of a fortified fur trade post disappeared. The new depot building was a square structure with sides about 100 feet, or 30 metres, long. The side facing the river was three storeys high and the three remaining sides were two storeys

4 York Factory in 1821. The main building is the "Old Octagon."
National Archives of Canada, C-1918.

high. There were no bastions or defensive stockades at the new factory. Instead, in front of the depot there was a large square, used as gardens, open on the river side and flanked by a fur warehouse, the summer mess, the depot itself, a dwelling for visiting officers, a saleshop, and the Red River Settlement warehouse. Outside this main square of the factory, subsidiary buildings were arranged around a network of wooden walkways much like the streets of a small village.

The main functions of the post after 1821 in addition to storage and transhipment were the manufacture of trade goods and supplies, and administration of the fur trade in the Hudson's Bay Company's Northern Department, which included most of the North-West. The officers stationed at York were responsible for much of the voluminous paperwork of the trade: personnel records, accounts, and correspondence. In addition the post had to be kept running and made as self-sufficient as possible, and much of the labour of company employees stationed there was taken up with provision-

5 Letitia Hargrave's "great swell": York Factory in the 1850s.
Provincial Archives of Manitoba, Rupert's Land Collection, No. 13.

ing, cutting firewood and lumber, constructing necessary buildings, and performing other such support activities for the factory.

The key to York's position in company operations, however, remained the fact that the Hayes River was the best route to the interior. The transport capacity of the York Factory main line had been strained even before 1821, and despite attempts to build a winter road, improve portages, and build subsidiary depots inland, this remained the case. York's centrality to the fur trade in western Canada depended in large measure on the absence of an alternative to shipping goods and furs through its warehouses. In the late 1850s an alternative was found. American railroads and steamboats offered connections as far west as St. Paul in the Minnesota Territory by the mid-1850s, and in 1858 a trial shipment of goods for Red River was sent out via St. Paul. In 1859 a steamboat was launched on the Red River, making it even easier and cheaper to ship goods to Fort Garry through American territory. By 1860 virtually the entire "outfit," or annual shipment of trade

goods and supplies, for posts in the Saskatchewan District was sent through St. Paul and Fort Garry.[13]

During the 1860s fewer and fewer goods were shipped through York Factory, and increasingly its administrative responsibilities and manufacturing activities were shifted to Red River. The number of employees stationed at York reflected this change. Its complement of 63 men in 1864-65 had been pared to 40 by 1869-70. York Factory remained an important post, but by 1870 its heyday had clearly passed. Indeed most historians feel the heyday of the fur trade in general had passed. By the 1870s the North-West was no longer primarily fur trade country, and agriculture, not furs, was to be its dominant enterprise.

It is sometimes forgotten how old settlements like York Factory are. The first posts were built in the area in 1682 at a time when there were no permanent settlements of Europeans in the rest of Canada outside the St. Lawrence River Valley and the Maritimes. As one author has pointed out, it is as old a community as Philadelphia.[14] At the time Joseph Colen began construction of a new factory in 1789 it was already over a century old. Not surprisingly, the community had already changed considerably from its early years. Between 1789 and 1870 life at the post continued to change, sometimes in response to its new functions and conditions in the fur trade and sometimes due to external factors. It should be remembered that in 1789 the French Revolution had just begun, the Industrial Revolution was beginning to gather steam in Britain, and in North America the colony of Quebec had not yet been separated into Upper and Lower Canada. By 1870 British North America had become the Dominion of Canada, the United States of America had just undergone the convulsions of a civil war, and Britain was at the height of the Victorian era. It is important to keep in mind that not

6 *Top left* Joseph Colen.
National Archives of Canada, C-1801.
7 *Top right* James Hargrave.
Provincial Archives of British Columbia, HP4244.
8 *Bottom left* Letitia Hargrave.
Provincial Archives of British Columbia, HP4243.
9 *Bottom right* William Mactavish.
Provincial Archives of British Columbia, HP4246.

only was York Factory a different place in 1789 than in 1830 or 1870, but so was the rest of the world.

Many definitions of social history exist, but most social historians ultimately are interested in "reconstructing the kind of life lived by the ordinary people of the past"[15] — in what changed in these people's experiences and behaviour and what did not, and in both cases, why. What follows is an examination of the lives of Hudson's Bay Company employees at York Factory in the late 18th and 19th centuries that, it is hoped, will give readers a sense of everyday life in that community.

Officers in charge at York Factory, 1786-1870

1786-1794	Joseph Colen
1794-1795	George Sutherland (Colen on furlough)
1795-1798	Joseph Colen
1798-1802	John Ballenden
1802-1809	John McNab
1809-1815	William Hemmings Cook
1815-1819	James Swain
1819-1821	Adam Snodie
1821-1829	John George McTavish
1829-1830	Robert Miles
1830-1834	A.H. Christie
1834-1839	James Hargrave
1839-1840	Nicol Finlayson (Hargrave on furlough)
1840-1851	James Hargrave
1851-1856	William Mactavish
1856-1858	James Hargrave
1858-1864	James Clare
1865-1869	Joseph Wilson
1869-1870	Samuel Parson

Social Structure and Social Relations

The earliest writers on the fur trade in western Canada were, for the most part, fur traders themselves. Most recognized that their readers were interested in more than the ledger sheets of the trade and that the fur trade was more than just a commercial undertaking: it was a way of life as well.[1] Subsequently authors often ignored or downplayed the fur trade as a social system and concentrated on the economic and business history of the trade. In recent years, however, attention has slowly been turning back to the study of "fur trade society."[2]

At least one resident of York Factory considered it to be the closest post of all to the ideal of fur trade society.[3] In 1849 Letitia Hargrave, the wife of Chief Factor James Hargrave, pronounced York Factory to be "by far the most respectable place in the Territory."[4] The exact reasons for her opinion can only be guessed at, but York Factory was unusual in several respects. At most posts the complement of men was usually too small to make many distinctions of social status practical. If the officer in charge of a small post kept to the practice of dining only with fellow officers, he would dine alone or with his family for most of the year. At other large posts, like Upper and Lower Fort Garry, the many people resident nearby who were not employed directly by the Hudson's Bay Company made it more difficult for company officers and their families simply to assume positions of social pre-eminence. York Factory's size, the range of occupations represented there, its remoteness, and the fact that virtually all its residents were either casual or permanent employees of the Hudson's Bay Company meant that fur trade society may well have achieved its fullest elaboration there.

Respectability at York meant a society that was organized around a system of ranks roughly analogous to those of military organizations.[5] Fur trade society was hierarchical, with employees divided into two basic groups: "officers" or "gentlemen," and "men" or "servants."[6] The great dividing line was where one dined and with whom. The right to dine in the officers' mess was the one sure test of status and the prerogative was eagerly sought and carefully guarded.[7]

Within the two broad social groupings of officers and men there were further sub-divisions of status and influence. Officers were divided into "commissioned officers" and "salaried officers" or clerks, postmasters, surgeon-clerks, sloop masters, and others. Commissioned officers were distinguished from other officers by title — they were either chief factors or chief traders — and by the way in which they were paid. A portion of the annual profits of the fur trade was set aside to form a fund for the payment of senior officers, with a chief factor receiving twice the share of a chief trader. Chief factors were senior to chief traders, and both were subordinate to the governor and London committee.[8]

Salaried officers ranked beneath commissioned officers. Amongst such officers, rank and influence were probably best indicated by wage rates. Senior clerks at £100 per annum or more were important and powerful figures. Apprentice clerks, on the other hand, were paid as little as £20 or £25 per annum: scarcely more than labourers and less than some tradesmen. Surgeons and sloop masters were often paid as much as senior clerks in recognition of their specialized knowledge. A few at York, notably James Hackland, a sloop master, and William Todd, a surgeon, rose to commissioned-officer status, but many chose to serve only a single contract before returning to Britain. They tended to be well-paid "sojourners," and as such probably did not wield the kind of influence their salaries suggest. Salaried officers also included postmasters and apprentice postmasters. Apprentice postmasters were described as "the lowest rank for a gentleman."[9] However, some were the sons of company officers, and if they showed talent they could expect quick promotion and more illustrious careers than a beginning at the lowest rank of gentleman might imply. Postmasters at York, on the other hand, were usually promoted from the ranks. Some, through long service, were accorded the status of clerks, and one particularly able man, William Anderson, rose from a labourer in 1833 to a chief trader in 1864 after passing through the ranks of the postmasters. In spite of these exceptions, most postmasters at York could aspire to no higher status, and despite the ability and experience that was the reason for their promotion, their status in post society may not have been as great as that of well-connected apprentice postmasters.[10]

Hierarchy amongst company servants is no less complex. At the base of post society were middlemen[11] and labourers. These job titles were to some extent interchangeable, and a middleman was liable to be required to do the work of a general labourer in winter just as a labourer might be requested to pull an oar in summer. In neither case were they hired for anything other than their willingness to perform unskilled physical labour. At a post like York Factory their work varied from manning the York boats to cutting wood and loading and unloading ships. With the exception of apprentices, no other servants received lower wages on average even including gratuities, the extra payments the company offered to certain employees for extra work.[12] Also, middlemen and labourers formed the most numerous category of servant in the Northern Department throughout the 19th century,[13] but at York Factory this was not necessarily the case. The size of this unskilled labour force varied widely at York. It ranged from a high of about half the work force in 1824-25 and again in 1864-65 to a low of about one-third in the late 1830s and early 1840s. Comparatively speaking, labourers did not form such a large part of society at York as they did elsewhere in the North-West.

Apprentices formed another segment of the servants employed at York Factory. They were almost always recruited from amongst the children of company employees, and while never numerous, they helped to keep the company supplied with the skilled tradesmen it needed.Their wages were low, ranging from £8 per annum in the first year of apprenticeship to £16 per annum in the seventh and final year. Even in this final year they were paid less than labourers or middlemen but, like apprentice clerks and apprentice postmasters, their position in the social hierarchy is difficult to define as they had better prospects than many whose wages were higher. In time most would serve as tradesmen though a few were taken on as apprentice labourers, which meant that they had little to look forward to after completing their apprenticeships aside from a small increase in pay.

York Factory's work force also included men whose special skills were rewarded with higher wages than those of labourers, but whose skills and wages were not those of tradesmen. The sloops stationed at York required crews. The boat brigades needed bowsmen and steersmen and guides. Sawyers and fishermen kept the post supplied with sawn timber for building and fish for provisions. There was always a small, but far from unimportant, group of servants providing semi-skilled labour for the post. Some, generally guides and interpreters, achieved a status very similar to that of the most experienced tradesmen or even the bottom ranks of the officers.[14] However, guides and interpreters were rarely listed as part of York's permanent work force, and they were usually posted in more remote areas like the Athabasca or Mackenzie River districts.[15]

On the whole, the best paid and most influential servants at York Factory were the tradesmen. They made up a large proportion of the total work force at York — usually between a quarter and a third of all servants stationed there (*see* Figure 11).[16] Probably at no other post did tradesmen figure so prominently in the population.[17] The reason for this was that in addition to the usual maintenance and provisioning of a large post, which required carpenters, joiners, stewards, cooks, bakers, and the like, York was expected to produce a wide range of trade goods and post supplies. As well, tradesmen at York trained apprentices, managed work parties in the summer, and controlled the operations of their workshops. Not surprisingly, their wages could exceed those of apprentice clerks and apprentice postmasters and approach those of postmasters.

Permanent company employees did not make up York's entire population. Some Homeguard Cree were employed there on a seasonal basis. Also, at any given time a certain number of men lived and worked there, but their wages were not charged to the factory. These men, listed on general charges and not always counted as part of the permanent work force, were usually new recruits waiting for assignment to interior posts, or old employees waiting for passage home to Britain. Neither of these groups, however, particularly affected the general social hierarchy of York Factory.

There was little or no overt questioning of the system of social distinctions, although company servants were quite capable of resisting what they felt was unfair treatment and even of organizing to press for higher wages and better living conditions. The social structure at York Factory resembled that of pre-industrial or *ancien régime* Europe with its "firm distinctions between persons [that] made some superior, most inferior," and its "various gradations, all authoritatively established and generally recognized."[18] According to historian Philip Goldring, York Factory was a place where

> *everybody found reason to be grateful for superiority over someone else. In the little chapel at York the Chief Factor's household sat alone in a corner to be "secluded & apart from the vulgar," while "the Mess" or unmarried officers and clerks also sat in a little group, "& the men w^d not share the [pews] with the Indians, the Fort Indians won't sit beside the tent ones & so forth."*[19]

It was probably this careful attention to status that made York seem "by far the most respectable place in the Territory."[20]

The social system so clearly portrayed in the seating pattern of the chapel was reproduced elsewhere in the post. Not only did employees eat their meals in messes divided by rank, they were fed differently, given different allowances of alcohol, sugar, and other luxuries, housed separately, and even accorded different leisure time in a complex system of ascending privilege.

Not all social distinctions or social tensions at posts like York Factory derived from the hierarchy of rank and privilege created by the Hudson's Bay Company. Fur trade historians have paid considerable attention to conflicts within the ranks of company officers and to the differing origins of company employees. Company officers argued over trade policy and territory, over power and influence, or even over which post had the best claim to a given hunter's trade. It has even been suggested that in the period after 1821, some officers formed a faction opposed to Governor George Simpson, who ran the company's North American operations between 1820 and 1860, and his favourites. This opposition faction differed from Simpson and his supporters on virtually every issue facing the fur trade from the treatment of wives married "à la façon du pays" to the support of missionaries.[21]

Other historians have examined the importance of the ethnic origins of company employees.[22] The Hudson's Bay Company recruited employees from a number of areas, and company officials frequently attributed general cultural characteristics to the employees recruited from a particular area: Orkneymen were reputed to be docile and frugal, and Lower Canadians, volatile but hardy. Whether or not these cultural and physical traits were correctly attributed to the various ethnic groups that made up the company's work force, there is some evidence to suggest that company employees formed strong social ties and, equally, aversions on the basis of their places of origin. At every encampment the brigade Robert Clouston travelled with "divided itself by mutual consent ... the Iroquois had a fire; the French Canadians had a fire," and Clouston, as an officer, had a fire to himself.[23] In 1790 one man asked to be recalled if "any Person from the Orkney Isles should be placed over me," and some English employees demanded that they be given first pick of the rations before the Orkneymen.[24]

Society at Hudson's Bay Company posts, especially at the larger posts like York Factory, was divided vertically along lines of rank or status and again horizontally by ethnicity, personality, and a variety of other less formal distinctions. It was important to try to ensure that any conflict or anti-social or criminal behaviour was effectively dealt with and controlled.

This was done by encouraging a system of social relations marked by both discipline and deference.

This system of social relations was maintained in a number of ways. Perhaps the most important was that the Hudson's Bay Company purposely recruited employees who were already used to accepting that life dictated inequalities of rank and wealth. As early as 1702, new servants were sought in the Orkneys. Joseph Myatt, the officer in charge of Albany in 1727, wrote that the problem with servants recruited in London was that they were "so well acquainted with the ways and debaucheries of the town."[25] English labourers and tradesmen acquired a reputation for complaining about the work expected of company servants, and as a result they were often viewed as troublemakers.[26] Over the course of the 18th century, few Englishmen were hired except as tradesmen or officers, and after 1821 they appeared less and less frequently even in those capacities (see Tables 1 and 2). Through most of the 18th century, Orkneymen dominated Hudson's Bay Company service largely because of their willingness to accept the wages and work conditions, and because they were viewed as more sober, frugal, and docile than English servants.[27] In the late 18th and early 19th centuries the company also began to recruit more Lower Canadians. While viewed as less frugal and less temperate than Orkneymen, they too were seen as being willing to accept the hierarchical structure of post society. Recruits from other Scottish islands and mainland Scotland were also viewed as controllable. By contrast, some English farm servants hired in 1836 were found to be "insolent, indolent, and mischevious," and the Norwegians recruited in the mid-1850s were described as "disorderly, impracticable men over whom we can exercise no controul."[28] While the composition of the work force at York Factory differed somewhat from that of the company's service as a whole, it did reflect a preference for servants from the Orkneys, Scotland, Lower Canada, and Rupert's Land itself.

According to Governor Simpson, carefully selecting recruitment areas and attempting to balance numbers of employees from different areas had the added advantage of simplifying control of the work force. He felt that antipathy between groups made the formation of "leagues and cabals which might be dangerous to the peace of the Country" more difficult.[29]

Discipline was also made easier by the fact that most posts were pre-eminently "company towns." Prior to 1821, employees could desert to the North West Company or XY Company, but this was not easily accomplished. York's isolation made desertion particularly difficult. In March 1816 an employee named George Gorn did desert from York Factory to escape punishment for theft. He did not get far, however, and was brought back a day later. Gorn remained disgruntled and a month later deserted again. This time he was not so lucky: when found three days later he was suffering from such badly frozen toes that nine had to be amputated.[30] In 1795 John Ward and Peter Sabbeston, two inland employees, deserted after being brought to York Factory for censure by the council at York. Ward's crimes were not mentioned, but Sabbeston had been fined £25 for refusing orders and striking Charles Isham, his master at Swan River House. The enormity of this breach of discipline in the council's eyes was indicated by the fact that Sabbeston's fine was equivalent to one year's wages. Both men were struck from duty and would have been sent home by the supply ship had they not robbed the factory and set off inland on the night of 31 August 1795. Ward and Sabbeston were more successful than Gorn, and they reached a Canadian post at Jack River near Playgreen Lake. When a North West Company employee, Joseph Le Rocher, arrived at York claiming to be a deserter, plans were quickly put in place to exchange him for Ward and Sabbeston. An exchange was eventually completed, and after returning to York, Sabbeston actually proved to be a satisfactory employee. Yet in spite of his change of heart, both Ward and he were sent home on the next supply ship.[31] The examples of Gorn, Sabbeston, and Ward did not end desertion, but they did show that it was not a very practical way to evade discipline. Once they had reached the North-West, most employees had no alternative to company service.

This in turn gave company officers considerable power. Senior or commissioned officers may not have enjoyed great status outside the Hudson's Bay Company's territories, but in the North-West their powers were considerable.[32] Miles Macdonell, the officer in charge of Lord Selkirk's first settlement party, described the powers of William Auld, then superintendent of the Northern Department, as follows:

> *You now compose in your person so many characters & functions civil, secular & clerical that you will be a match for the Devil himself — there can be no such thing as getting to the unguarded side of you — you only want* military *to make you invincible —* [33]

The officers in charge of posts like York were very conscious of their status and dignity, and were careful not to compromise either. Dr. Helmcken, a visitor at York, offered the following account of the transformation of James Hargrave's behaviour once he arrived at the factory:

> *Now altho Hargrave ... had been so very familiar and affable on board, no sooner did he set foot ashore than he became dignified cold and distant! Like an admiral, who may be pleasant and urbane ashore, but the moment his foot touches the deck, he is the*

Table 1
Distribution of York Factory Permanent Work Force by Place of Origin: Officers

	1824-25		1829-30		1834-35		1839-40		1844-45	
	n	%	n	%	n	%	n	%	n	%
Orkney	2	20	1	20	2	33.3	2	28.5	2	33.3
Shetland										
Hebrides										
Mainland Scotland	2	20			1	16.7	2	28.5	3	50.0
England except London	1	10	2	40	1	16.7	1	14.3		
London	2	20			1	16.7				
Other Britain	1	10					1	14.3		
Upper and Lower Canada	1	10	1	20						
Rupert's Land	1	10	1	20	1	16.7	1	14.3	1	16.7
Other European										
Total	10	100	5	100	6	100.1	7	99.9	6	100.0

Source: Canada. National Archives. Manuscript Division, MG20, Hudson's Bay Company Archives (hereafter cited as HBCA), B.239/g/1-46, Abstracts of Servants Accounts, 1821-71; some missing information was supplied by Philip Goldring from the data base he prepared for Parks.

Table 2
Distribution of York Factory Permanent Work Force by Place of Origin: Tradesmen

	1824-25		1829-30		1834-35		1839-40		1844-45	
	n	%	n	%	n	%	n	%	n	%
Orkney	7	43.8	3	20	3	30	8	57.1	5	50
Shetland									1	10
Hebrides										
Mainland Scotland			3	20	2	20	2	14.3		
England except London										
London							1	7.1		
Other Britain										
Upper and Lower Canada	9	56.3	9	60	5	50	2	14.3	2	20
Rupert's Land							1	7.1	2	20
Other European										
Total	16	100.1	15	100	10	100	14	99.9	10	100

* Norwegians.

Source: HBCA, 239/g/1-46.

Table 1
(continued)

1849-50 n	1849-50 %	1854-55 n	1854-55 %	1859-60 n	1859-60 %	1864-65 n	1864-65 %	1869-70 n	1869-70 %	Cumulative n	Cumulative %
3	37.5	1	14.3	4	50.0	4	50	1	14.3	22	30.6
		1	14.3							1	1.4
										–	–
1	12.5	1	14.3	1	12.5	2	25	1	14.3	14	19.4
2	25.0							1	14.3	8	11.1
		2	28.5	2	25.0	2	25	1	14.3	10	13.9
										2	2.8
1	12.5							1	14.3	4	5.6
1	12.5	2	28.5	1	12.5			2	28.5	11	15.3
										–	
8	100.0	7	99.9	8	100.0	8	100	7	100.0	72	100.1

Table 2
(continued)

1849-50 n	1849-50 %	1854-55 n	1854-55 %	1859-60 n	1859-60 %	1864-65 n	1864-65 %	1869-70 n	1869-70 %	Cumulative n	Cumulative %
6	54.5	6	54.5	7	50.0	2	22.2	5	41.7	52	42.6
						2	22.2	2	16.7	5	4.1
						1	11.1	1	8.3	2	1.6
1	9.1	2	18.2	1	7.1	2	22.2	1	8.3	14	11.5
										1	.8
										–	
										–	
				1	7.1					26	23.0
4	36.4	3	27.3	3	21.4	2	22.1	3	25.0	18	14.8
				2*	14.3					2	1.6
11	100.0	11	100.0	14	99.9	9	99.9	12	100.0	122	100.0

Table 3
Distribution of York Factory Permanent Work force by Place of Origin: Skilled and Unskilled Labour

	1824-25		1829-30		1834-35		1839-40		1844-45	
	n	%	n	%	n	%	n	%	n	%
Orkney	21	58.3	9	52.9	16	59.3	11	58.8	11	57.9
Shetland										
Hebrides	·				2	7.4	4	25.0	4	21.1
Mainland Scotland	2	5.6			1	3.7				
England except London	1	2.8	1	5.9					1	5.3
London										
Other Britain	1	2.8	1	5.9						
Upper and Lower Canada	8	22.2	3	17.6	6	22.2			3	15.8
Rupert's Land	2	5.6	3	17.6	2	7.4	1	6.3		
Other European	1	2.8								
Total	36	100.1	17	99.9	27	100.0	16	100.1	19	100.1

* In 1864-65 five employees were listed as being from the ships *Prince Arthur* or *Prince of Wales*. Only one man, Henry Tuggey, continued on in company service, allowing his home parish to be identified.

Source: HBCA, B.239/g/1-46.

admiral — discipline prevails, and he may or may not be a tyrant. Hargrave was nevertheless kind in his way, but ... he had to go into harness at once.[34]

Salaried officers, too, had considerable disciplinary responsibilities. As a result, efforts were made to try to ensure that officers were "socially as well as administratively superior to their men."[35] Most officers were certain that good discipline could only be maintained if they did not allow themselves to become too close to the men. George Simpson McTavish's father, a former chief factor, advised him, "On no account be familiar with the men as they soon lose respect for an officer who forgets his position."[36]

Not all officers were willing or able to maintain this social distance. Joseph Colen, for example, felt obliged to send Thomas Wiegan, a writer, or junior clerk, off to work amongst the men as a punishment: "[Wiegan's] delight is to associate with the common labourers, with whom he would be

Table 3
(continued)

1849-50		1854-55		1859-60		1864-65		1869-70		Cumulative	
n	%	n	%	n	%	n	%	n	%	n	%
12	50.0	6	25.0	5	21.7	17	43.6	9	45.0	117	47.8
4	16.7	4	16.7	4	17.4	6	15.4	4	20.0	22	9.0
3	12.5	9	37.5	5	21.7	9	23.1	1	5.0	37	15.1
2	8.3	3	12.5	1	4.3			1	5.0	10	4.1
1	4.2			2	8.7	1	2.6	1	5.0	8	3.3
										2	.8
1	4.2					1	2.6			22	9.0
1	4.2	2	8.3	6	26.1	5	12.8	4	20.0	26	10.6
										1	.4
24	100.1	24	100.0	23	99.9	39*	100.1	20	100.0	245	100.1

in a continual state of intoxication could he but get Liquor." Weigan's "indiscretions [were] so glaring, that he is become the butt and ridicule to men and natives,"[37] which undermined the status and authority of officers in general. The problem posed by officers like Wiegan was not simply one of personal immorality. Such behaviour also affected relations between officers and men in a community where authority was displayed in a direct and often physical manner.

York Factory was not an idyllic community in which crime, dereliction of duty, and anti-social behaviour were unknown. Over the years the Hudson's Bay Company and its senior officers experimented with a wide variety of punishments ranging from flogging to fines to jailing offenders. What is perhaps most striking about the various attempts to institute some sort of system of punishment was how haphazard they were. Punishments were anything but consistent, with the sole exception that minor transgressions like insolence usually brought the culprit a pummelling from the nearest superior.

Throughout the 18th and 19th centuries, officers' feet and fists provided the basic means of enforcing discipline at York Factory and elsewhere in the company's service. An officer who did not maintain his distance from the men threatened the system in which virtually everyone was subject to chastisement by someone of a higher rank because unless officers were to be chosen simply for their strength, the person receiving the beating had to be willing to endure it without fighting back. Without this consent, day-to-day discipline at the post might well have collapsed.[38] Similarly, an officer who might have preferred not to strike an insolent employee ran the risk in not doing so of losing his influence.

References to officers hitting servants became less frequent in the York Factory journals after 1821, and attempts were made to control the use of this sanction. Certainly company servants were prepared to protest what they saw as unwarranted beatings. As early as 1819 the steersman of a York boat refused to return inland with Mr. Dears, the officer in charge of the brigade, after Dears had struck the steersman across the back with a sabre, presumably with the flat of the blade. The steersman had not been "guilty of any impropriety of Conduct," and the journal entry clearly implies that Dears had overstepped his authority.[39] However, Letitia Hargrave revealed that officers were loathe to give up this prerogative entirely. She found it "remarkable how ready gentlemen are with their hands here." Her husband and her brothers were quite willing to "belabor" tradesmen and labourers who annoyed them, but her comments contrast with her husband's advice to his subordinates, whom he was quick to censure for tendencies towards violence.[40]

Even junior officers might be threatened with physical discipline, though it is not clear whether or not such threats were ever acted upon. Dr. Gillespie, the surgeon, and William Mactavish, the post accountant, both threatened to thrash R.M. Ballantyne when he was an apprentice clerk for his conceited or "stylish" behaviour. Gillespie even threatened to increase the indignity of the beating by making it public.[41] Letitia Hargrave's letters suggest that the system of rank at York Factory constituted a definite pecking, or perhaps more accurately thrashing, order.

When officers wished to battle servants without invoking the prerogative of rank, they sometimes specifically put aside such distinctions. An officer, Richard Grant, once felt impelled to battle the cantankerous tinsmith John Beith after Beith accused the Hudson's Bay Company of swindling the Indians. When Beith seemed unwilling to fight back, Grant took off his jacket, threw it on the ground, and announced that "there lay coat and commission."[42]

More serious crimes warranted more formal punishment than a cuff or a kick. At York Factory severe punishments were rare. Indeed, the last recorded case of a servant being whipped for theft occurred in 1797.

> *In the Evening Donald Laughton was punished for Theft — He has been frequently detected in pilfering from his fellow Servants — as well as stealing things from out of the Ware House — His sentence was to be tyed to the beaver press — and every one of his fellow Servants giving him a stroke — on his bare back with a heind [sic] Whip — which was executed on him accordingly.[43]*

Two canoemen from the Peace River district who were brought down to York Factory in 1825 were accused of theft and desertion. Neither had enough money to pay a fine so it was decided that they be

> *immediately Hand Cuffed and in that situation that they be publickly exposed during one full day on the roof of the Factory, afterwards that they be imprisoned during one week, fed on bread and water, and in winter that one of each be sent to winter among the Europeans at Churchill & Severn Forts.[44]*

The punishments the canoemen received more or less exhausted all the non-financial sanctions available to the officers at York. Confinement to quarters or to the launch house or some similarly unpleasant residence, with the added indignity of being put in irons, was effective punishment.[45] Short rations were also used as a punishment. One disgruntled employee was "scowered into obedience by a regimen of Bacon & Oatmeal & not a little chastized by the Musketoos (for he led a Sylvan life)."[46] Transfer to another post away from friends or family or to an unpopular post was also used occasionally to discipline the men.[47]

For most offences serious enough to deserve formal punishment, fines were imposed. As early as 1792 the London committee established the principle that fines were to be levied for "neglect of duty or other gross misconduct." It was felt that they were "the best mode to be adopted in order to keep up a proper subordination."[48] Fines were to be imposed by the governor and council, and reviewed by the London committee.[49] Occasionally fines were declared to be excessive in the view of the committee and were lowered.[50] Ordinarily, though, fines were confirmed if imposed with "that calm equanimity without which the administration of Justice must degenerate into tyranny."[51] From the 1790s on, minutes of the council at York and later the Northern Council frequently refer to fines levied for everything from desertion to excessive consumption of provisions. Nor were fines applied only to servants; company officers, including commissioned officers, were fined on occasion.[52]

In certain exceptional cases employees were sent home as a disciplinary measure, though the London committee frowned upon this practice:

> In some instances, men have been sent home on very trifling grounds, by which a considerable loss, has been incurred of money paid in advance of wages, in expenses in bringing the men to and from the post of embarkation, in the expense of their passage, & their wages for several months during which no useful service could be expected from them.[53]

For the most part the company and its senior officers were prepared to see all but the most recalcitrant employees serve out their terms.[54]

Though far from common, more serious crimes like murder, attempted murder, manslaughter, or assault presented the Hudson's Bay Company and its senior officers with problems they were hard pressed to solve. It was not until 1822 that it became a matter of policy that capital crimes committed in Rupert's Land should be tried in Upper Canada.[55] Prior to 1822 it was far from clear what courts, if any, had jurisdiction over Rupert's Land and what could be done to prosecute serious offenders other than send them back to Britain. Even when it was determined that Upper Canadian courts had jurisdiction in Rupert's Land, it was by no means simple to prosecute anyone, as the accused and all witnesses either had to travel to Upper Canada or swear affidavits. In 1839 Adam Thom was appointed to judge cases at Red River, but it was not until 1854 that a circuit court was established at Norway House to try civil and criminal cases there.[56] In any event the records at York Factory give no indication that courts in Upper Canada or elsewhere in the North-West were used to deal with criminal cases that occurred at the factory.

The confusion over how to try serious criminal cases was made even greater by the question of whether or not the company had any legal jurisdiction over native peoples, or if company officers even wished such jurisdiction. Elsewhere in the North-West some officers attempted on occasion to punish Indians for actions taken against the company or its employees. Punishments were deeply resented, and after one such incident in 1803 the London committee flatly informed its officers that "forebearance" in the treatment of Indians accused of crimes was only prudent.[57] At York Factory such forebearance was called for in 1796. Two York Factory Indians were reputed to have killed a North West Company trader, Robert Thompson. Having heard that the two men had taken up residence at York, North West Company officials wrote to Joseph Colen requesting that the

Indians be seized and sent inland to a North West Company post as prisoners. Some of Colen's fellow officers were prepared to go along with this plan, but he overruled them.

> *I considered that it would be an act of imprudence to pursue the plan for ... numbers of Indians would soon assemble and over-match any force [we] could send with the Captive, they would not only rescue their Chief but resent the insult offered him — and it would be a miracle, if any of those who had him in Charge, escaped the fate of Mr. Thompson. — ... for by committing such an act, [we] would be declaring open hostilities against the Indians, and expose all the Honble Company's Servants Inland to their resentment.*[58]

In a bizarre sequel that June, Joseph Le Rocher arrived at York Factory claiming to be a deserter from the North West Company. As he was still under contract to the North West Company he was only engaged conditionally. Three days later Le Rocher attempted to kill one of the Indians who had killed Thompson, and only the timely intervention of another company employee kept Le Rocher from success. Early in July Le Rocher attempted to kill another Indian, who was related to the Indians who had killed Thompson. This time Le Rocher was handcuffed and placed under guard while Colen attempted to learn what had prompted these attacks. Fellow servants revealed that Le Rocher had entered Hudson's Bay Company service with the specific intention of revenging his former master's death, and that if successful, his debts to the North West Company would be cancelled.[59] Ten days later he was sent back inland to be turned over to the North West Company in return for Ward and Sabbeston, deserters from the Hudson's Bay Company. Colen's limited powers when faced with a serious crime like attempted murder were obvious. Not only could he do nothing about the Indians who had killed Thompson, but he could only send Le Rocher back to the North West Company.

In cases that involved only Indians, Hudson's Bay Company officials were even more reluctant to intervene in any way. When an Indian named Abishabis, or Abbis Shabbish, proclaimed a new religion in the early 1840s and later murdered five members of the York Factory band, James Hargrave remained uninvolved. Abishabis then went to Severn, where he apparently so terrified the local Indians that they would not leave the post. This finally forced John Cromartie, the interpreter in charge of Severn, to seize Abishabis in order to send him to York as a prisoner, resolving his problem if not Hargrave's. It was a great relief all round when one of the Severn Indians killed Abishabis as he was about to be shipped off to York. Letitia Hargrave neatly summed up the feelings of most company officers when she remarked that "the Indians have their own laws and we dont interfere."[60]

In the 1840s and 1850s some native prisoners were sent to York Factory or its outposts from Red River. Their punishment was effectively that of banishment for one or two years to Trout Lake, Severn, Churchill, or in one case, York Factory. Some committed further thefts, but the behaviour of most was "quite exemplary." Indeed, a number ended up being hired as labourers at Churchill and Severn after their sentences had been served.[61] The one prisoner held at York Factory was Atasawapoh. A mixed-blood from the Saskatchewan District, he had killed a Canadian in a quarrel. A jail was built at York in 1841 to confine him, and he spent a year picking oakum, making dog harnesses, and sewing tent covers before being exiled to Ungava. Despite the drudgery of the work and a prison diet of pemmican, biscuit, and water that gave him scurvy at one point, he appears to have been a model prisoner.[62] Not only did he profess remorse, but he did not complain about being exiled to Ungava. The latter punishment seems rather harsh, but as James Hargrave noted, it would have been unwise to let Atasawapoh return to the Saskatchewan District where his victim's friends might have sought revenge.[63]

Amongst company employees at York the most common crime was pilferage of goods. In 1791, for example, sloopers made off with the mainsail of the factory sloop "to make trowsers." Such minor thefts were typically the sort of problem officers at York had to face.[64] Careful rules about who could enter storerooms and close supervision of the loading and unloading of supply ships prevented most serious thefts. Indeed, when thefts occurred from packages and chests landed at York, the officers in charge there were not above suggesting that the crimes had been committed on board ship — not at York Factory.[65] As Chief Trader James Clare argued, in a small community like York Factory, where everyone's activities were subject to the scrutiny of others, few thefts were likely to go unnoticed and unreported. The closest thing to a major scandal at York was the firing of Captain John Richards, commander of the annual supply ship, after he was caught with illicit furs in 1801. The London committee had no doubt that these furs had been obtained from employees at York and demanded that the practice stop.[66] Richard's crime was unusual in that clandestine trading in furs was not often reported in the 19th century, unlike the period up to the 1770s. After 1801 the chests of homeward-bound employees were sometimes searched, but it was rarely reported that furs were found.

Generally speaking, minor infractions of post discipline were dealt with by a blow or two from an officer or tradesman, or in cases that were deemed slightly more serious, with a fine. The latter appears to have been adequate sanction for all but the most "refractory servants," or for all but those rare occasions when thefts were more than pilferage or crimes were violent. The use of fines to punish employees of all ranks was admirably suited to the fur trade, given the motives most Hudson's Bay Company employees had for taking up their careers in the fur trade.

Adventure, the desire to escape problems at home, and other personal reasons may have prompted some to join the Hudson's Bay Company's service. Some, like parish- and charity-school boys, probably had little choice in the matter. However, most who could choose were motivated by economic reasons. As one clerk at York wrote:

Shut up in this solitary corner, time of necessity hangs heavy on our hands, and I must own that nothing but the want of a sufficiency to support me in Canada prevents me from leaving this desert and again joining my dear relations.[67]

Wage rates changed considerably for all ranks over the course of the 18th and 19th centuries, and at any given time wages varied in their attractiveness compared to what could be earned at equivalent jobs in Scotland or the Canadas,[68] but what was almost always true was that, as the company provided room and board for its employees, they enjoyed disposable incomes far greater than those of men doing similar work in either Britain or Canada. Frugal employees could save large portions of their incomes. Letitia Hargrave reported in 1842, with some incredulity, that her cook, Robert Garson, had saved £300 over 27 years of service at wages of only £17 per annum. Not only had he saved well over half his income, but his net worth was as great as her brother Dugald Mactavish despite their considerable differences in wages and status.[69] Garson's savings were not unusual, at least for Orkneymen, many of whom saved 70 per cent or more of their wages.[70] Orkneymen had reputations for being particularly careful with their money, but other company employees also managed to save substantial amounts when motivated to accumulate enough capital to purchase a farm or to set up a small business in Britain or Canada.[71]

For them company service was a means to an end. Many had to serve out more than one contract to acquire the capital resources they desired though, so such individuals were not necessarily those who served the shortest periods of time. Other men, including many company officers, some residents of Rupert's Land, and those who married and established families in the North-West, came to see their employment in the fur trade as a life-long career. Individuals with 15 or more years of service were not uncommon at a post like York Factory, and some, like Robert Garson, continued to work

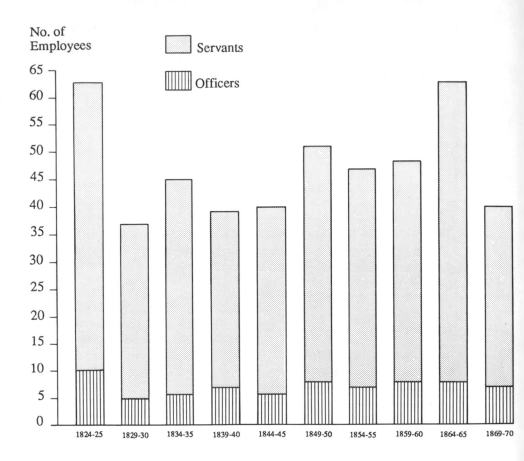

10 Size of the permanent work force at York Factory.
Source: Canada, National Archives, Manuscript Division, MG20, Hudson's Bay Company
Archives, B.239/g/1-46, Abstracts of Servants Accounts, 1821-71.
Drawing by C. Piper.

No. of Employees

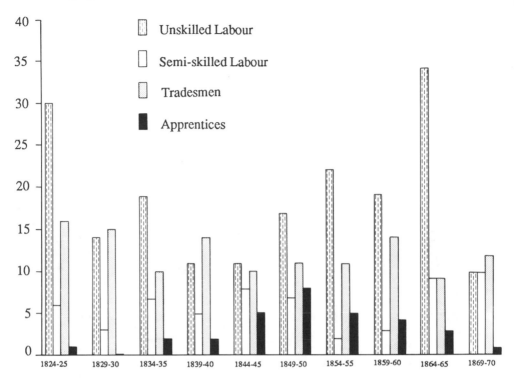

11   York Factory servants by occupation. Semi-skilled labourers included those with country skills: fishermen, sailors, interpreters, bowsmen, steersmen, guides, sloopers, boatmen, cattle keepers, and sawyers. Tradesmen included carpenters, blacksmiths, butlers, bakers, coopers, tailors, masons, cooks, mates, boatbuilders, storemen, tinsmiths, joiners, stewards, store porters, hatters, and armourers.

Source: Canada, National Archives, Manuscript Division, MG20, Hudson's Bay Company Archives, B.239/g/1-46, Abstracts of Servants Accounts, 1821-71.

Drawing by C. Piper.

Table 4
Mean of Years of Experience of York Factory Permanent Work Force

	n *	mean	median		n *	mean	median
		1824-25				**1829-30**	
Officers	10	8.7	7.0		5	10.6	10.0
Tradesmen	16	5.9	4.5		15	7.5	9.0
Other Servants	37	6.3	5.0		17	10.4	9.0
		1834-35				**1839-40**	
Officers	6	7.8	7		7	11.9	7.0
Tradesmen	10	12.5	14		14	8.6	7.0
Other Servants	29	6.1	5		18	7.5	5.0
		1844-45				**1849-50**	
Officers	6	10.7	4.5		8	11.6	6.0
Tradesmen	10	13.1	14.5		10 **	12.3	10.5
Other Servants	24	6.1	4.0		32	4.5	4.0
		1854-55				**1859-60**	
Officers	7	11.7	10		8	11.0	10.5
Tradesmen	11	12.2	9		14	8.9	5.5
Other Servants	29	4.6	3		26 +	4.7	2.0
		1864-65				**1869-70**	
Officers	8	13.5	10.5		7	6.7	5.0
Tradesmen	9	7.8	5.0		12	9.8	9.5
Other Servants	45 +	4.4	3.0		21	7.9	4.0

*   Number of employees.
** In 1849-50 George Flett, the schooner mate, drowned. No years of service were listed for him.
\+ In 1859-60 and 1864-65 John Dunning was carried on the York Factory books as a "blind labourer." No years of service were listed for him.

Source: HBCA, B.239/g/1-46

Table 5
Distribution of All Employees of All Ranks
by Place of Origin, 1824-70 *

	n	%
Orkney	193	41.1
Shetland	28	6.0
Hebrides	39	8.3
Mainland Scotland	38	8.1
England except London	17	3.6
London	10	2.1
Other Britain	4	.9
Upper and Lower Canada	54	11.5
Rupert's Land	84	17.9
Other European	3	.6
Total	470	100.1
All Scotland		63.5
England		5.7
The Canadas		11.5
Rupert's Land		17.9
Other		1.5

* As in Tables 1 to 4, this cumulative distribution of employees by place of origin is based on five-year samples. Because some employees served for longer than five years, a number of individuals have been counted more than once.

Source: HBCA, B.239/g/1-46.

year after year despite savings that would have enabled them to retire in some comfort. Others found company service not to their liking, and there were always those who served out no more than one contract. These employees probably left company service with no less a sense of relief than company officials felt on seeing them depart.

From 1830 to 1880, while the largest single group of company employees as a whole was always those with only one or two years of experience, the mean number of years of service was "considerably above the minimum five-year term of European recruits, and more than double the minimum three-year term for North American engagés."[72] While there was always a high turnover in employees, a large proportion of the work force at any given time had long experience in the fur trade.[73]

After 1821 the work force at York Factory was, if anything, even more likely to be experienced than the company's employees as a whole.[74] With the exception of a period during the 1850s and early 1860s when large numbers of new recruits were stationed at York, the typical resident of York Factory was serving on his second contract or even a subsequent one. The company seems to have been especially careful to keep a corps of very experienced employees amongst the officers and tradesmen at York. The other ranks of the work force were on average considerably less experienced, but even amongst the labourers there were always a significant number of men with ten years of service or more (*see* Table 4).

The size of the complement of men at York Factory changed a good deal over time (Figs. 10 and 11). The large number of men of all ranks stationed at York in 1824-25 reflects the inflated size of the work force of the Hudson's Bay Company after its amalgamation with the North West Company in 1821. Governor Simpson's attempts through the 1830s and early 1840s to pare down the size of the work force are evident at York Factory, as is the renewed growth of the service in the 1850s and 1860s.[75] Yet while the numbers of employees stationed at York fluctuated widely, the numbers of officers remained relatively constant (Fig. 10). The numbers of tradesmen stationed there also changed very little, whereas the numbers of unskilled and semi-skilled employees changed dramatically (Fig. 11). This suggests that the administrative and manufacturing functions of York Factory changed less than its transportation and warehousing responsibilities.

Most notable about the employees at York Factory is the degree to which Orkneymen dominated all ranks. Although Orkneymen were more likely to serve as tradesmen or unskilled and semi-skilled labourers, they also formed the largest single group of officers (Tables 1 to 3). Over 40 per cent of all employees of all ranks stationed at York were Orkneymen (Table 5). If one adds men from the Hebrides, Shetland, and mainland Scotland to the Orkneymen, well over 60 per cent of the work force was Scottish. By comparison, the next largest group of employees, natives of Rupert's Land, made up less than 18 per cent of the total. In this respect the community at York Factory almost exactly reverses the pattern of company service as a whole: from at least 1850 on, natives of Rupert's Land were usually the largest category of permanent servants except amongst unskilled labourers.[76]

The overwhelming numbers of Scottish employees at York may very well have had an impact on how the community developed. When other British employees are added to the Scottish officers and servants, they total just under 70 per cent of the work force. This may explain, at least in part, why so often social change at York appears to reflect changes in British society in the 18th and 19th centuries, and why it might have appeared so respectable in Letitia Hargrave's eyes in comparison to what she knew of other fur trade communities. Quite probably no other post was so British in its population.

Work

The revolution in work patterns and production methods that transformed British society in the late 18th and 19th centuries had little direct impact on fur trade communities like York Factory. The Hudson's Bay Company did operate steamboats on inland waterways from the 1860s on, but steam power was not applied to fur trade operations. For the most part the fur trade relied on human and domestic animal muscle as a power source.[1]

Work at York Factory remained essentially pre-industrial in character. In 1844 a Scottish friend of James Hargrave referred to York in jest as a "heavy, lumbering, lazy" sort of place quite out of touch with the "velocified" pace of life and work in Britain.[2] Like many jokes the observation contained a grain of truth. York Factory was not completely isolated from the forces of social change, but many features of life there changed only slowly. Work at York Factory remained much closer to the patterns of work in 17th- and early-18th-century Britain than to labour in the mills and factories of industrialized Britain.

At a post like York Factory, most work required little or no division of labour and could be pursued without regard to what others were doing. Work like hunting, fishing, cutting wood, or even manufacturing barrels might involve a number of subsidiary jobs, but these could usually be accomplished by the same worker. As a result, work could only be measured in terms of output over relatively long periods like the week or month or season or, in some instances, the entire year.[3] Because of this, workers enjoyed a fair degree of control over how they budgeted their time and effort, and the working day could be lengthened or shortened as needed to keep up output. Moreover, within any given workday, time could be taken off work for any number of reasons. This meant that the general pattern of work at York Factory, as in pre-industrial Britain, was one of alternating periods of idleness or near idleness and bursts of intensive effort.[4] This did not mean that York was an unproductive place, nor that the men stationed there were lazy. What it did mean was that work was organized on different principles and was carried on at a different pace using different methods from those characteristic of much of 19th-century Britain.

There is little evidence that York Factory residents maintained work traditions like St. Monday, an added day of rest and usually alcoholic relaxation claimed by many tradesmen in England into the 19th century. Charles Kitson, a carpenter at York in 1792, once informed Joseph Colen that "it was against his Religion to work on a Monday,"[5] but this was unusual. On the other hand, much of the work of the post took place well away from the prying eyes of officers. Most work was directly supervised by a tradesman or an experienced labourer who may well have turned a blind eye to a casual approach to work on Mondays or any other day so long as overall production did not reflect badly on his abilities. Post journals also include many references to idle or incompetent tradesmen and labourers and to the difficulties of trying to ensure that work was done promptly and well. For example, Colen moved to the new York Factory in 1792 before it was completed to keep an eye on the carpenters, Kitson and Henry Gaines, who was as troublesome as Kitson. Presumably without Colen to oversee their work they would have celebrated St. Tuesday and St. Wednesday as well.[6]

In some cases a lack of attention to work may have been no more than a personal idiosyncracy or a devious scheme to get oneself sent home as incompetent. Faced with an absolute refusal to do any work, officers could do little if threats, fines, or fists failed. One individual named Hugh Wilson refused all work and rendered himself so disgusting and such a nuisance that Joseph Colen had no choice but to send him home. Wilson took to his bed for days on end and refused to get up even "to ease nature." His personal habits were so unbearable that he was moved first to a bed in the guard room, and then outside into a tent.[7] Finally at shiptime he was sent home.

Not all idleness was a matter of individual preference. Until the late 19th century the Hudson's Bay Company as a matter of policy preferred to maintain a larger-than-necessary permanent work force to meet seasonal demands for extra labour rather than try to hire large numbers of temporary workers for the summer and fall shipping seasons.[8] As a result employees were often under-employed or given make-work projects. In the late 18th century David Thompson confessed that his work as clerk and accountant at

York Factory could be completed in a few days and the rest of his year was spent at the more agreeable pursuit of hunting "Geese, Ducks and white Grouse."[9] As the administrative responsibilities of York Factory grew, clerks found that they had to spend longer hours at their desks than Thompson, but even so they were allowed the privilege of leaving their work for a turn on their snowshoes or a bit of hunting when they felt like it. Company servants could always be put to work hunting or cutting wood or even doing tasks with little obvious value. Periodic attempts were made to arrest riverbank erosion at York throughout the 18th and much of the 19th centuries. None worked, but as late as 1840, men were were still facing the riverbank with stones: a laborious but ultimately futile job.[10] The 40-foot lookout tower James Hargrave had built in 1840-41 incurred the displeasure of Governor Simpson, who saw it as an enormous make-work project. He suspected that the only justification for the lookout was that it provided a pleasant place above the mosquitoes for an after-dinner pipe.[11]

Nevertheless, despite a work force for whom work often had to be found, and the occasional lazy employee, York Factory was not an unproductive place. Tradesmen and labourers may have been able to adjust their workdays and pace of work to suit themselves, but their output was carefully recorded, and overall their levels of work and skill were subject to the scrutiny of the officer in charge of York, as well as the governor and the London committee.[12]

The irregular pace of work over days and weeks was part of a broader, seasonal pattern of labour. Company employees of all ranks worked at a variety of tasks over the course of the year, often in spite of the formal occupational title given to them in company account books. Officers were expected to hunt for provisions, supervise work or the saleshop, and keep records as required. Tradesmen generally worked at their trades between mid-October and early April — less than half the year. At other times they, too, supervised others' work, packed and stored goods, helped with post repairs and construction, and carried out other assigned tasks. Labourers were expected to cut wood, salt geese, and work on boats as circumstances dictated.[13] In this respect as well, work at York resembled work in pre-industrial Britain.[14]

Work at York was roughly divided into two seasons. The summer work season, which stretched between April and mid-October, was the period of most intensive effort as employees struggled to load and unload the supply ship, pack furs from the interior, and arrange shipments inland. During the fall and winter the pace slackened as most were engaged in producing trade

12 Annual supply ships had to anchor at Five Fathom Hole (far right),
more than eight kilometres from York Factory.
National Archives of Canada, C-1916.

goods for the following year or supplying York with firewood, fish, meat,
and other provisions.

The exertions of employees at shiptime were often enormous. When the
ship's arrival was delayed or bad weather interfered with loading and
unloading cargo, the workday could span both day and night. In 1847 when
troops were sent to Red River the capacity of York's work force was
strained almost to the breaking point. After his men unloaded two supply
ships James Hargrave was moved to comment that

> *we have at length closed a shipping season attended with more*
> *labor and anxiety than I have ever hitherto experienced at this*
> *Depot.... the labor has been unremitting — by day and by night —*
> *on Sunday and weekday.... and amidst storm and rain. My poor*
> *people have wrought as I have never seen servants work before. —*
> *many of them are invalids and the whole are so thoroughly ex-*
> *hausted that they will require some days rest before I can get them*
> *into "harness" again.*[15]

Even in ordinary years the summer workday could stretch from "four in the morning until Six, Seven, or Eight at Night," although 12-hour days from 6 a.m. to 6 p.m. "with intervals of 40 Minutes for Breakfast and 1 Hour for Dinner" were more common. The winter workday was much shorter. Usually beginning in November the men were served breakfast at 6:30 a.m. and began work at 7:15. Dinner was served between noon and 1:00 p.m. and the workday ended at 5:15. However, these hours were only approximate; work was limited to the daylight hours beginning as early as light would permit and ending when the light failed.[16]

Thus, in effect, the workday at York was a function not of "clock" time, but of "nature's" time.[17] Attempts were made, however, to impose the greater discipline of clock time on work at York Factory. At large posts, like York, bells had been used from at least the mid-18th century to divide the day into work and meal periods.[18] The use of a bell to signal changes in work routine seems to have been borrowed from naval practice, and as in the navy, the bell was a symbol of a disciplined and punctual work force. The Reverend William Mason, a missionary at York, observed that the bell helped to ensure that the business of the post was carried out with "the strictest regularity."[19] For officers like George Simpson McTavish, strict regularity in work was felt to be very important.

> *Surrounded by miles of swamp, neighbours a couple of hundred miles distant, communication with the outside world limited to four regular packets, namely, Winter, Spring, Summer, ship [or] Fall, the living conditions were only made tolerable by the efficient moral discipline of the officers in charge. With idleness or laxity of government, men would have soon lost the grip on themselves, and become as uninspiring as the native. Therefore, after years of experience, the routine was carried on with proverbial clock-like accuracy, and to the best advantage of health, work, exercise and pastime. Regular hours of work were as essential in the wilds as in business city marts and factories....[20]*

Nevertheless, work at York Factory was not conducted with clock-like regularity however much the officers wished that it were.

In part, the persistence of pre-industrial work habits may be attributed to the degree of control fur trade employees were able to exercise over their own working lives and not simply to the inability to find useful applications of steam power or mass-production techniques to the fur trade. Although post society was hierarchical and quasi-military in form, tradesmen and labourers were not entirely powerless. With varying degrees of success they were able to resist changes in the fur trade that threatened their wages and to demand certain rights and privileges that made post life more tolerable and even, by the standards of the time, comfortable. Individually and collectively they protested what they considered to be unfair treatment, and on occasion they could force at least partial redress of their grievances.

The difficulties the Hudson's Bay Company had with recruiting sufficient numbers of skilled employees meant that senior officers were advised not to dismiss servants without good cause. It also meant that disgruntled employees could seriously hinder future recruitment on their return home when they came from small, close-knit communities like Lower Canadian seigneuries or Scottish islands. In the 1790s, a period of great upheaval at York Factory, Orcadian servants threatened to disrupt recruitment if their demands for better treatment were not met:

> *unless your honors send out a larger stock of English Provisions — I am fearful very few men will enter your Honors Service hereafter; and had it not been for the News of a war, the Chief Part of this Place [York] intended to make Application to return for no other reason than their wanting Common Necessaries for many months which almost disables them from doing their duty.*[21]

Such threats were not idle, for a Mr. Watt in Kirkwall in the Orkneys was actively trying to discourage potential employees from signing on with tales of the horrors of life on Hudson Bay. Fifteen years later it was revealed that the tactic was extended to try to force the company to raise wages.

> *We are fully informed of the Combination that prevails in the Orkneys between the men formerly in our Service as well as those who are now actually in our employ & their Relations & friends with the view of preventing our being supplied with the number of hands wanted for our Service, with the intention of obliging our Chiefs to raise the wages of the men who are in the Service at an exorbitant rate —*[22]

The company was forced to offer higher wages to new employees signing on in Stromness the following year, and the wages of old employees signing new contracts were also increased.[23] The increased wages offered employees in 1806 reflected not just the success of the Orkney "combination" though, but also rising wage rates, which made previous salary levels less attractive, in Britain during the Napoleonic Wars. Groups of employees could also threaten to resign en masse as a means of securing concessions from the company. Canadian employees used this tactic to protest the "rough usage they received being so few, and the partiality shewn to the other men" in 1791.[24]

The most concerted attempt to influence wage rates and work conditions through collective action took place in the late 1780s and early 1790s. The problem began in 1787 with attempts by bowsmen and steersmen to use the threat of resigning to secure additional wages. The London committee refused to accede to their "extravagant Demands" and suggested that they be sent home if they pressed these demands or if they refused "to go where ... ordered."[25] At first Joseph Colen was reluctant to order skilled canoemen home as he claimed that they intended to sign on with Canadian fur trade companies as soon as they arrived back in Britain. If too many steersmen left company service at once "they might attempt something daring ... for gratitude for past favors is treated by them as Chimeras, and their own interest is the only God they worship."[26] He also felt that the attempt to force higher wages was running out of steam as "Thomas Robinson (the person who wrote for 15£ p year or home two years ago)" had "begged to remain in the Country" and had agreed to a three-year contract at £8 per annum for the first two years and £10 for the final year.[27] Robinson's agreement to terms and the contracts signed by other experienced employees made Colen hope "that the main link of the Chain is broken on which all their dependance hung."[28] The summer of 1790 was quiet, but over the winter the canoemen apparently devised a scheme to push more forcefully for higher wages. Colen wrote that

> *most [were] inclinable to return for two years only — that their times might expire at once: — and as the chief part are Steersmen — they suppose their leaving the Service all at once it will greatly distress the Inland Trade. — if not totally stop it.*[29]

James Morrowick, "the principle [*sic*] Ring-leader" of the combination, revealed that the canoemen had taken an oath to act together to support their demands.[30] Morrowick had returned to the interior despite a majority vote of the governing council at York to send him home. Colen slyly suggested that if Morrowick had gone inland, it was with the connivance of William Tomison, the governor of the company's inland operations at the time.

In 1792 the focus of the conflict shifted away from wages alone. The surveyor Philip Turnor was to be sent on an exploratory journey up the Nelson River in search of a shorter route to the Athabasca. A number of men refused to undertake the journey, probably because of the difficulties that river presented to paddlers.[31] Their leader was identified as James Linklater, and it was decided to make an example of him. When he informed the council at York that he would be "damn'd if he did go," he was immediately dismissed from company service and placed on half rations until the ship arrived to return him to Britain.[32] Linklater's fate caused the rest of the canoemen to swallow their objections to voyaging on the Nelson River.

The following year the London committee advised the council at York on how it wished to deal with these growing labour difficulties.

> *In the case of Combinations among the servants ... send such refractory servants home if their Contracts are expired & the Fine imposed on them by your Council shall be duly observed by us & they shall never again be employed by us encourage young Hands & bring them forward as occasion may require as Steersmen at the usual pay of £15 to £20 p Ann but you shod. studiously avoid that their Contracts expire not all at the same time.[33]*

One steersman, Laughton Taylor, was discharged from company service for announcing that he would not go inland "unless every Officer who went Inland were ordered to do the same duty as himself."[34] However, Taylor's view was unusual. Such open resentment of officers' prerogatives was rarely expressed in fur trade records. Of much greater significance was the men's resistance to taking boats into the interior in place of canoes. Substituting boats for canoes promised a substantial saving in manpower,[35] but it also threatened to undermine the privileged position of steersmen and canoe builders, and would mean that skilled canoemen would either have to learn new skills or be replaced. Not surprisingly, one man who suggested that boats could be taken inland with ease was threatened with "rough usage."[36] In 1794 the conflict reached a crisis of sorts. Colen himself took the first York boats inland to Gordon House so as to avoid problems with the men and the experiment was successful.[37]

Still, the canoemen were successful in forcing the company to adjust their pay. The route inland from York Factory to Buckingham House on the North Saskatchewan River was divided into four sections from York Factory to Hill River, Hill River to Deep Water Lake, Deep Water Lake to Cumberland House, and Cumberland House to Buckingham House. Trip bonuses were offered for the completion of each stage. The pilot of the brigade received 20 shillings; steersmen, 15 shillings; bowsmen, 15 shillings; and middlemen, 10 shillings. The section from Hill River to Deep Water Lake was so difficult and included so many portages that bonuses were doubled for it.[38] In addition the basic wage of bowsmen was raised to £14 per annum not including bonuses, and both bowsmen and steersmen were promised that they would receive wages as such, even if they were not formally listed on the company books in those positions.[39]

Attempts to prevent the introduction of York boats on inland routes had failed, but the company was forced to pay bonuses to everyone working on the brigades, and the principle was established that extra or unusually demanding work was to be rewarded with payments over and above those of a regular labourer. Nor were these gains ephemeral. Bow and steersmen continued to receive extra wages whether they worked on York boats or canoes. Moreover, the company continued to pay bonuses and gratuities over and above regularly contracted wages to reward employees doing extra labour or serving in remote districts.[40]

Colen felt that the campaign of bow and steersmen to resist the introduction of boats and to secure higher wages was encouraged and perhaps even led by William Tomison.[41] Tomison did disagree with the policy of substituting boats for canoes, in part because it threatened to reduce the number of men stationed at inland posts to oppose the Canadians. Nevertheless, there is no reason to assume that the canoemen were simply manipulated by Tomison and that they were incapable of organizing themselves to defend their position and to obtain concessions.

The threat of strikes and refusal to perform a particular duty was a powerful weapon on occasion. In the 1850s, employees were recruited in Norway. Through an error in translation of the standard employee contract, Norwegian recruits were led to believe that they could resign from company service after giving one year's notice of their intention to do so. This provision was not in the English version of the contract. Unless a person proved unfit or was dismissed, employees were expected to serve out their contracts. The company alone could terminate the contract before its completion. The Norwegian servants were not a great success at York, nor were many of them happy with the conditions of work there.

By the summer of 1858, problems reached a head. In July, 16 Norwegian servants refused to do any further duty and went on "strike." James Clare, then officer in charge at York, stopped their wages but confessed that he had no other "means to enforce discipline." It was even feared that the strike would spread to the Orkneymen once they realized Clare's "total inability effectually to punish such open mutiny."[42] Clare decided to go aboard the annual supply ship with a translator to explain the correct wording of the contract to new Norwegian recruits. Those who were unwilling to accept the terms of the English version of the contract were offered passage home and release from their contracts. Sixteen of the 34 new Norwegian recruits took up this offer when Clare refused to raise their wages to equal those paid to new Orkney recruits. The remaining Norwegians were then angered to discover that the company would not supply them with free blankets, tea, and sugar as they claimed had been promised. Eleven more resigned and in the end only seven of the 34 Norwegian recruits were landed at York. While the company refused to alter its contract provisions, it was equally powerless to hold the Norwegians to that contract. In the end the company suffered a heavy loss on its experiment with hiring in Norway, losing the cost of the men's passage and their advance wages, and in 1859 Norwegian recruitment was abandoned.[43]

The difficulties with discontented Norwegian servants began a period of strained relations with the larger work force. Through the late 1850s and early 1860s labour difficulties beset the inland canoe brigades.[44] At York Factory the permanent work force was also dissatisfied, and James Clare reported that "combinations" had been formed to press grievances. In 1863 Clare wrote that he had been

> *induced to send a few men from this place who have shown a most dis-satisfied spirit and expressed to me their determination to do no work after the departure of the ship, in the event of their not being permitted to retire: — I have had some trouble with my men this season as on some trifling pretext of infringement of the circulars issued by the Company or promises made to them by the Agents, they have formed into Combinations refusing to work if their demands were not complied with; they seem to be understanding the power they have in their hands when acting in a body, I trust however by gradually weeding out and getting rid of the more troublesome characters to be able to put matters on a better footing in time.[45]*

Weeding out "troublemakers" was virtually the only response officers could make to threats to refuse work. Clare's replacement at York, Joseph Wilson, explained that the old policy of fining servants guilty of refusing orders had lost much of its former effectiveness. Only those prudent enough to have amassed savings feared fines, and he implied that they were not the sort of employee needing correction.[46] It was not until 1867 that "European servants whose contracts have expired ... appeared generally desirous either to re-engage in the service or to proceed to Red River"[47] — a sign that at least temporarily York's labour problems were abating.

Company servants at York also used their power to protest living conditions and unwarrantedly violent treatment by officers — occasionally with success. In 1798, for example, a number of officers pushed William Cooper, the labourer cleaning their "guard room," outdoors after he had spoken to them "in an insolent manner." He fell and cut his cheek, whereupon the tradesmen and labourers immediately gathered in the factory yard to protest such ill-usage at the hands of officers. The protest had continued for two days when John Ballenden, the officer then in charge of York, attempted to "reason" with the men. His suggestion that their behaviour was unwarranted and that they were guilty of impropriety was not accepted. As a result, despite Ballenden's misgivings, the officers involved had to give the men a public, albeit far from gracious, apology before the men would consent to obey orders again.[48] Similarly, attempts were made to improve living conditions at York in the 1790s and in the first decades of the 19th century following a period of agitation by company servants for improvements in food supplies and complaints about the heavy reliance in the winter diet on salt venison.[49]

This willingness to protest living conditions was never far from the surface at York Factory, and from time to time it boiled over into confrontations between officers and men. In 1858 the scarcity of country provisions led to protests over the quantity of salt provisions given to the men. John Moar, an assistant boatbuilder, was one of the leading protestors. When James Hargrave reproved Moar "for the carelessness and indifference with which he performed his duty to the Company, in comparison with the eagerness with which he urged his claims to better Rations, better cookery and other matters that he considered 'his Rights,'" Moar was far from chastened. He informed Hargrave that as Hargrave "had injured his character as a Tradesmen he would work no longer for the Company." Moar demanded to be sent home, and when Hargrave suggested that he go to Churchill instead, Moar replied that "he would not go unless sent as a prisoner." Hargrave's ill-timed criticism of Moar's work habits resulted in Moar's having to be sent home even though his contract had not been completed.[50]

Hargrave's experience with Moar is indicative of the independence and degree of control over their work that many fur trade employees, especially tradesmen, claimed. On occasion employees could protest successfully against infringement of their "rights" and extract better work conditions and wages from their employer. Despite the hierarchical structure at York Factory, company servants were far from powerless.

In the past the ability of company servants to organize themselves to protect their interests and to preserve a degree of autonomy has been largely ignored, but it would be unwise to make too much of it. "Combinations" of servants and even individual resistance to orders were relatively rare. Joseph Colen's belief that the labour problems of the early 1790s were leading to a crisis "which is to determine whether the Chief and Officers are to rule the men — or the men to have the sole command over their superiors"[51] owed more to the anxieties of the time than to any evidence that company employees planned to overturn established authority. The unrest at York and among company employees inland in the 1790s occurred at a time when British workers were becoming increasingly aware of their rights and economic power and when the democratic and republican ideals of the American and French revolutions influenced many. Nevertheless, Laughton Taylor's demand that officers do the same duty as canoemen is one of the rare occasions when the system of social distinction upon which fur trade communities like York were organized was openly challenged by a company servant.

Indeed, a large proportion of employees of all ranks appear to have found their employment by the Hudson's Bay Company satisfactory enough to re-engage, and although average lengths of service varied over time, they remained high enough to suggest a reasonably contented work force.[52] This also suggests that, notwithstanding occasional recruitment problems, the company was reasonably satisfied with the quality of its employees.

However diligent and able the permanent work force was, they did not perform all the necessary work of the post. At York there were two main sources of labour that could be used on a temporary basis: the families of employees and the local Cree population. The labour of wives and children was important to York Factory despite the concern shown by Governor Simpson and the London committee that payments for their labour be properly noted and that dependents not become an excessive drain on supplies.[53] In fact, wives and children worked to earn these supplies. Children collected the produce from the post gardens and did other odd jobs about the post. The wives of company employees in addition to their domestic responsibilities often trapped small fur-bearing animals like martens and rabbits. They also made snowshoes and tracking shoes, and helped to clean and prepare furs. They sewed bags, oil cloths, and boat covers, and repaired buffalo robes.[54] In 1802 the council at York suggested that they were virtually employees of the Hudson's Bay Company — a position the London committee did not dispute too vigorously, simply contenting itself with trying to limit the number of wives present at its posts.[55]

The Homeguard Cree also supplied temporary labour. In many cases their work was similar to that of employees' wives, but they also did much of the hunting for York and provided it with a large proportion of its country provisions. The goose hunt in particular was almost exclusively the preserve of Indian hunters, and they were responsible for hunting much of the caribou, ducks, and other waterfowl consumed at the post. They often carried the correspondence packets between posts, and they occasionally helped with haying, rafting wood, transporting geese or fish in from other camps, and loading and unloading boats at shiptime.[56] In fact, there were very few aspects of work at York Factory in which the local Cree did not take a hand on occasion.

Canoe brigades formed another major source of work for the York Factory Cree. From the late 1820s on, transportation of goods between York Factory and Norway House relied heavily on the Hayes River Indian brigades. Native freighters proved reliable, honest, and efficient, and observers like Donald Ross, long the officer in charge of Norway House, and Governor Simpson compared their work favourably with that of the company's permanent employees and tripmen from Red River.[57] It would have been extremely difficult to maintain York Factory without the aid of temporary labour from the York Factory Cree.

Both permanent employees and the temporary work force, hired as needed, operated within a system of work that remained firmly pre-industrial. The working life of a tradesman or labourer at York would not have been much different from that of a fellow tradesman or labourer in the Orkneys or Lower Canada throughout most of the 19th century. The same cannot be said if the comparison were made with a factory operative from Manchester. The thoughts of company servants were never recorded as assiduously as their purchases in the saleshop, but they too might have drawn a distinction between "lumbering" York and "velocified" Britain.

Leisure

Most people believe that the struggle for survival in fur trade settlements was so all-consuming that little time was left for leisure or recreational activities. Even sports historians take the view that "in the pioneer settlements of the Europeans, play was relatively unimportant compared with the serious work of survival."[1] Company records from York Factory, however, indicate that employees enjoyed a lively and varied recreational life. Far from abandoning the sports, games, and other leisure activities common in Britain, company men retained their interest in familiar diversions and discovered new recreational activities to while away their substantial leisure hours.

Early fur trade records do not always make it clear what days were celebrated as holidays, and practices may have varied considerably from post to post or at the whim of officers in charge. By the late 18th century though, most holidays at York Factory were celebrated on a regular basis. At York Coronation Day, St. Georges' Day, Easter, and the Christmas season between Christmas Eve and New Year's Day were normally treated as holidays. Other holidays like Guy Fawkes Day, the king or queen's birthday, and later, St. Andrew's Day were also celebrated as holidays on occasion. In all, these holidays constituted about 10 to 14 days of the year. In addition company employees were normally not required to work on Sundays, whether or not religious services were held. Although some missionaries complained that Sundays were not treated as days of rest in the fur trade, their comments appear to have been directed primarily at canoe and boat brigades, which frequently travelled on Sundays, and not at practices at bayside posts. Between Sundays and other holidays, about 60 to 65 days of the year were days off work at York Factory from the late 18th century on, or about one-sixth of the year.

By the 19th century, holidays were even more extensive for most residents of York. Although there is a reference to Saturdays being treated as half-holidays at Prince of Wales's Fort as early as 1749, it cannot be determined if this custom extended to York.[2] Nevertheless, a private journal kept at York in 1829 indicates that Saturdays were treated as full holidays, and both R.M. Ballantyne and the Reverend William Mason suggest that officers at York in the 1840s and 1850s were granted Wednesdays as holidays as well.[3] This extra day of rest was given in compensation for the longer hours of work officers put in during the winter months compared to tradesmen and labourers. Even if a four-day work week was not the practice year round at York, sanctioned holidays there may well have amounted to as much as one-third of the year by the mid-19th century.

In addition to their regular holidays, company men's work hours were not particularly onerous, and most had their evenings free, especially during the period when the factory operated on winter work hours. In addition, since work was seasonal and task-oriented, work patterns in the fur trade were marked by periods of intense effort followed by periods of reduced effort. For example, the time between the departure of the supply ship in early September until mid-October when winter work hours began was described as a "leisure season" during which York Factory residents "had [their] time entirely at [their] own disposal."[4] While this comment undoubtedly exaggerates the freedom of choice company men exercised during this time of the year, many managed to appropriate for themselves unsanctioned leisure time since much of the work of the post could not be supervised directly by officers.

Company employees in the 18th century probably had less leisure time than workingmen in Britain. It has been estimated that in pre-industrial Britain as much as "one day in three was a holiday of some kind."[5] By the 19th century, however, the extensive calendar of religious feast days and other traditional holidays had been "considerably pruned, both by employers and the church" until in the 1830s in England only Sundays and eight statutory half-holidays remained.[6] In Britain a Saturday half-holiday was gradually re-introduced, but as late as the 1870s many English workers had not secured a five-and-a-half-day work week.[7] It is somewhat ironic that fur trade employees appreciably expanded their leisure time at the same time as workers in Britain saw their leisure time eroded.

Leisure was an important part of life at York Factory and any attempt to reconstruct company employees' way of life needs to consider how they used their leisure time.

Competitive sports did not play a particularly large role in the leisure activities of company men, but some sports were played at York Factory. The most frequently mentioned sport at York was football, which one author described as the "national game of the North-West."[8] Football was played as early as New Year's Day 1734 at Prince of Wales's Fort at Churchill,[9] and the game remained a frequent part of the Christmas–New Year's holiday season at the bayside posts throughout the 18th and early 19th centuries. At York Factory it was not mentioned until 1776, but thereafter it was often described as part of the Christmas holiday celebrations until well into the 19th century.[10] In the 1840s post journals at York Factory stop mentioning football games, which may have become so commonplace that those who kept these journals did not bother to note them.[11]

The games at York were spirited affairs, though alcohol and frigid temperatures could stop even eager players. The journal entry for 25 December 1823 reads:

Ther 30 below Zero

Stormy weather as has been the usual custom at this place part of the Men and some of the Gentlemen turned out to a game of football which was not kept up with much spirit probably from the Severity of the Weather combined with a previous too free use of the Bottle....,[12]

Otherwise the games tended to be "warmly contested," as well they might be considering that on occasion prizes of substantial quantities of alcohol were offered to the victors: Chief Factor John George McTavish, for example, had put up a two-gallon keg of rum as a prize the previous Christmas.[13] Indeed, there was a close connection between football and drink at York, and some officers may have disapproved of it in consequence. In 1845 James Hargrave indicated that he only permitted a game of football as a reward for men's "moderate ... use of spirits" that Christmas.[14]

It is not clear under what rules, if any, the games were played. In Britain it was not until the late 19th century that football separated into its characteristic forms of soccer and rugby, and rules were codified. Until then there were as many versions of football as there were towns that played it. The only common characteristics were that it was played with some sort of ball, and it was violent and dangerous. A French observer remarked, while watching a football game in 1829, that "if Englishmen called this playing, it would be impossible to say what they would call fighting."[15]

As a large proportion of the participants in any game at York Factory were Orkneymen, their game probably resembled that played at Kirkwall on New Year's Day.

Regularly as the day [New Year's] recurs there is a gathering of the populace intent on preserving one curious and time-honoured custom from extinction. The game — which should have ended with the era of cockfighting — is virtually a trial of strength, of pushing and wrestling power between "up the street" and "down the street," the grand object of the belligerents being to propel the ball to one or the other end of town. Broad Street, where the struggle commences under the shadow of St. Magnus [Cathedral], becomes the centre of attraction about noon-tide. Sailors and porters arrive in formidable force from the purlieus of the harbour, tradesmen gather in groups, and even hoary-headed men, feeling the old glow of combative blood in their veins, hasten to the scene of anticipated contest. At one o'clock a signal pistol-shot is fired, the ball is tossed into the air from the steps of the old cross, and around it, soon as it bumps on the ground, there immediately gathers from all sides a dense and surging crowd. The wrestling and struggling mass sways hither and thither, sometimes revolving like a maëlstrom, and at others stationary in a grim deadlock. At intervals, the ball, as if flying for dear life, makes a spasmodic bound from the crowd; but a sudden headlong rush encloses it again, and so the struggle continues as before. For onlookers it is exciting to observe the fierce red-hot faces of the combatants, while the only appearance of good-humour displayed is a grim smile flickering fitfully across an upturned visage.... Heavy known-down blows, both foul and fair, are freely given and received. The struggle seldom lasts much longer than an hour, and when the seamen and porters win the day, they place the ball, as a trophy of conquest, on the top-mast of the largest ship in the harbour....[16]

Even if the numbers of participants were fewer at York Factory, the game would have been as boisterous and exciting, and may well have been a useful safety-valve for social tensions. Discipline in the fur trade was often physical, and company servants had little choice but to submit. When the officers joined football games it gave servants a chance to retaliate in a way that implied no threat to the structure of post society.[17]

Other than football games, few competitive sports are mentioned in post records. There are infrequent mentions of races at York Factory. In the summer of 1825 a race was held between "the Govrs New Boat and Montreal light Canoe eight men each win by the former a very near thing," and George Simpson McTavish described racing dog-drawn carrioles on frozen rivers at Christmas in the 1880s.[18] It was also customary to hold target-shooting competitions on St. Georges' Day, which Samuel Hearne, the explorer and company officer, noted served the dual purpose of sport and improving levels of marksmanship.[19]

Fights were mentioned quite frequently in York Factory journals but few were athletic contests. It has been suggested that after 1821 the champions of canoe brigades sought each other out upon their arrival at York Factory or Norway House to settle "the unofficial heavyweight championship" of the North-West, and some brigade champions like Paulet Paul achieved almost mythic fame as fighters.[20] Although some of Paul's most memorable battles ocurred at York Factory, York's residents themselves were at most spectators at these events. Boxing apparently appealed more to tripmen and sailors than to permanent company employees stationed at York whose fights were more brawls than sport.

Sedentary games had their devotees at York Factory. Whist was a popular card game among some officers. James Hargrave was "a good player" and a willing instructor of beginners, and William Mactavish was "a great whist player."[21] James Hargrave also played chess, and Donald Ross at Norway House thought enough of his talents to request "a few lessons from your right reverend wisdom on the subject."[22] Checkers were also popular, and amongst company servants "every apartment possesse[d] its well-thumbed pack of cards, its rude cribbage-board, and sets of wooden dominoes."[23]

Gambling, though rarely mentioned, would have been a part of many games. Much as officers criticized their native customers for gambling away their furs,[24] sport and recreation in Britain in the 18th and 19th centuries were closely tied to betting. Company journals contain the odd reference to gambling games like dice, and Ten Shilling Creek reportedly got its name from a wager.[25] Two York residents attempted to set up raffles of their property as money-making schemes, but neither raffle produced the desired result. In one case a watch was put up as the prize but several participants did not pay and James Hargrave refused to pursue the defaulters.[26] The second proposed raffle never got off the ground. Hargrave refused to allow a retiring officer to raffle his gun among the men, apparently on the grounds that it was unseemly for an officer to try to raise money by such an expedient.[27]

Hunting and fishing were both recreations and work at York Factory. For much of the 18th century, provisions, not recreation, were the main object of hunting and fishing which were usually treated as work activities. There was little sport in hiding immobile for hours on end on frozen marshes waiting to shoot geese or in setting nets under river ice. In the 18th century when company men did engage in hunting and trapping outside of work hours it was usually to acquire furs, which were either kept for personal use or traded to the company as a means of supplementing income.

The company itself did little to encourage trapping by its employees since it was felt the activity often led to private or illicit trade. Company officers and men often traded furs with ships' captains on their own account, and a thriving contraband trade in furs was well established by the mid-18th century. In 1770 the salaries of officers in charge of posts were raised and bonuses offered on the total volume of trade to discourage this illicit trade, and in 1825 most of the direct economic incentive for private trapping was removed when the company decreed that employees' furs would be purchased at rates no higher than the Indian standard.[28] In addition, employees wishing to procure furs for their own use after 1841 had to pay prices equivalent to the highest prices paid for prime furs of the same type at the London fur auctions.[29] Still, George Simpson McTavish mentioned that junior clerks found the few extra pounds they could earn trapping were welcome additions to their slim budgets.[30] Others, like William Mactavish, used the money they received from trapping for more altruistic purposes. He simply turned in the furs he trapped and requested that their value be set aside to support needy Indians.[31]

Hunting, like trapping, became in the 19th century more a spare-time activity of officers than of tradesmen or labourers. While hunting for provisions remained an important work activity, it was also viewed as valuable exercise. Officers were encouraged to hunt "for the sake of their health," though undoubtedly many simply enjoyed the activity.[32] The exercise entailed in hunting was simply an added attraction to the thrill of the chase, and few officers hunted animals that did not provide adequate sport.[33]

In the case of fishing the distinction between fishing as work and fishing as recreation seems to have been based on technique. Most of the fish used as provisions at York were caught using nets, scarcely a sporting proposition. Angling for fish, however, was a different matter. Although it was not mentioned in post records as often as hunting or trapping, some York residents were avid fishermen. Once again most were officers — especially senior officers who could take time off work without risk of censure and who could arrange the necessary boats and crews to transport themselves to favoured fishing spots like Ten Shilling Creek. It was also senior officers who could afford the elaborate equipment of rods, reels, and flies that

13 The duck hunter. Warehouse shelves at York Factory were recently found to include several painted boards, probably executed in the late 18th century. Now restored, they offer lively pictures of everyday life at the post.

gentleman followers of Izaak Walton required.[34] The object of most sport fishing at York was the speckled trout found in Ten Shilling Creek, but which George Simpson McTavish revealed did not always behave in a sporting fashion.

At some point in the 1880s McTavish was talked into fishing with Chief Factor Fortescue.

> *Mr. Fortescue had a beautiful imported rod, with fancy tackle, and a book of fly hooks that would have delighted an entomologist. I was very much afraid that I would have very little chance of catching anything against such a handicap, as my outfit consisted of a small sapling cut from the woods, a stout piece of cord, a large unadorned hook, and for bait a piece of salt pork.*

Despite his crude equipment McTavish immediately landed three or four trout, whereupon Fortescue attempted to teach him how to fish properly. On his first cast with Fortescue's rod he got a bite, causing Fortescue to demonstrate how to play the fish. McTavish returned to the use of his own gear while Fortescue struggled to land the trout.

> *When the time came for us to head for home, I had caught nineteen, and Mr. Fortescue one, showing that the trout, thank goodness, had not yet become civilized. They wanted no gaudy attraction to stimulate their appetites. They were after the substance of a chunk of salt pork, and despised such small allurements as a colored figment of imagination in the shape of an imported fly.[35]*

Snowshoeing was enjoyed as both a pleasant form of exercise and as a necessary adjunct to winter hunting. R.M. Ballantyne's descriptions of "rambles" on snowshoes leave a strong impression of the pleasure young officers derived from this pastime, although much of their enjoyment came from the accidents that befell beginners.[36] Canoeing and boating were also seen as enjoyable diversions, though not, one suspects, by those who earned their livings in such craft. York Factory records also include a few references to skating, usually in concert with reports of injury.[37] The risks attached to skating on uneven river ice with skate blades that were strapped onto shoes or boots must have been considerable, and it is unlikely it ever attracted more than a handful of participants at York. As one York resident wrote,

> *As to skating here it is but very poor for we only had a week or so of it in the fall of the year & that was far from being good as the Ice was by no means so smooth as the polished surface of a mirr[or] so that I enjoyed but little of it.[38]*

Swimming was also mentioned when it resulted in some misadventure. Unlike skating, however, bathing accidents were mortal. Two girls drowned while swimming in 1799:

> *About noon several young Women who had been in the habbits of bathing in the River two of whom unfortunately drowned in sight of the Parents and Relations about 100 yards distant above the Factory — Every exertion was made by our People to save them, but arrived too late to afford them any assistance. However one was picked up, about an hour afterwards and every means was used as prescribed the the Human Society for restoring to Life — but without the least Symtom of Effect.[39]*

In 1821 an employee named Haldane Snodie also

met with [an] untimely end by going into the river to relive himself
from the extreme heat of the weather, he unfortunately gote out of
his deepth, and is supposed was seized by the cramp; he immedi-
ately sunk to the bottom and appeared no more.[40]

Swimming, skating, hunting, fishing, trapping, snowshoeing, and boating all provided residents of York with opportunities for recreation. Although in some cases it is hard to separate recreation from work, the lakes, rivers, and woods around York offered fur traders considerable scope for leisure activities. However, not all of the diversions of fur trade life depended on these natural resources or on active physical activities. Leisure at York had a more intellectual side as well.

Despite their isolation many traders attempted to keep abreast of the political news of the day, and they were not unaware of at least some current academic debates. Visitors were often astonished by the range and number of books available at posts and by the eagerness with which traders took up intellectual questions.[41] Many had distinctly scholarly tastes. Samuel Hearne, for example, was a religious sceptic who drew his beliefs from Voltaire's *Philosophical Dictionary*.[42] James Hargrave read translations of Homer, Euripedes, Herodotus, and Livy.[43] Indeed, the oldest book collected from the York and Moose Factory libraries in 1924 was a Latin copy of the *Epistles of Pliny the Younger* dated 1678.[44] Nor were such intellectual tastes only exhibited by remarkable individuals. Reading, conversation, debate, and in some cases writing were regular parts of fur trade life and came to be shared by all levels of company employees, though not all subjects were discussed with equal eagerness. The Reverend J.P. Gardiner noted in 1861 that the men at York Factory were "willing to talk on any subject — science, politics — anything rather than practical Christianity."[45]

Opinions on political questions appear frequently in letters and journals. Donald Ross at Norway House particularly enjoyed discussing political events with James Hargrave. Both Ross and Hargrave rejected radical political reform, but supported more moderate democratic changes. Ross, for example, suspected that the British Parliamentary Reform Act of 1832 had been carried by unlawful means, but that on this occasion the ends justified the means.[46] Hargrave, for his part, found his enjoyment of "Alison's History of Europe during the French Revolutionary War" marred because it was "a little too *Tory* for me in its politics."[47] Of course political opinion varied, and Governor Simpson for one suspected most company officers, unlike Ross and Hargrave, were prone to "narrow ... illiberal ideas."[48]

Given their great interest in politics and the affairs of the outside world, news in any form was eagerly sought. Newspapers were sent annually from

England and Scotland to posts and individual subscribers. News could then be shared either by distilling the essence of the papers' contents into letters sent to friends or actually shipping the newspapers on to others. York's position as the central depot meant that it also acted as a distribution centre for news and newspapers throughout the North-West.[49] Employees there were fortunate; they do not seem to have had the kind of longing for news that led a trader in the Mackenzie District to mourn: "I am as usually the case with me in this miserable and distant part of the country, a bankrupt for news of any kind. Where My friend shall I glean any? from Indians, animals or Fowls of the air."[50]

When James Hargrave was a clerk he spent much of the "leisure season" — between the departure of the supply ship and the onset of winter — reading his way through the piles of newspapers, magazines, and books the ship had delivered to York.

> *Many of these are Scotch papers, and my evenings are now chiefly spent in perusing them. With such amusement this period is indeed the pleasantest season of the year with me. With an armfull of them by my side on a chair, I tumble myself down on a sopha or across my bed, and in a short time, transported in spirit to the Cacton [Calton] Hill of 'Auld Reekie' or imagining myself Saundering about the Blue-berry covered Hill of Galashields I soon lose all thought of the Land of forest and flood through which my present pilgrimage runs.[51]*

Like newspapers and magazines, books were widely available at York Factory and many residents were avid readers and collectors. The company itself sent books to its posts as part of its long-held desire "to promote Virtue and discourage Vice." In the 18th century this generally meant prayer books, Bibles, collections of sermons, technical treatises on navigation, and in 1794, "Primers and Spelling Books" to teach employee's children.[52] Small collections of books were carried on post inventories as company property, but the sort of books provided suggest they were sent to York with practical and moral purposes in mind rather than as a recreational resource.

Private book collections were more common and included more diverse materials. These collections varied in size from a few volumes to Joseph Colen's large personal library of 1400 volumes.[53] Company records from the late 18th century on include many individual's private book orders. Most were similar to the following requests:

> *Mr. William Moore — The works of Josephus and the new Edition of Harris's Voyages*

> *Peter Fidler — Heath's Royal Navigation or Astronomen*
>   *Accuratia*
> *David Thompson — Robertson's Elements of Navigation,*
>   *the last Edition in two Volumes.*[54]

These choices were not exactly frivolous and suggest self-improvement was a major motivation in fur trade reading habits. Works of fiction or poetry were not entirely ignored though. David Thompson purchased *Paradise Lost* in 1792, and Peter Fidler, another surveyor and explorer, brought Mrs. Radcliffe's gothic thriller *The Mysteries of Udolpho* in 1795.[55]

Nineteenth-century book orders give some idea of the eclectic tastes of fur trade readers. In 1841 James Hargrave, for example, ordered "Rose's Translation of Orlanda Furiosa, Percy's Relics of Antient English Poetry, Washington Irving's Astoria, Cowpers Translation of the Illiad & Odyssy, The Subaltern, Bracebridge Hall, Arabian History, Translations of Euripedes, Herodotus and Levy [*sic*]."[56] Hargrave's reading tastes were more elevated than most. Donald Ross, who enjoyed discussing books with Hargrave, described his purchases of reading material in 1833:

> *you wish to tantalise me with the prospect of having a peep into your Book Case — but I meant to have played you a nice trick on the same score last fall when I desired that you would examine the condition of my box from home, that package contained a variety of fine things — such as* Logan's Highlands & Highlanders — *Hoods* Comic Annual, Friendships Offering, *the* Literary Souvenir, *the* Penny Magazine, *the* Saturday Magazine, *the* Penny Cyclopedia, *the* Olio, *the* Mirror, *the* Literary Gazette *and the* Atlas; *What a feast for a hungry book worm? — next year if my letters get home I expect in addition to the continuation of these — the whole of* Sir Watty's *[Walter Scott's]* Novels — *besides other such fineries such as* Robinson Crusoe *and the* Pilgrim's Progress. *— ... I dare say you will think it altogether a strange selection — but I have already got a good stock of standard works — to resort to when I am in the mood — .*[57]

Ross admitted his taste was for "light reading," but suggested that his reading choices were philosophically sound — at least according to Benthamite Utilitarianism:

> *a man should regulate his reading much in the same manner as he does his other appetites and propensities — by enjoying that which affords him the greatest share of satisfaction, providing that its tendency is not to injure himself or any one else —.*[58]

The book-collecting habits of tradesmen and labourers are more difficult to describe since there are so few references to their owning or ordering books. The Reverend Gardiner attempted in 1859 to provide all new recruits to the fur trade with Bibles and prayer books during their stays at York Factory. He discovered that one in four had a Bible already, but none had prayer books.[59] Bibles were probably relatively common but other books that were owned by company servants are largely unknown. Tradesmen and labourers at York were often literate, and a few tantalizing clues as to their book-buying and reading habits can be found. Joseph Colen for example, complained in 1792 that the men at York had read Edward Umfreville's *Present State of Hudson Bay*, and under its influence they "bid difiance [*sic*] to all order" in the belief that the company had no power to fine them or regulate their conduct.[60] The book order of William Drever, a carpenter at York in 1834, also survives. Drever requested the following volumes:

1 Copy Housepainter & Colourman's Guide } *By P.F. Fingay*
1 Do The Varnishers Guide
1 Do the Cabinet Makers Do By G.A. Siddons
1 Do The Builders Practical Do } *By John Nicholson*
1 Do The Millwrights Do } *Esq. Civil Engineer*
1 Do The Young Mans Book of Knowledge
1 Do The Cottagers of Glenburniel
1 Do The Cottagers on the Cliff
1 Do The Sequel to Ditto[61]

Like those of company officers, his reading tastes were shaped largely by a desire for self-improvement but not exclusively so, as his purchase of novels indicates.

Of greater significance in bringing reading material to all sections of post society was the development of subscription libraries. The first organized collection of books in the North-West for which the title library is warranted was probably the library established at Red River about 1816. It consisted of 200 volumes in 1822, to which Peter Fidler's collection of some 500 volumes was added when he died in December 1822.[62] This library was largely based on company and individual philanthropy, but most post libraries followed a different pattern.

The model for these libraries was the library at Fort Vancouver. A collection of technical volumes on subjects like gunnery and law had existed at Fort Vancouver from at least 1825, but Dr. William Tolmie, who had been sent to Fort McLoughlin in the Columbia District in 1833, raised the idea of creating a subscription library. After Tolmie discussed the scheme with fellow clerks and Chief Factor McLoughlin, "a circulating library of papers, magazines, and some books" was established in 1836.[63]

The library was kept at a central location, Fort Vancouver, but included subscribers from small subsidiary posts who sent for the material they wanted and returned it when convenient. Once a year subscribers met to order books, magazines, and newspapers for the following year. The order was sent by canoe to York and then on to London, where the company secretary placed the order with London book dealers. The following year the material was shipped back to Fort Vancouver, and the account of the "Columbia Library" was debited. The idea proved to be popular. It spread first to the Mackenzie District in the 1840s and then in the 1850s to York and Moose Factories.

The initial meeting to establish a library at York Factory was held on 18 February 1856. "A sufficient sum to purchase 200 vols was at once subscribed and Laws & regulations were made — Mr Clare — Dr Beddome — Mr Anderson, Mr Watson and myself [William Mason] were present."[64] The other officers at York also supported the plan, donating money and promising to subscribe.

York Factory's officers were the library's first supporters, but it was intended to serve the entire community. Mason felt it would be "a great blessing to the Establishment when carried out upon sound principles and I sincerely hope it will succeed and prosper — The present inmates are much given to reading & I only wish I had my books which were left at Red River Settlement to lend to them."[65] The library was opened on 1 November 1856 "for the benefit of all classes." Mason, for one, "was pleased to see many of the servants enter their names as annual subscribers of 5s/– & some 10s'–. May it be the means of creating a thirst for the knowledge of eternal things."[66] Knowledge of eternal things was certainly procurable in the library, which consisted of 133 volumes in addition to a number of publications from the Religious Tract Society.[67]

From these small beginnings a large and popular institution developed that served not only York but also its outposts. When George Simpson McTavish described the library in the late 1880s it probably resembled the library of the 1850s and 1860s in most respects aside from size.

> *York Factory was fortunate in having a goodly collection of books, amounting to nineteen hundred volumes when I left in 1889.... The duty of librarian fell to the apprentice clerk for more reasons than one, the chief however being that the ten shillings fee, otherwise to be paid from his first year's salary of twenty pounds, was allowed for his services, and meant much to him. The higher officers paid*

one pound, the clerks ten shillings and the mechanics and labourers five shillings annually, the same rate applying ... to post managers and men in the district and adjoining ones. The books covered many fields of knowledge, selection being made from catalogues received from London by the ship, at an annual meeting, held prior to the departure of the Winter packet which carried the next year's order to England via Winnipeg. The men had a representative, but dependence was placed almost entirely on the officers, who tried to get the best, and most for the available funds.[68]

The available funds were used first of all to bring collections of popular periodicals like *Punch* or *Chamber's Journal* up to date and to add to series of popular 19th-century writers. Adventure stories were purchased for the men, but officers took care to ensure that "no trash" was acquired, feeling they "could not afford to get worthless books."[69]

The library was opened on Saturday nights, officially for one hour after the ringing of the post bell signalled the end of the workday, but in practice until everyone had searched the shelves for his week's selection of reading material. The library was in disarray when McTavish took responsibility for it, previous librarians having neglected to keep good records of its holdings or the locations of books loaned out. Clearly, however, it was not simply a large collection of books, but an organized library for which books and periodicals were systematically collected.[70]

Surviving catalogues of fur trade libraries give some indication of the holdings of York's library and thus of its subscribers' reading tastes. Post libraries contained some reference works such as encyclopedias, dictionaries, Bartlett's *Familiar Quotations*, and so on. Magazines like *Punch*, *Chamber's Journal*, *Cornhill Magazine*, and the *Monthly Review* were common. Histories, mainly ancient, military, and British, formed a large part of the collections, along with a fair amount of religious material — primarily tracts and biographies. Works on natural history, science, travel, and exploration were also represented. However, the bulk of the collections was literary: Shakespearean drama, the poetry of Burns, Byron, Longfellow, and Tennyson; and novels by Scott, Dickens, Disraeli, Bulwer-Lytton, Thackeray, Trollope, and Stevenson.[71] Reading tastes at York Factory did not differ much from those in Britain.

Library holdings were quite conventional, reflecting the control over the operation of libraries exerted by missionaries and company officers. Officers had a disproportionate influence on the selection of books, they managed the library, and they, along with William Mason, provided the impetus to establish a library as well. What was different about the library at York Factory was the attempt to attract subscribers from amongst the tradesmen and labourers through special lower subscription fees and the purchase of books designed to appeal to non-officers. The Mackenzie District Library by contrast charged £1 to join it and a yearly subscription fee of £1.[72] At these rates most labourers and apprentices would have been hard pressed to join.

William Mason clearly thought that one of the great advantages of including tradesmen and labourers in the library scheme was that it provided yet another means of encouraging religious knowledge and, perhaps, belief. The London committee and company officers promoted the library and encouraged reading as a recreation as a means of "civilizing" the men's recreations. It provided in their eyes a more desirable recreational alternative to the cruder pleasures of drink, gambling, or fighting. The opinions of company servants on all this interest in their moral and personal improvement are unrecorded; most were probably quite happy, though, to have access to a library.

While many spent their leisure hours reading, some residents of York turned to writing. The literature of travel and exploration owes a lot to XY, North West, and Hudson's Bay Company employees, many of whom lived and worked for at least portions of their careers at York. James Isham, Andrew Graham, Joseph Robson, Henry Kelsey, Anthony Henday, David Thompson, and Edward Umfreville were all authors who lived for a time at York. In the 19th century two residents of York became published authors, one of poetry and the other of adventure novels. However, their residence at York and their use of their fur trade experiences as inspiration are about the only parallels in their writing careers.

Dr. William Smellie, the surgeon at York Factory from 1845 to 1849, produced a volume of poetry that was published in 1855. Smellie used the unlikely nom de plume of "The Scald," perhaps attempting to cast himself and his poems in the mould of the heroic tales told by Old Norse poets. Entitled *The Sea; Sketches of a Voyage to Hudson's Bay; and Other Poems*, Smellie's book contains what one hopes is the only attempt to describe arriving at York Factory in rhyming couplets.

> *A Mongrel crew they were as e'er pulled o'er*
> *In boat of six from any stranger shore —*
> *Canadians, Metifs, Crees, Hebridean Gaels,*
> *And wandering natives of Orcadian dales.*
> *The Indian garb those motley settlers wear,*
> *Gaudy yet homely, makes a stranger stare;*

The garnished mocassin of tawdry show,
The scarlet sash, and moose or grey capot,
With ornamental work for various needs,
Tinsel of quills, and party coloured beads.[73]

Smellie admitted that "the poems now offered to the public have neither the charm of romantic narrative, nor the zest of humourous description, to recommend them to the general reader"; however, he hoped that they might afford some "gratification to more reflective minds." They had, after all, provided him with the pleasure "of the hours spent in dalliance with the Muse."[74]

Smellie apparently did not dally as profitably with his muse as Robert Michael Ballantyne did. Indeed, Ballantyne dallied a bit too much as his contributions to work at York Factory were not highly regarded. William Mactavish thought "it would have been a better joke, since they are determined to have a farce, to have sent out, either Mr. McKenzie's or Mr. Finlayson's coat and trowsers stuffed with straw" than Ballantyne.[75] Despite an undistinguished career as a clerk at York Factory, Fort Garry, and Tadoussac between 1841 and 1847, Ballantyne was to have a distinguished career as an author of boys' adventure novels. His novels *Ungava*, *The Young Fur Traders*, and *Hudson Bay* were all based on his experiences in the employ of the Hudson's Bay Company, although some fellow officers found them rather fanciful.[76] In these and other books set in equally exotic locales, Ballantyne offered his adoring public of Victorian schoolboys a heady mixture of morality, imperialism, and romantic adventure.

Intellectual life at York Factory was not limited to literary pursuits, and many developed interests in scientific pursuits. York Factory residents made significant contributions to scientific knowledge in several fields, most notably natural history and geography. In the 18th century, individuals like Thomas Hutchins and Andrew Graham provided considerable material for Thomas Pennant's *Arctic Zoology*, an early and most important work in the field. Henry Kelsey, Anthony Henday, and David Thompson were all important explorers, and Thompson's map-making and surveying skills are justly famous. By the 19th century York's residents made more modest contributions to knowledge, though a kind of amateur interest in natural history, astronomy, and other sciences remained strong. In addition company employees, partially on their own initiative and partially at the behest of the company and outside organizations like the Smithsonian Institution, Audubon Society, and Royal Society, collected meteorological data, geographical information, and innumerable natural history specimens.

Some personal research involved subjects on the fringes of respectable scientific opinion. William Mactavish and Dr. Tolmie for a time became interested in phrenology, which led Mactavish into making "himself acquainted with the notions of every one who has got into difficulties with Church or State for being too far in advance of the world."[77] It was, no doubt, good training for a future governor of Assiniboia.

Some experiments were more like pranks or parlour tricks, like shooting frozen balls of mercury through planks.[78] More serious experiments on the effects of cold temperatures were tried, including a test of the different freezing points of rum, brandy, and mercury in 1792.[79] Tests of the post's thermometers in 1836 indicated that they were not calibrated properly. The mercury in them only registered about 32 degrees below zero Fahrenheit when it began to freeze, not 40 below as it should have. As a result James Hargrave suspected that much of the meteorological data collected at York was not as accurate as it ought to have been.[80]

At about the same time, the permafrost layer at York was studied. A pit was dug into the permafrost, but after eleven days of labour with pickaxes and hatchets, digging was abandoned. It was decided to bore through the frozen ground instead.

> *The depth of the pit dug was 13-1/2 feet, 3 of which were through thawed ground on the surface, and the depth bored from the bottom of the Pit till they reached the unfrozen clay was 7 feet, making in all 20-1/2 feet from the surface to the bottom of the permanently frozen ground.... The Temperature of the thawed clay immediately below the frost, was ascertained to be 33° from two examinations of what was brought up by the Auger.... Wood at 9 feet, and a Musile shell at 13 feet from the surface were found in a state of perfect preservation.*[81]

The purpose of this experiment, aside from satisfying a vague curiosity, is unclear and it was not repeated.

Residents at York Factory had some interest in astronomical phenomena. In 1821 York boasted, in addition to a terrestial globe, "1 Celestial Globe 14 Inch diameter" and "1 Telescope with Stand complete."[82] Eclipses of both sun and moon were mentioned in the post journals,[83] but more as interesting and unusual occurrences than as the subjects of intense scientific interest. Nevertheless, the period of a lunar eclipse was closely noted,[84] and during a solar eclipse someone carefully observed that the temperature reading on the post thermometer dropped five degrees, from 9 to 14°F below zero.[85] The appearance of Halley's Comet in 1835 sparked considerable interest:

> *Halley's Comet ... was first noticed about 8 p.m. among the princi-*
> *pal stars in the Constellation of Ursa Major. In appearance it*
> *resembled a star of the first magnitude but less brilliant and*
> *surrounded by a pale halo, with a tail pointing in an easterly*
> *direction. This is stated by Astronomers to be its first appearance*
> *since 1759, as it requires 75-1/2 years to perform its full circuit. It*
> *is to be regretted that there are no instruments at the factory by*
> *which its altitude could be ascertained.*[86]

It was in the area of natural history that fur traders probably made their greatest scientific contributions. Virtually every fur trade author included a lengthy section on the flora and fauna of the North-West in his book, and post journals and correspondence are filled with observations on animal population and unusual behaviour, like partridges producing eggs in February or plover appearing before geese in the spring.[87] Some tried to tame animals and keep them as pets or domestic animals. The Hargraves, for example, kept a great horned owl in the nursery yard with their other pets: a large setter, a cat, and two Dandy Dinmonts.[88] On a grander scale, plans were made to domesticate caribou for use as draught animals on the winter road between York Factory and Norway House, but nothing came of the scheme.[89]

Attempts were also made to ship live specimens home. Smaller mammals like beaver could be shipped to England,[90] but large animals like buffalo proved to be exceedingly difficult to export. After years of failed attempts two buffalo were finally put on board ship in 1844 along with 26 hundredweight of hay as fodder.[91] It seems either that the buffalo survived, or that it was deemed too expensive to continue shipping them, since no further references were made to buffalo arriving at York for transport to England. Certainly previous attempts to ship buffalo from York had been dismal failures.

> *There are two unfortunate Buffaloes on their way to the ship,*
> *where as usual they will meet their doom. Two years ago there*
> *were 3, all of them were literally hunted to death. Wilson sent all*
> *the Indians & Orkney men to catch & put them on board the*
> *Schooner. Instead of enclosing them in a circle, the whole party*
> *chased them through the Fort till the poor creatures lay down. I*
> *never saw such a hunt, & no one attempted to enlighten the people.*
> *One died before it got on board the ship, the others immediately*
> *after. Next news was a lamentation from London on the difficulties*
> *of a sea voyage to these animals. The anchor had not been raised*
> *when they died. But of course we said nothing about their ex-*

periences on land. This year long instructions have come as to their treatment & provender. I daresay they will do, as at any rate Mr Wilson will not require to chase them, having each an immense log of wood tied to its collar, which it can scarcely move with. Every step they take they must drag this weight after them so that they will not run much.[92]

Collecting dead specimens presented fewer difficulties than shipping live animals. In most cases specimens were collected for individuals or institutions in Britain or the United States,[93] but some fur traders acquired their own collections.

Stuffing birds and animals became so popular that the Hudson's Bay Company had lengthy instructions for the proper procedures to follow written up and included in a notebook.[94] Birds and mammals were the most common specimens collected, but shells, eggs, plants, shrubs, bushes, and seeds were also shipped to Britain from York Factory.[95] Company employees at York found much to interest themselves and to enjoy in nature. They were amateurs, but their collecting activities and observations of natural phenomena were not without value both for scientists of the day and, in some instances, modern scholars.[96] Above all, the widespread interest in natural history and science, like the library, private book collections, and writers found at York Factory, indicates a more active intellectual culture than most have assumed existed at fur trade posts.

However, leisure at York Factory had a darker side. Alcohol caused serious social problems that affected the lives of officers and servants and interfered with the operations of the factory. While most of the attention to alcohol consumption in the fur trade has focussed on its impact on native peoples, the drinking habits of traders themselves are worthy of some scrutiny.

Excessive drinking created considerable social tension at York Factory. It led to dereliction of duty by both officers and men as well as to arguments and physical violence.[97] Social events were frequently marred by the effects of heavy drinking, and even church services were disrupted by drunken men on occasion.[98] Worst of all, it could result in accidents and deaths, and on rare occasions, theft, assault, and murder.[99] Care should be taken, however, not to overstate the problems caused by alcohol. Recent research on causes of mortality at York Factory indicates that alcoholism was not a major cause of death there during the period between 1714 and 1801.[100] Alcohol abuse was cited as the primary cause of death in only two cases during this period — a far cry from the notion that " 'Brandy-death' was common, and known in Rupert's Land as a Northwester's Death."[101]

Alcohol also served important functions at York and other company posts. It was a major item of trade, and it was used extensively to reward dangerous or demanding work and to mark achievements such as the shooting of the first goose of the year. It was an important part of most social gatherings as well as holidays and other celebrations, and while fur traders were not known for their moderation, not all celebrations degenerated into drunken revels.

A certain amount of alcohol was always shipped from England for consumption at posts, but individuals also imported their own personal stocks. Donald Ross, for example, earned Letitia Hargrave's censure by importing ten gallons of whiskey and ordering eight more gallons of brandy from York Factory for himself and his wife.[102] When alcohol was unavailable from England or post stocks, or cost more than some could afford, ingenious employees produced their own alcoholic potions. In the 1790s when war interrupted shipments from England, Joseph Colen assumed the role of distiller and produced supplies of spirits for the inland trade. In fact, he appears to have produced a kind of handbook on distilling for the company.[103] Company employees also tinkered with imported spirits to suit their tastes. Shrub, a drink usually made from rum mixed with orange or lemon juice and sugar, was particularly popular at York. In 1827, for example, 168-3/4 gallons of shrub were made up at York for consumption there.[104] Substandard liquor supplies from England were ingeniously doctored to make them more fit for consumption: "assisted the Coopers in starting the Bungs of the Porter Casks and putting therein some plumbs and fresh Hopes the whole of the Porter as it came from England not deserving Warehouse Room."[105]

Even before the union of the Hudson's Bay and North West companies, the importance of reducing the trade in alcohol with Indians had been discussed. Alcohol's baneful effects on fur traders themselves was also recognized. The first concerted efforts to reduce alcohol consumption in the North-West occurred at the time of the union of the companies and initially were directed at the Indian trade. The minutes of council for 1822 ordered that officers reduce the amount of alcohol given to natives as gifts by one-half and that the practice of trading furs for alcohol be abolished.[106] During the 1840s these regulations were further reinforced by a total ban on giving alcohol to natives as gifts or in trade at the bayside posts of Churchill, Severn, and York.[107] Soon attempts were made to extend controls to company employees. The standing rules and regulations established that no one in company service, whatever his rank, would be allowed to purchase more than two gallons of spirits and four gallons of wine from depot supplies in any given year.[108] In the 1850s such old company traditions as the regales of rum given to tripmen on arrival at York and on leaving the factory to return home came under attack. Despite resistance the regale was changed from a gift of rum to a gift of tea and sugar.[109] At the same time attempts to encourage voluntary temperance were gaining strength. From the 1830s, post journals began to mention that holiday celebrations were marked by moderation, and the men's decision not to consume all the alcohol they were allowed was noted with approval.[110] Although in 1841 it was decided to reduce presents of rum from one to one-half pint a day for major celebrations,[111] James Hargrave felt voluntary temperance showed even better results:

> *it is pleasing to observe that scarcely a single instance of intoxication was to be found among the whole party of upwards of thirty servants, and this marked improvement in their conduct has arisen from their being persuaded of the evil consequence of indulgence in regard to their healths, rather than from being restrained from purchasing. Scarcely any of them in course of the season having purchased one half of the quantity permitted them by council and the greater portion not more than one quarter.[112]*

Missionaries at York Factory also encouraged temperance. The Reverend Gardiner in particular made special exhortations every Christmas season on the subject, apparently without much effect.[113] According to his journals, Christmas festivities at York continued to rely heavily on alcohol into the 1860s[114] despite Hargrave's belief that drunkenness was declining.

Gardiner's teetotal principles may have made his judgement of drinking practices at York unnecessarily harsh. Certainly from at least the 1840s on, the heavy drinking traditions of fur trade society were under attack. Officers, missionaries, and the governor and committee of the Hudson's Bay Company all tried to alter drinking habits by regulation, example, or moral suasion. The campaign against excessive drinking in the fur trade paralleled a similar movement in Britain and relied on many of the same tactics. The fact that heavy drinking was under attack on both sides of the Atlantic underlines the need to compare drinking customs in the fur trade with practices elsewhere. Alcoholism and binge drinking were certainly problems at York, and large quantities of alcohol were consumed there. Indeed, drinking was one of the most common leisure pastimes in the fur trade. Company employees' drinking habits, nevertheless, were not unusual. In 18th- and 19th-century Britain alcohol consumption was also high and drunkenness was commonplace at all levels of society. As Samuel Johnson remarked, "all the decent people in Litchfield got drunk every night, and were not the worse thought of."[115] Compared to the London of "Gin Lane," where gin-sellers advertised their wares with the slogan "drunk for a penny, dead drunk for twopence, and straw for nothing," alcohol consumption at York seems rather modest. By the mid-19th century the temperance movement had succeeded in making drunkenness less respectable; still, as historian G.M. Trevelyan wrote, "when Queen Victoria died, drinking was still a great evil from the top to the bottom of society," though less so "than when she came to the throne."[116] Although it is sometimes noted that some company employees purchased ten or more gallons of spirits a year in the early 18th century,[117] this in fact translates into a weekly consumption rate of about one and a half pints, or 750 millilitres, of brandy or rum. Stated another way, this constitutes an average daily consumption of about 3.5 fluid ounces, or 110 millilitres, of spirits: slightly higher but roughly comparable to average rates of alcohol consumption in modern Canada.[118] Company employees also drank beer and wine, which would have increased their total alcohol intake, but from the mid-18th century on, their consumption of spirits probably fell. According to Andrew Graham, the fur trade author, by the 1760s "to prevent immoderate drinking no person is allowed to buy more than six gallons of English brandy per annum.... one quart at one time."[119] Later alcohol purchases were restricted still further, making it unlikely that the consumption rates of the early 18th century were ever reached again.

Company employees developed special holiday traditions that often served to underline the ties that bound the community together. During the early 1790s Guy Fawkes Day was generally celebrated as a holiday. The men were given time off during the day, and in the evening they had a large bonfire and fireworks. These amusements produced a horrifying accident in 1795:

> In the Evening the Men had a bondfire and were diverting themselves as usual when a mellancholly accident befel my nephew Thomas Colen, who had indiscreetly put a number of fire Works into his breast Pockets which took fire. — The consequences that ensued was dreadfull all his Cloaths were blown to pieces, and himself exhibited one of the most shocking spectacles I ever beheld, his body, hands, arms, neck, and face are dreadfully mutulated — part of the bones of his fingers, and Ribs are bare — [120]

Thomas Colen survived his injuries, but it seems Guy Fawkes celebrations did not, for York Factory journals make no further references to bonfires and fireworks on 5 November.

England's and Scotland's national days were also celebrated at York Factory. In the 1790s St. George's Day, 23 April, was generally marked by target shooting for prizes, but in 1797 it was abandoned due to the shortage of gunpowder and the custom seems to have been dropped.[121] By the mid-19th century, St. George's Day was only marked by an extra allowance of rum.[122] St. Andrew's Day, 30 November, was adopted as a holiday after the influx of Scots officers into Hudson's Bay Company service in 1821. The day was marked by an extra rum allowance and sometimes a dance in the evening, but the normal work of the post was carried on for at least part of the day.[123]

Significant events during the course of the year were also turned into holidays. Shiptime, in addition to being a time of hard work, was also a time of celebration. The departure of the ship for England was occasion for merry-making:

> *About noon [Captain Ball] embarked for the vessel accompanied by all the passengers, also Mr. Miles and myself who went on board to spend the day with them. After dining with them and demolishing nearly a dozen of the Old Boys wine, we bade them farewell and returned ashore with about a half dozen more bottles for amusement on the way. These, to tell the whole truth, were also near a close before we reached the Launch end; and having had a pretty strong breeze ahead on coming up the river, either that notion or the wine must still have been in our noodles when we got ashore, from the zig-zag course we made on steering up from the shore to the gate of the Fort. We however found that the gentlemen who had remained ashore were also improving the occasion as comfortably as we had been doing, — so to it we went again; and at this moment I have just made my retreat good, with just as much sober sense left me as to be able to sit down and add a few lines to my Journal.[124]*

Often the ship's departure was used as an occasion for balls, which the Reverend Gardiner noted with disapproval might last until three o'clock in the morning and which were "productive of much evil" in his eyes.[125] Even the arrival or departure of prominent company officials was used as an excuse for a dance on occasion.[126]

The Christmas holidays were the most important festivities at York Factory. They ran from Christmas Eve to New Year's Day, though on occasion their effects lingered on. In 1848 Robert Wilson sprained his ankle while dancing on Christmas Day and did not reappear at the officers' mess table until February. He was still limping from his injury at the end of

14 A Christmas dance in Batchelors' Hall in the 1840s is depicted in
R.M. Ballantyne's *Hudson Bay; or, Everyday Life in the
Wilds of North America.*
Hudson's Bay Company Archives, Provincial Archives of Manitoba.

March.[127] Wilson's case was an extreme one, and most had recovered health
and sobriety within a day or two.

The holiday season was marked by unusual indulgence in more than just
alcohol. It was an occasion for football, hunting excursions, dances, over-
eating, pranks, and horseplay. According to R.M. Ballantyne's description
of Christmas at York Factory, the day began in "Bachelors' Hall," the
residence of unmarried officers, with pillow fights, people being locked into
rooms, and other such boyish amusements.[128] Games and pranks and hunting expeditions were only preliminaries to the real business of the day:

Christmas dinner and then a ball. New Year's Eve was celebrated in much the same way. Extra food rations were always handed out to the men on Christmas Eve and again at New Year's. Depending upon the state of supplies, foods might vary, but the list for 1829 is not untypical: "1/2 lbs Raisins, 1/4 lb Butter, 1/8 lbs Tea, 2 lbs Sugar, 2 lbs Grease, 1 lb Flour, 1 lb Salt Pork, 1-1/2 lb Fresh Do., 1 fresh Goose, 1 Rabbit, 1 pint Rum and 1/2 pint molasses. — And the same extra allowce. will likewise be delivered to them new year's day."[129] With these supplies company servants could produce reasonable facsimiles of traditional British Christmas dinners, including pudding and roast goose, though rabbit apparently had to replace vegetables. Officers enjoyed even more lavish fare with roast goose and beef, salt pork, partridges, and port and Madeira wine.[130]

After the dinner it was customary for a dance to be held that attracted the entire community of York Factory — officers and men, their families, and the Homeguard Cree. The balls were exciting events. Music was usually provided by fiddlers, and the dances were mostly Scottish reels at which the Indian women were not particularly accomplished, but which they enjoyed immensely. An interesting feature of the balls was the tradition that developed of company employees lining up to be kissed in turn by all the Indian women present.[131]

Not everyone found equal enjoyment at these dances. Letitia Hargrave was an infrequent participant, finding post balls "humbling" affairs at which

> *40 squaws old and young with their hair plaited in long tails, nothing on their heads but their ever-lasting blankets smelling of smoke and everything obnoxious. Babies almost newly born & in their cradles were with their mothers & all nursing them in the face of everyone....*[132]

If Letitia Hargrave was offended by the behaviour of Indian women, the Reverend Gardiner was distressed by the alcohol consumption, sexual promiscuity, and late hours. In 1858 he refused to allow his servant to go to the New Year's Eve ball. She defied him and went anyway. He refused to have her back so she went to live with the Homeguard Cree across the river where, according to Gardiner, she supported herself as a "common prostitute."[133] Gardiner also worried about the pressure the balls exerted on the suggestible to slip from the path of virtue: peer pressure often encouraged drunkenness and other excesses.[134] Gardiner seems, however, to have reserved a particular dislike for the balls' impact on his domestic arrangements:

> *The festivities of the season end to day & I am really glad of it. We have not been able to sleep any night since Christmas day till*

15 *Opposite* and **16** *above*   The fiddler and dancers.

about four o clock in the morning. The dances are held in the carpenter's shop & we can hear the dancing as plain as if it was only next door: & all night long some intoxicated persons were walking past the house, one night while we were taking supper two fell against our front door, the door burst open & the two men fell inside. It is very painful to witness so much immorality....[135]

In addition to a dance and the traditional football game, New Year's Day was celebrated by a salute with firearms and visiting around the post.

Early in the morning the clerks visit the gentlemen in charge, & each gets a tumbler full of "Old man's milk" a punch made of equal parts of Brandy & milk with spices &c — the gentleman in Charge then meets all the servants in the Carpenter's shop & gives two glasses of Brandy or wine to each the servants go out & the Indians are then received first the men then the women & these also get two glasses of spirits — the servants then visit the clerks & each house in the Fort & the Clerks visit each of the men & this visiting goes on till 4 oclock in the after noon & sometimes till late in the evening, each giving the other grog.[136]

Such activities served to reinforce the communal ties of post society, and despite Gardiner's disapproval, served an important social function beyond mere diversion.

The historian Joseph Strutt suggested in 1801 that in order to form a true impression of people it is necessary to examine them at play as well as at work.[137] The study of leisure activities at fur trade posts like York Factory reveals a hitherto largely unsuspected side of fur trade life. It was not a life of uninterrupted toil, and company employees enjoyed a wide variety of intellectual, sporting, and recreational pursuits. These pursuits were generally similar to leisure activities in 18th- and 19th-century Britain, and like popular recreation there, helped to dissipate social tension and underline social cohesiveness, as well as providing considerable pleasure.

Accidents, Disease, and Medical Care

Perceptions of the risks to one's health entailed in a career in the Hudson's Bay Company's service varied greatly. Samuel Hearne described Prince of Wales's Fort, York's close neighbour on the bay, as "the healthiest part in the known world."[1] York Factory, on the other hand, never received the same sort of testimonial. Some even suspected that York was "unfavourable to the constitution of its inhabitants."[2]

It is difficult to judge the accuracy of such subjective opinions. There are no general surveys of mortality rates — the standard test of health conditions in a community — in the fur trade. As a result it may well be that York Factory was less healthy a settlement than many other fur trade posts. This does not mean, however, that the fur trade was particularly risky as a career.

A recent study has indicated that at York Factory between 1714 and 1801, 64 company employees died while stationed there. It has been estimated that the death rate at York for this period was about 0.015 persons per year. This mortality rate compares favourably with mortality rates among young adult males in other colonial communities such as 18th-century Massachusetts, where the mortality rate for men between the ages of about 20 and 40 years has been computed at 0.03 persons per year.[3] Unfortunately, population mobility and other problems preclude establishing meaningful mortality rates for the 19th-century population of York.

Nevertheless, there is no compelling evidence to suggest that health risks at York Factory increased significantly for the largely European population of company employees working there in the 19th century. The same is not necessarily true for the population of native people in the York Factory area. Beginning with the smallpox epidemic of 1781-82, the Cree had their numbers seriously depleted by the epidemic and infectious diseases inadvertently introduced among them by contact with whites. In general though it would appear that while mortality rates among company employees at York were considerably higher than modern mortality rates in Canada, they were not unusually high either for other colonial communities or for 18th- and early-19th-century Britain for that matter.[4]

For company employees, accidents were probably the single most common cause of death. Most accidental deaths were caused by drowning, which was the most serious occupational hazard in the fur trade.[5] A few drownings occurred as a result of swimming, but most were work accidents. Unpredictable weather and dangerous shoals made the area around the mouth of the Hayes River on Hudson Bay hazardous, and travel on the rivers around York required caution as well.

There were other hazards at York too. Individuals who became lost were in some danger. John Smith, a sailor, died of exposure in the fall of 1791 after being stranded in a boat accident. Although safe on shore, he was unable to find his way to the factory, and the following spring his waistcoat and pocketknife were found in a small stand of trees about 18 miles from the factory.[6] Most experienced employees travelled properly prepared and had acquired some knowledge of woodcraft. They recognized the warning signs of frostbite,[7] made sure they were properly clothed, and at least knew that if they did become lost within earshot of the post, the ringing of the factory bell would lead them home. Inexperienced men were in the most danger and were most likely to venture out in bad weather or without proper clothing and equipment.[8]

James McDonald, a new recruit in 1858, paid a heavy price for his inexperience:

> he had been sent with our lumbering party to some distance from the Factory ... and a few weeks after arriving at their wintering grounds lost himself in the woods, and, although a diligent search was made for him by his companions, it was not 'till seven days after that he was found starving and severely frozen; ... Dr. McLeod immediately started to render what assistance might be in his power, I regret to say on the doctor's return he reported that he had been obliged to Amputate both feet....[9]

Even experienced hands with considerable knowledge of woodcraft could fall victim to bad luck and perhaps personal recklessness.

> It is with much pain that I have to mention this day the loss of poor Nepinawasis, an Indian lad retained at the Factory as an Assistant

Dog-Driver and hunter during the Winter. After his arrival last Eveng. as above noted, he spent the night in dancg. and amusements among his companions and it was not till this Morning about sunrise that he was found absent from his usual quarters. On searching, however, his body was found on the outside of the Fort Pickets perfectly lifeless and hard frozen, among the Snow. It would seem that he had gone out on some necessary occasion, and being as I am now informed Subject to epileptic fits, there is every reason for thinking that he had been seized with one, and so sank down, unfortunately in a place where there was little chance of his being found in time to save his life. — The people say that he had been drinking, but was far from being helplessly intoxicated.[10]

York Factory, like most fur trade posts, was built almost entirely from wood, and fire was a very real danger there. On several occasions forest fires threatened the factory, some caused by human carelessness and others by violent thunderstorms. Thunderstorms in 1802, for example, set the woods on fire across the river from York,[11] and a bolt of lightning struck the mainmast of the post's brig, *The Beaver*. It shattered the mast and threw captain and crew to the deck "as if they had been Electrified." Luckily they recovered their senses in time to put out the fire the lightning caused.[12]

York Factory also had several fires in the factory itself. Most were chimney fires, and only rarely did a fire burn out of control as in 1822 when the carpenter's shop burned down.[13] The success York residents had in controlling the threat of fire can be attributed to several sensible precautionary measures. The substitution of stoves for open fireplaces and the regular sweeping of chimneys and stovepipes in the early 19th century lessened the risk of fire. Gunpowder was stored away from other buildings in a specially constructed magazine, and cookrooms and workshops where fires were necessary were separated from other buildings. Nevertheless, fire remained a serious concern. After Fort Pelly burned to the ground in 1843, Letitia Hargrave remarked that her husband was liable to "kill himself with fear for York" lest the same thing happen there.[14]

Some of the work at York was hazardous as well. Hunting accidents and injuries sustained cutting timber and firewood occurred with some regularity. Few were fatal, however, and most victims, if they survived the initial accident, were successfully treated by post surgeons whose surgical skills were more than adequate for stitching and dressing wounds or amputating fingers or toes in more serious cases. However, problems could arise if complications set in, and William Bakie died in 1801 when, after badly cutting himself with a hatchet, he came down with scurvy as well.[15]

Often these accidents were the result of carelessness or foolhardy behaviour, as in the case of a post sawyer who froze his fingers badly enough that one had to be amputated. According to the journal entry the poor man lost his finger because he "would persevere to work at the pitsaw with naked hands while the Therms. stood at -28 to demonstrate to his comrades how hardy he was."[16] Other accidents were simply freakish and attributable more to bad luck than error. One man, for example, was killed when he put an old gun barrel that unfortunately still contained powder into the blacksmith's forge to rework the metal.[17]

While accidents were the major cause of death and injury, they were accepted as an inevitable hazard of life and do not appear to have caused an unusually high mortality rate at York. The perception that life at York was "unfavourable to the constitution of its inhabitants" rested not on the risk of drowning or slicing one's foot open with an axe, but on the chance of illness. Although post records are often vague about identifying diseases and symptoms were only imperfectly recorded, a brief descriptive account of the incidence of disease and its treatment is possible.

Some illness at York appears to have been primarily psychological. William Mactavish, for example, appears to have been prone to depression. His responsibilities as the post accountant were unusually heavy. The prospect of keeping York's voluminous account books straight was enough, he confessed, to produce "a fit of the Blue Devils of about 6 weeks duration" during which he had "not energy enough to copy them."[18] According to Letitia Hargrave, his health suffered every year after the ship sailed: "Willie was much longer in getting well after the ship sailed than usual. Indeed it is only within the last 3 weeks that he has been able to eat."[19]

William Mactavish's depressions were less tragic in their consequences than in the case of a labourer David Harvey. Harvey accidentally shot and killed the son of Samuel Grey, a fisherman, in 1850.

> *The unfortunate man [Harvey] ... had neither eaten nor apparently slept since, — and appeared to be sunk in such a state of Melancholy — He was accordingly ordered to be removed from the house where it happened and placed along with some of his most intimate friends by means of whose conversation it was hoped that he might recover from the Mental agony under which he evidently suffered. — This course seemed to be producing its effects as he began to converse, and at the hour of dinner today, he told them that he intended to take a walk. — A short time afterwards however, his Capot, Vest, Belt, and Gloves, were discovered alongside the Water Hole on the River, and as he was found missing it was*

*evident that he had watched his opportunity when the people were
absent from the Plantation and had destroyed himself by drowning.
He had apparently had this object ... on his mind for some time; for
during the Forenoon he is now said to have repeatedly asked
whether the dinner hour was near; but most unhappily without
exciting any suspicion of his purpose.*[20]

On occasion someone at York became so violent that some form of
restraint was needed. In the 18th century this usually meant being chained
to one's bed. Such treatment often worked since some employees who were
declared insane seem actually to have been suffering from delirium tre-
mens.[21] In 1793 an even more sophisticated means of restraining those who
threatened violence became available when some "straight waistcoats" were
sent to York from London.[22] On at least one occasion, however, physical
restraint could not be used because the insane man was an officer and thus
a "gentleman." The structure of fur trade society made it impossible to
consider clapping an officer in irons, and for the better part of one whole
year Donald McKay disrupted life at York and terrified its residents. Posted
to York Factory in the vague capacity of "Gentleman at Large" in 1798, he
quickly proved to be impossible for John Ballenden, then the officer in
charge of York, to control. Ballenden's problems with McKay began with
an argument over a servant. Although McKay had always been allowed
someone to cut his firewood and "do anything he wants," he demanded that
one of the post's tailors be sent to act exclusively as his servant. Ballenden
remarked that "His launching out into such gusts of passion without the
least provication [*sic*] makes me think at times he is deranged in his
mind."[23]

Ballenden's words were prophetic for McKay's outburst over the servant
was not the end of his odd behaviour. He soon refused to dine with the other
officers and requested that his provisions be served out separately.[24] He
then complained of the wine he was served, sending a bottle of it to
Ballenden to taste and preserving "a phial full to shew the Gentlemen of the
Committee."[25] Ballenden, apparently anxious to placate McKay, agreed
that "having been shaken in the Bottle, it was not quite fine." McKay was
given another bottle of wine, which he accepted with ill grace, suggesting
that "we wanted to *poison* him and further that when he was up in my room
a Week ago, *something was put into his Glass for that purpose.*"[26]

By May, McKay had taken to leaving insulting notes directed at Ballenden around the post. One, which he dropped into the York Factory courtyard, read in part:

Advertisement
Whereas a Street Scrub writer, and is Supposed to
be a pickpocket, has made his Escape from
Billingsgate in June 1795, and fled to York
Factory Hudson's Bay N. Amc. This is to give
Notice to any person or persons who may
apprehend the said miscreant will receive one
Hundred Guineas Reward by applying to C — No 6
Northumberland Street Strand....

Mark read and Digest this
You toad poxed faced Vagabond
Your Note is dabed with Cheat,
& your face may be served the same.

That same evening, as on the two preceding evenings, immediately after the factory bell was rung at 8 o'clock "a Gun [was] fired from one of the Windows of Mr MacKay's Appartment."[27] The threatening and violent aspect of McKay's insanity continued throughout the summer. He warned one man that he would not allow anyone to come closer to his rooms than the "Corner of the Men's House."[28] He also threatened to burn his own residence down and paraded about the factory yard with sword and pistols, challenging everyone to fight.[29] At long last, on 15 September 1799, he was shipped back to England on the departing supply ship. What is most interesting about this case is not the form McKay's insanity took, but the sense that because he was a gentleman, nothing was done about his illness except to wait for the ship to send him home.[30]

Employees' medical problems were sometimes attributed to mental unbalance or imagination when in fact this was not the case. In 1841 William Spence, a fisherman, became ill. He was subject to "frequent fits of incoherency and idle talk about an Indian female for whom he has formed a foolish attachment."[31] He had no obvious ailment, so his illness was put down to a "decided alienation of the mind."[32] When he finally died, however, the post surgeon found that Spence had been suffering from "congestion of the brain" and, more importantly, "gangrene of the bowels."[33] Whatever the surgeon meant by these terms, clearly poor Spence was not just suffering from a psychological complaint.

It is sometimes suggested that suicide, murder, depression, and alcoholism — all indicators of mental problems — were common in the fur trade.[34] York Factory records suggest on the contrary that company employees bore the strains of life in the fur trade fairly well. In the 18th century, murder, suicide, and alcoholism were not major causes of death at York,[35] and 19th-century records offer a similar pattern. Mental health at

York Factory may have been better than at more isolated and lonely outposts, but it is at least as likely that the mental rigours of the fur trade have been exaggerated.

On the other hand, the journals and correspondence from York Factory reveal that residents were subject to a bewildering array of physical diseases. Many were simply the common ailments of 18th- and 19th-century life and may be passed over quickly: dropsy, gout, rheumatism, sciatica, epilepsy, lung inflammation, piles, and ophthalmia. Interestingly, venereal diseases were mentioned less frequently in 19th-century as opposed to 18th-century records. In part this may have been the result of attempts to screen out venereal-disease carriers prior to their departure for the North-West,[36] and to the use of mercury in treating syphilis.

Of far greater import were epidemic diseases. In 1856 a particularly virulent form of erysipelas, or St. Anthony's Fire, was reported at York Factory.[37] In 1846, freight boat crews from Red River brought an epidemic of measles that resulted in the death of 31 Indians and wreaked havoc on the company's transportation system.[38] Influenza epidemics struck York four times, with the epidemic of 1845 having particularly deleterious "effects on the physical strength of the Convalescents."[39] Scarlet fever killed two children at York in 1864, and many children died as a result of "water on the brain" in 1834-35.[40] There were typhus outbreaks at York Factory in 1843 and 1863.[41] In 1843 the typhus was combined with brain fever and bowel complaints. Only one man died, but the business of the factory was brought to a virtual standstill.[42] In 1863 only 27 of 73 new recruits for the fur trade could travel inland. The rest had to remain at York in quarantine as a result of typhus.[43] Between September and December six men died as a result of the disease.[44]

The most intriguing epidemic at York was "York Factory Disease." It first appeared in the spring of 1834 and did not entirely disappear until 1837. Described as a form of "dyspepsia" or "colic," it was rarely fatal, but it forced James Hargrave and the other factory officers to be evacuated from York Factory in 1836.[45] The company was worried enough by the disruption it caused that an enquiry into its causes and possible cure was ordered. The enquiry began by examining cooking utensils, but found no evidence that copper or lead poisoning was the cause of the problem. Instead it was suggested that the disease, which struck officers at York, was caused by the long hours they spent in an over-heated office keeping accounts. Increased record-keeping responsibilities combined with Governor Simpson's policy of pruning manpower had increased the workload of York's officers in the late 1820s and early 1830s, ending an earlier tradition of officers spending much of the winter outdoors hunting and snowshoeing. The other suggested cause of the disease was the indifferent quality of York cooking, which too often spoiled otherwise palatable and nutritious food. The report of the enquiry recommended that officers be encouraged to take exercise during the day and that the temperature of the accounting office be kept lower so as to prevent "a languid State of the System, with loss of Tone in the Stomach."[46]

The disease was not reported again, and it remains something of a mystery. Neither colic nor dyspepsia are unusual medical complaints anywhere, and they are certainly not limited to York Factory. Digestive complaints were fairly common at York both before and after the appearance of the York Factory disease, and it may well have been nothing more than a more virulent form of a general medical problem.

The most serious disease at York Factory was scurvy. Between 1714 and 1801 nine men died from scurvy, making it the most common cause of death there after drowning.[47] Although occasional references to its appearance can be found as late as the 1840s,[48] it was primarily a problem before 1821. Antiscorbutics were known and used at company posts from the early 18th century. This use of antiscorbutics helped to control outbreaks of scurvy at some posts like Prince of Wales's Fort,[49] but York Factory was not so lucky. The reasons for this can only be guessed at, but it is likely that the failure to fully exploit the potential food resource of fish at York prior to the 1820s played a significant role in the greater incidence of scurvy there than at Prince of Wales's Fort.

In years when supplies of country, or locally acquired, provisions were low and scurvy made its appearance, the results can only be described as harrowing:

It is impossible to express my anxiety having so many disabled Men around me, others daily falling bad and no fresh provisions to be got so much distress us, that I know not what to do — God I hope will send speedy relief. —

The Scurvy rages, with violence and some Men are so Bad it is [with] difficulty [that] they are removed from their beds — Scarcely one person at this place but is tainted with this disorder — and It is almost impossible to describe the malady that rages amongst us which is attended with a kind of putrifaction the Teeth loosen Gums swell, A quantity of loose dark flesh is cut off daily from the afflicted before they can take any kind of Subsistance The Patients Legs swell which are much discoloured they are disabled and contracted in their Limbs as to render them objects of Comis-

seration — Their breath is so offensive as to be utmost unbearable; and a lowness of spirits attends the whole afflicted....[50]

In the 18th and early 19th centuries the causes of disease were imperfectly understood. People knew that individual diseases had individual causes, but concepts of these causes were often confused and somewhat contradictory. Nevertheless, sensible treatment of some diseases based on empirical observation of what worked and what did not were often arrived at without fully understanding why the treatment worked. The treatment of scurvy is a useful illustration of this process. Vitamin C was neither isolated nor was its chemical identity established until 1932, yet Francis Bacon had noted as early as 1627 that oranges could help cure the disease.[51]

At posts like York Factory an empirical approach to disease treatment and prevention was also followed. The campaign to rid the factory of scurvy was based on three measures: exercise, cleanliness, and the use of antiscorbutics and other improvements to diet. All three sorts of measures undoubtedly had health benefits and were based on observation, though in the case of scurvy only the third measure actually addressed the real cause of the disease.

Indolence and inactivity were often suggested as at least predisposing men to scurvy. One employee named Robert Wilson was accused of rejoicing in his illness "as it exempts him from any work."[52] Robert Hudson, a clerk at York in 1790, was described as "the first and only instance" Joseph Colen had seen "of an Officer being afflicted with that disorder, brought on, entirely thro' his inactivity." Hudson eventually died from scurvy in April of 1790.[53] However, the reason why officers were less likely to contract scurvy had nothing to do with their activity. Their diet was more varied and depended less on salt provisions than that of tradesmen and labourers, making officers less prone to the disease.

Improving the cleanliness of the factory and the personal hygiene of the men also became an important preoccupation. Joseph Colen was convinced the men's personal habits were largely to blame for the prevalence of scurvy at York.

> *Six in the Sick List; part of whom very bad with the Scurvy, but so indolent that notwithstanding their health in a great measure depends on keeping themselves clean, they cannot be prevailed on, even to wash their hands and face oftener than once a week, and some of them not as frequent, and I am credibly informed, here are many men at this place that has not done this office unless compelled to it for many Months together, and that is, as often as they wash their Linen, but to prevent this trouble, they have got into the habit of wearing flannel Shirts, which they wear from the begin-*

ning of October, till the warmth of the sun the May following
obliges them to lay such filthy apparel aside.[54]

Colen and the surgeon instituted a plan whereby "conspicuous" offenders were to be awakened at "five O'Clock in the morning, in order that they may clean themselves by the time the rest of the men go to their work."[55] The London committee supported this policy and added some coercive weight to the plan.

We observe that your Men, according to your Report, keep them-
selves exceedingly filthy, it is therefore, very easy to account for
the Scurvy, making such progress amongst the Men — a triffling
Fine ought to be imposed on those, who do not clean themselves,
at least once a Week on Sundays—.[56]

Periodic attention was also paid to cleaning up the factory itself. Cleaning of the men's houses and their bed places was encouraged "to prevent if possible the encroachments of Disease," and in 1825 the London committee urged Governor Simpson to consult with the surgeon at York on "proper regulations to ensure cleanliness both in the persons of the Men and their houses."[57]

Dietary reform was taken up by the Hudson's Bay Company, although in many respects diet in the fur trade was superior to 18th- and early-19th-century diet in Britain, particularly for tradesmen and labourers. Imported provisions from Britain, however, were all too often indifferent in quality at best and completely unusable at worst, making the threat of scurvy worse if supplies of country produce failed. Throughout the 18th century, officers in charge of company posts complained about provisions that were short weight, putrid and decaying, or infected with maggots. Suggestions that such food was *"unwholesome and unfit for human Eating,"*[58] while undoubtedly true, had little apparent effect until the 1790s, when the London committee began to treat such complaints more seriously. Irish beef, for example, was much disliked, and the committee promised to stop shipping it.[59] The committee also sent out new types of food — like rice and Dutch cheese — as experiments in an effort to find more nutritious food and ones that would keep better.[60] In general, food supplies from Britain were more bountiful and of better quality than had been the case for some time.

In addition to improved food supplies, new types of antiscorbutic were shipped to York. Drawing on the experience of the navy and the East India Company, "Red Cabbage in vinegared Pickle" and "Essence of Malt" were sent to York as being "the best remedy for the Sea and Land Scurvy ever Discovered."[61] Careful instructions described how to use the malt most effectively:

At some of our factories, they have made beer of it, this is contrary
to the very Intention, we sent it for, it is only to be taken medici-
nally & prepared thus — 4 oz of the Essense, are to be desolved in
a pint of boiling Water & drank at two Seperate Draught in the
forenoon, by those only who are afflicted with the scurvy, without
the mixture of Hops which medical Men say here, destroy its virtue
as an antiscorbutic—.[62]

Other antiscorbutics like lemon crystals and sauerkraut also were used.

Similarly, efforts were made to find locally available antiscorbutics. Cranberries, in particular, were collected diligently to serve during the winter and spring, and the meagre supply of vegetables from the post garden was pressed into service.[63] Ironically the latter were preserved for post use at the expense of the supply ships' sailors, who had been accustomed to commit "depradations" on the post garden for fresh food for their voyage home.[64]

Some dietary innovations were more psychological than anything else. At the orders of the post surgeon, wine and grog were dispensed to the men ostensibly to prevent scurvy, but in fact to cheer "drooping spirits."[65] The men themselves had great faith in the medicinal value of alcohol. One employee reputedly drank a hogshead of English porter and some gallons of port wine in addition to consuming a supply of lemon salts, essence of malt, and cranberries as a sort of personal cure.[66] Yet despite all these efforts scurvy was not really controlled at York until the mid-1820s, when large supplies of fish were added to employees' winter and spring diet. These fish were frozen almost as soon as they were caught and brought in enormous numbers to York where they helped to avoid excessive reliance on pre-served foods like salt beef and pork in the winter diet.

Encouraging exercise and improving personal hygiene and nutrition formed important parts of the company's attempts to control diseases like scurvy and the York Factory disease. However, not all illness could be treated or prevented with such reforms, and surgeons were normally sta-tioned at York as part of the regular complement of officers there. Although accorded the status of officers and gentlemen, their position in the post hierarchy was somewhat ambiguous. In the 18th century the surgeon was usually the highest-paid employee at York after the officer in charge there and his deputy. After 1821, surgeons' wages varied more; still they were always among the best-paid officers at the post. This would suggest that they were important figures in post society and that their medical skills and services were highly regarded, but this does not always seem to have been the case.

In the 18th century, post surgeons were often viewed by officers in charge of York and other posts as malcontents and illicit traders.[67] The London committee itself suspected that surgeons' duties were not overly onerous and that their ample spare time ought to be turned to alternative activities like acting as schoolmasters.[68] Indeed after 1821, surgeons were hired to serve as both clerks and doctors.[69] Between 1821 and 1870 few surgeons at York served more than two or three years, making most essentially well-paid sojourners.[70]

The quality of the medical care they offered was also sometimes called into question. William Smellie, for example, failed to distinguish himself as either a clerk or a surgeon, and Governor Simpson remarked that the company could easily dispense with his services in both capacities.[71] Indeed many post surgeons were recruited as much for their availability as for their skills. Often the ship's surgeon on the annual supply ship was offered a contract to stay on at York to replace a homeward-bound surgeon.

Not all surgeons were recruited in such haphazard fashion, and some showed genuine initiative and skill in the conduct of their duties. William Todd is given much of the credit for halting the spread of the smallpox epidemic of 1837-38 by instituting a vigorous campaign of vaccination among the Indians and company employees of the Swan River District, where he was posted after he left York.[72] A vaccination program was also carried out at York Factory and in its surrounding district,[73] but most medical problems at York required less sophisticated treatments.

Dr. William Smellie's medical notebook for 1846-47 has survived. Although his skills as a doctor were not highly regarded at York, his notebook suggests the post of surgeon at York did not require extraordinary competence. Over 13 months he treated 136 patients, a leisurely rate of about ten patients a month.[74] The surgery he performed was generally minor: extracting teeth, lancing infections, and stitching cuts. He did, however, also have to amputate a toe, set a fractured finger and a wrist, and draw fluid from the abdomen of a man. In all, 30 of his patients had suffered some sort of accidental injury. Almost half of his other patients, 44 in number, suffered from dysentery, diarrhoea, constipation, gastric pain, or other digestive problems. Most of these patients were treated with calomel, jalap, powdered rhubarb, or cream of tartar, and all recovered. The bulk of his other cases consisted of coughs and colds, vomiting, headaches (including a couple of hangovers), or general aches and pains. These he treated much the same way, with emetics and purgatives, or less frequently, with ointments, poultices, or bleeding. Only a handful of his cases appear to have been either serious or mysterious enough in cause to have required anything more than a rudimentary knowledge of medicine to treat. Indeed the two most startling features of his notebook were how mundane most complaints were and the fact that nearly one-third of his patients were not regular residents of York at all but Indians, boatmen, and others visiting the post.[75]

Mortality figures and available medical evidence do not suggest that company employees faced great risk in taking up careers in the fur trade. If York Factory was seen as an unhealthy posting, it was so primarily by comparison with other posts. Moreover, there may have been some comfort in the notion that most accidental injuries and illnesses at York were not beyond the ability of even indifferently trained post surgeons to treat. At least York Factory residents did not face the situation that prevailed in most of the rest of the North-West, where "if a man gets ill, he goes on till he gets better; and if he doesn't get better, he dies."[76]

Education and Religion

In the 18th century, company territories were rarely visited by outsiders, and organizations other than the company itself had little influence on post life. During the 19th century, however, the North-West became much less isolated and new influences came to bear on fur trade communities, especially major centres like York Factory. At York, post society became increasingly complex and new social institutions took root. The most important of these were a system of schooling and job training for company employees and their children, and the construction of a church and the settlement of a resident missionary there.

Numerous studies of the history of education in the North-West have been written.[1] Most of these begin with the first attempts to provide formal training for children in skills like reading, writing, and basic arithmetic. It has been pointed out, however, that such studies are based on a narrow conception of education as formal schooling.[2] Indian children were taught language and other necessary social and survival skills without recourse to primers or spelling books, and so too were the children born to company employees and their native spouses. Company employees also were encouraged to learn Indian languages and to acquire practical skills in hunting, fishing, and trapping, but there is little evidence that any sort of formal training in such matters was offered at company posts.

As early as 1710 Henry Kelsey produced a dictionary of Indian words and phrases that the company had printed for use at York Factory,[3] and other such educational materials were occasionally prepared, but there is no record of their being used in any systematic fashion to train junior officers for their duties. Throughout most of the 18th century the company preferred to hire men whose job skills were already acquired, and if special skills were required, that they be taught by the simple but effective technique of learning by doing. Similarly, the children of company employees were not seen as a potential source of new recruits, and with very few exceptions it was assumed that they would be reabsorbed back into Indian society.

This laissez-faire approach to education and job training prevailed until the late 18th century. The creation of inland posts greatly increased the Hudson's Bay Company's demand for labour at a time when recruitment in Britain was becoming more difficult and more expensive. The American War of Independence and later wars with revolutionary and Napoleonic France increased competition for able-bodied and skilled employees and drove wage rates up. The company responded by increasing its wages and by broadening its recruiting efforts to include Canadian, Highland Scots, Irishmen, and others in addition to the Orkneymen upon whom it had so long relied. The company also realized that the children of its employees at company posts might serve as a large and hitherto almost completely unexploited source of new recruits.

At the same time, company employees themselves were increasingly eager to find places for their children in their employer's service. Many had grave misgivings about their children adopting an Indian way of life that they viewed as primitive, heathen, and dangerous.[4] Paralleling changes noted by historians of the family in 18th-century Britain, fur trade fathers, beginning with officers and then extending down through the ranks, were prepared to make larger financial and emotional investments in their children.[5] Some established annuities to support their wives and children after they left company service or in the event of their deaths. Others tried to find husbands for their daughters among their fellows and to settle their sons in careers either with the company or outside the fur trade. Some sort of education and job training that could be provided at company posts came to be seen as a valuable means of achieving all of these objects.

The first tentative steps away from a policy of laissez-faire and in the direction of a more formal system of schooling at company posts occurred in 1794 when the London committee shipped "one hundred Primers or Spelling Books for the use of the Children" to York Factory. In its annual letter the committee remarked that it hoped "much good will be the result of your care & Attention to [the children's] Improvement."[6]

The use made of these educational materials is unrecorded, but they were also sent to other bayside posts and at Moose Factory records refer to children being "at their Books" in the late 1790s.[7] At about the same time the company began to offer apprenticeships in trades to children of its employees. The earliest such apprenticeships at York were confirmed by the London committee in 1801: "George Ross Son of the late Mr Malcolm Ross John Inkster & Joseph Cook may be entered on the Companys Books as Apprentices & allowed £6 pr Ann each."[8]

In 1806 the London committee proposed the creation of formal schools at its bayside posts and clearly stated the advantages it expected from the scheme:

> *Wishing you to cultivate as much as possible an intimate connection with the Natives all over the Country & to facilitate your intercourse with them, which must of course prove advantageous to the Company, we have thought it would be adviseable, to instruct the Children belonging to our Servants in the principles of Religion & teach them from their youth, reading, writing Arithmetic & Accounts, which we should hope would attach them to our service & in a few years become a small Colony of very useful hands.[9]*

The response from York Factory was swift and favourable:

> *This benevolent proposition of your Honors ought to excite grateful sensations in the hearts of your servants & doubly excite them in the promotion of your concerns.... [the] Schoolmaster ought to be steady & if of advanced age his success might be greater, [for] the sending of Children to the Factory will depend upon the compliance of the Parents.[10]*

Despite this reply the London committee had some difficulty in settling upon a plan. The following year it outlined its concerns and offered an interim measure:

> *we now send a parcel of books which are necessary & we hope that the Surgeons at the different factories, who must have much leisure time, will cheerfully engage in this useful service, — they must not suppose that it requires any very particular qualifications or study, to engage in this service — while his pupils are learning, with a very little attention, he will always find himself sufficiently prepar'd for their progressive improvement — .[11]*

Although the committee felt that teaching did not require any special qualifications, those who took on the task were promised some small remuneration for their efforts.[12]

That fall a school was begun at York Factory, though not under the supervision of the surgeon. On 14 October 1807 a Mr. Garrock commenced work as the schoolmaster and continued in that occupation intermittently over the winter and spring.[13] Garrock may deserve the title of the first schoolmaster in western Canada, but he was not always attentive to his duties. Although referred to as a "diligent" teacher, he is mentioned as frequently in the post journal as being engaged in hunting and trapping, and by spring he was said to be "attentive to the Guns & traps ... and grows a good partridge hunter."[14]

The education offered at York Factory in 1807-08, while better than nothing, did not satisfy expectations. In 1807 the annual letter from York contained hopes for a less haphazard type of schooling:

> In the first instance it is the anxious desire of every parent that the happiness resulting from Education & Religion should be imparted without distinction to the Children of both sexes & that the female youth in particular should experience that delicacy & attention to their persons their peculiar situation requires — Native women as attendants on these young persons seems improper — their society would keep alive the Indian language & with it, its native superstition which ought to be obliterated from the mind with all possible care It is therefore humbly suggested that a female from England of suitable abilities & good moral character accompanying the schoolmaster would obviate the necessity of employing such attendants & the cleanliness of the Children & domestic Economy of the seminary under the superintendence of a respectable Matron, would, we have no doubt be equal to the wishes of your Honors & promise to the undertaking, that success, which could not be expected from a more limited regulation — The expenses necessarily incurred in forwarding this benevolent design, would, as far as your Honors thought proper be chearfully sustain'd by those whose children received the benefit of the institution — The residence of the Children & their instructors would be most convenient at a short distance from the Factory, where firewood & country provisions, could with little difficulty be procured on the spot — Many places of this kind are to be found — in the Vicinity of York & such retired situations would not only estrange the Children from their Indian acquaintence, but present other advantages friendly to the progress of Education morality & good order....[15]

The London committee was either unable or unwilling to hire matrons and clergymen for schools. It was also unsure of the value of creating a residential "seminary" separate from the factory. In 1809 it did suggest, though, that a school might be established at Cumberland House, which was more accessible to inland posts and which enjoyed ample supplies of country provisions.[16] However, the proposal was not acted upon, especially as a school was already operating at York Factory.

In 1808 this school was run by a Mr. Geddes. Initially it consisted of only four full-time students, Catherine Sinclair, John and Mary Bunn, and Harriet Ballandine, with Joseph Cook an occasional student. In June 1809 three more sons of William Hemmings Cook, the officer in charge at York, were enrolled in the school, and by August, eleven students were attending it.[17] The job of schoolmaster still appears to have been only a part-time occupation, and Geddes was frequently reported to be off hunting.[18] In his absence either the surgeon, Mr. Bunn, or James Dibble, another employee, officiated. Despite the lack of continuity in teachers, the London committee was informed that "the School Establishment is proceeding under the happiest presages of Success," and samples of the students' work were sent to the committee as proof of the students' "amelioration."[19] Some construction work was also carried out at York for school purposes including converting the former beer shed into a winter schoolroom.[20]

Despite this obvious local interest in the scheme, references to school operations in post records peter out. York's schoolmaster, Mr. Geddes, was still listed as employed in that capacity up to 1813 in personnel records, but whether or not the school continued to operate cannot be determined.[21] After 1813 the experiment of stationing schoolmasters at bayside posts was abandoned, and the Reverend John West reported in the 1820s that the company's former schoolmasters "were unhappily diverted from their original purpose, and became engaged as fur traders."[22] It is probable that the school at York, along with the schools at Moose, Albany, and Eastmain, were dropped as part of the austerity measures the company introduced in 1811 in order to compete more effectively with the Nor'Westers in the interior.

The practise of recruiting apprentices from among the children of company servants was not abandoned though, and apprenticeships continued to be offered at York Factory. By 1820, however, John West, an Anglican missionary appointed as chaplain to the Hudson's Bay Company, was struck by the numbers of children at York Factory who, he feared, were "going up in ignorance and idleness." West hoped that at least some of these children could "be maintained, clothed, and educated upon a regularly organized system," and he took one Indian boy inland with him to Red River from York Factory as a pupil.[23] West and his Anglican missionary successors at Red River eventually did establish a school there, and a handful of children were sent from York Factory to the Red River Academy, as the school came to be known, to be educated.[24]

Without a school at York itself, however, it was still difficult and expensive for parents to secure formal education for their children. It was still only the children of officers who were sent to Red River or Britain for schooling.[25] There was a need for a school at York, and in 1834, references to an evening school for tradesmen, labourers, and children begin to appear in post journals.[26] The journal entry for 21 October 1840 describes the operations of this school in some detail:

> *An Evening School conducted by William Anderson the Store Porter was this day opened for the instruction of the young apprentices under contracts to the company at this place which is also attended by all the children of the Tradesmen, and by such of the servants as are desirous of improving their education. — The hours of attendance are from 6 to 9 O'Clock — candles, likewise Paper, Pens and Books for the apprentices, are supplied them gratuitously, and it is hoped that the instruction thus afforded them will not only be of use to them individually but tend to render them more efficient servants to their employers when they come to years of maturity.*[27]

The evening school ran from the fall to the spring, roughly corresponding with the period of the year when the factory operated on shortened winter hours. At the end of the school year the apprentices were examined on their progress in reading, writing, and arithmetic, and on occasion "a few prizes were distributed among those who had shown the greatest and most rapid proficiency."[28]

The arrival of a resident missionary, William Mason, at York in 1854-55 meant the expansion of the school's operations. Until then the post's storekeepers had run the school, for which they received £5 per annum in extra pay.[29] Both Mason and his successor, the Reverend J.P. Gardiner, were eager to lend a hand with the school. At their instigation Indian men and women were included amongst the students, and Mrs. Mason organized and taught an infants' school.[30] The school was further expanded to run during the summer especially for the Indian children, and Bible and "conversational" classes were also added.[31] In addition a printing press was sent to York Factory for the use of missionaries in 1857, and a number of catechisms and other religious tracts were printed in syllabics there.[32]

Paralleling the development of the evening and mission schools at York Factory was the expansion of the company's apprenticeship training there. Apprenticeship policy was outlined in the minutes of council for the Northern Department in 1830.

> *That Chief Factors and Chief Traders in charge of Districts and*
> *Posts where regular Tradesmen are employed be authorised to*
> *engage strong healthy half breed Lads not under 14 years of Age*
> *as apprentices to be employed with those Tradesmen for the pur-*
> *pose of acquiring a Knowledge of their business on a term of not*
> *less than seven years at the following Wages which are considered*
> *sufficient to provide them with clothes and other personal neces-*
> *saries, viz: the 2 first years at £8 p annum, the next 2 years at £10*
> *p annum, the following 2 years at £12 p annum and the last year at*
> *£15, making the seven years apprenticeship an allowance of £75.*
> *— Such lads not to be employed with their Fathers nor in the*
> *Districts where their Fathers and families reside.*[33]

Between 1821 and 1870, twenty-six apprentice tradesmen and labourers learned their trades at York Factory. All but two of them were designated as "native" or born in the North-West in personnel records, meaning that well over 90 per cent of York's apprentices were the children of company employees. York was the most important centre for training apprentices in the Hudson's Bay Company's service, and although apprentices never made up more than a tiny fraction of the company's work force as a whole, apprenticeships were an important means of training and recruiting the children of company employees.[34] Indeed, James Hargrave once remarked that the principal tinsmith at York, William Baillie, had been "reared, educated and taught his trade at this factory."[35]

While schools and job training required the creation of new social institutions at York Factory, they had a practical purpose that grew out of the demands of the fur trade and the desire of fur trade fathers to settle their sons in careers and to improve their daughters' chances of marriage to fellow employees. The construction of a church at York Factory and the settlement of missionaries there reflects the new influence of outside organizations on post life in the 19th century.

The first entry in the earliest list of instructions to company officers in 1680 reads "In the first place Wee do strictly enjoyn you to have public prayers and reading of the Scriptures or some other religious Books wheresoever you shall be resident, at least on the Lord's days."[36] Throughout the 18th and early 19th centuries similar exhortations were delivered to officers in charge of posts, and the frequency with which proper celebration of the Sabbath was urged suggests that actual practice fell far short of the ideal envisioned by the London committee. Some officers took their religious responsibilities seriously, but for the most part Sunday was just a day of rest. Individual traders ranged in their beliefs from the devout to the sceptical to the indifferent.[37] There was no real effort made to convert the native population, a fact frequently mentioned by critics of the company and its officers. In 1811 Miles Macdonell remarked that after nearly a century and a half of contact between traders and Indians, there was not "the faintest idea of the true Deity to be found" among Indians.[38]

The appointment of John West as chaplain to the Hudson's Bay Company in 1820 was part of a major shift in company policy. Officially West was to minister to the white population of Red River and those posts that he visited in his travels, but West himself planned to extend his ministry to the Indian and mixed-blood population. Two years earlier, in 1818, a Roman Catholic mission had also been established at Red River with the support of Lord Selkirk. Clearly the company had no desire to play favourites with the Christian churches and allow the development of a single, company-supported church in the North-West. Its desire to let a number of different denominations establish missions was further underlined by its encouragement of Methodist missions in the 1840s.[39] However, it was the Anglican Church through the Church Missionary Society that dominated religious life at York Factory.

John West visited York Factory every year from his arrival there in 1820 to his departure for England in 1823. His impact was far greater at Red River, but each of his visits offered the residents of York Factory a chance to celebrate marriages, have their children baptized, and attend services celebrated by an ordained minister. Other missionaries also passed through York Factory, and up until the 1850s these visiting clergymen provided most of the religious instruction and services available at York. While they were frequent summer visitors, they were not residents of the factory. As a result, despite official encouragement of "the due observance of the Sabbath and the public reading of prayers,"[40] religious observance was erratic. Much depended on the views of the officers in charge of the posts at York and elsewhere if no missionary was resident.

This was not entirely satisfactory to either the Hudson's Bay Company, or at least a portion of its governing committee,[41] or the missionaries and the churches they represented. While the minutes of council for 1823 urged regular Sunday services and the supply of Bibles and prayer books to servants, John West remarked that Sunday services would be observed "only when convenient."[42] Nor were West's fears entirely groundless, for religious services were not always offered at York, though it was not entirely fair to characterize them as being offered only when convenient.[43]

In 1850 Bishop David Anderson of Rupert's Land broached the idea of establishing a church and settling a minister at York with the board of the

Society for the Propagation of the Gospel in Foreign Parts. The SPG was a similar organization to the Church Missionary Society with roughly parallel aims. In Rupert's Land the Church Missionary Society generally provided missionaries for work amongst the native peoples, whereas the SPG was more active in providing Anglican ministers for white congregations. At least initially it appears that the proposed church at York Factory was intended primarily for company employees and their families. Anderson requested a grant of £100 per annum from the SPG and offered to try to match this amount with funds from his diocese.[44]

The following year Anderson took up the proposal again after arranging added support for the scheme and deciding that a smaller subsidy would be sufficient to establish the church. Anderson now emphasized the plight of the Christian Indians at York, who added a petition of their own to his letter. The petition described their desire for religious instruction and their need for "the spiritual oversight of the Church."[45] Anderson pointed out that "It does seem hard that all the Clergymen, coming to the Country land at York, see the Indians there, & pass on to their destinations." Moreover, York was "an important Fort with many Clerks and servants of the Hudson's Bay Company without the means of grace among them."[46] Anderson also advised that York needed a clergyman who was "an unmarried man & one easily satisfied & contented with but little comforts — a man of self-denial & energy."[47]

No such person willing to go to York could be found in Britain so Anderson suggested that a student then attending St. John's Collegiate School in Red River be appointed to serve at York. The student was Robert McDonald, who had been studying for the ministry with Anderson for the past two and a half years and who was about to be ordained as a deacon. He had a number of valuable attributes as a potential minister at York, being acquainted with syllabics and able to speak some Cree. He was also willing to accept £50 per annum from the SPG with £100 from the company as a wage.[48] Unfortunately there were some difficulties that Anderson touched on in a private letter to the Reverend Mr. Hawkins, the secretary of the SPG:

Mr. McDonald was born in this Country but is European on his Fathers side & partly European on his Mother's — He does not therefore come under the Same Category as Mr. Budd, but is Country born, *not an Indian — I state this because often the other idea gets abroad, & the Ch Miss. Socy. in their Intelligencer speak of one Catechist as an* Indian, *to whom I had to explain the circumstance or he might naturally have been offended....*[49]

McDonald was acceptable to the SPG, but others were less sure of his suitability. The official history of the SPG merely states that "it was deemed advisable to send a clergyman of greater experience, and as such an one could not be obtained until 1854 ... the Mission was undertaken by the C.M.S."[50] Bishop Anderson later remarked:

> All thought him rather young & without the needful experience for such a charge.... The HHB Co have also made some objections on the ground of his being born in the Country, & therefore not of sufficient influence with the gentlemen of the service. Now my first thoughts were the poor Indian, & for him I still feel deeply. However I now am relieved from the responsibility, having done all in my power to send them a Minister.[51]

The Church Missionary Society was more successful at finding a minister for York Factory, and in 1854 they appointed the Reverend William Mason to the position. Mason had been James Evans's assistant at Norway House and had recently left the Methodist Church and been ordained as an Anglican minister. He was an experienced and capable missionary with an impressive knowledge of syllabics.

The next order of business was providing a church and accommodation for Mason and his family. As there was no house for him, Mason left his family at Red River, and as there was no church, a mess room was used in the interim for Sunday services.[52] Work was begun on a parsonage in the fall of 1854; it was completed the following summer,[53] and by 1855 Mason and his family were resident at York. On 16 September 1856 the foundations of a church were officially laid. Bishop Anderson presided over the ceremony that accompanied the laying of the foundation, and he named the church the Church of St. John of York.[54]

Even with a church and a parsonage the life of a missionary at York was far from idyllic. The cold was such that the church could only be used from late spring to early fall. York's residents had a distinctive manner of indicating when it was time to abandon services in the church: "Very cold in Church this morning. Most of the people took their books away — signifying they shd. not attend divine service again here this season."[55] During the winter, services were moved to an old mess room that was somewhat warmer. The cold was a common complaint of Mason and Gardiner. Mason once remarked that he had had a cup of tea freeze solid before he had finished it.[56] Gardiner and his wife seem to have been particularly affected by the rigours of their life. She was ill for most of their stay at York, and after being transferred to Churchill, Gardiner had to give up his mission

17   The Indian church at York Factory, designed by James Hargrave, was
completed in 1858.
Provincial Archives of Manitoba, J.A. Campbell Collection, No. 164.

there because his labours had produced "a great degree of Nervous Depression."[57]

The biggest problem facing the missionaries, though, was the indifference of most company employees to moral and religious exhortations and their disinclination to participate fully in religious services. Gardiner found that neither his good example nor his sermons could keep the men from celebrating Christmas with large quantities of alcohol, not prayer. Indeed, Gardiner was once told outright that he would not be troubled much by one sceptic's presence in church since "I never go there & I am just as good as many who do go."[58] According to Mason, officers attended services fairly regularly, but few servants did.[59] That the comforts of religion were only desired by a minority is borne out by the Reverend W.W. Kirby, stationed at York in 1870, who mentioned that of 53 people at York Factory, only about ten attended services.[60] Nor ought this to have been too surprising to York's missionaries since many of the men were Roman Catholics or Presbyterians after all.

The missionaries stationed at York did not discuss their work among the Homeguard Cree in much detail. Their journals and correspondence report no major triumphs in converting the native peoples of the area, and only modest success in involving the Homeguard in their mission school. It did become a tradition at York to hold an extra service on Sundays and religious holidays in Cree, but this was perhaps the single most obvious manifestation of missionary concern with York's native population.

In general, missionaries had little direct influence on post life. They had difficulty reaching those company employees who were not already Anglican or prominent enough to see it as politic to attend church services. Their attempts to influence behaviour, like Gardner's campaign to discourage holiday drinking, appear to have fallen upon deaf ears. What is most significant about the arrival of missionaries at York was that their presence there clearly indicated that the long isolation of company posts was coming to an end. The Hudson's Bay Company was no longer the only significant organization in the North-West, and post communities were no longer exclusively populated by company employees, their families, and the local native population. The missionary presence at York was a herald of further changes in post society, though these were changes that were not particularly noticeable until after 1870.

Standard of Living

Studies of standards of living in the past often raise as many questions as answers, but nothing could be more basic to the study of a community than how its residents clothed, housed, and fed themselves. Fortunately Hudson's Bay Company records are remarkably rich in the details they provide about the material culture of the fur trade. It is possible to describe in some detail the clothing, accommodation, and diet of company employees stationed at York Factory and to offer some cautious comparisons between their standard of living and the probable standard of living of individuals employed in similar occupations in Britain and Lower Canada. It is also possible to suggest the degree to which fur trade material culture represented a direct inheritance from the home communities of company employees, borrowing from native cultures, or innovation by traders themselves.

From about June to October company employees wore "common European dress."[1] The climate at most posts presented no unusual problems during those months, and thus there was no need to make many adaptations in European dress. For the most part, men wore shirts, trousers, jackets, shoes, and hats in various styles and combinations, though fashion did play a role in their choice of clothing. Company employees in the 1780s were described as wearing tight blue jackets with leather trousers, but by the 1840s, shirts, trousers, and capotes had to be cut to provide a "full roomy size ... as tight clothes are quite unsaleable among our laboring people."[2] In 1858 some embroidered flannel shirts were declared unsuitable for trade, "being of too inferior a quality and the embroidered pattern in bad taste for

Officers and not sufficiently showy to suit our voyageurs."[3] Tripmen had a reputation for showy dressing, but many company officers took equal interest in their wardrobes and appearance. Many ordered their clothing directly from British or Scottish tailors, though as befitted their status as men of business they purchased more formal attire. In 1828, for example, James Hargrave spent over £7 out of his salary of £100 for a frock coat, waistcoat, trousers, two lambswool cravats, and a fur seal cap along with tooth powder and a dozen cakes of scented soap.[4] In the 1780s William Tomison even kept a special scarlet vest to wear during his visits to York Factory. He put on the vest when he arrived and carefully stored it away when he returned inland.[5]

Company employees' "summer" clothing came from several sources. Until 1770 most clothing was inexpensive ready-made clothing purchased from ship captains' supplies of seamen's "slops." After 1770 the Hudson's Bay Company began to send out its own supplies of ready-made clothing, allowing employees to purchase shirts, shoes, gloves, and other items from the post saleshop. Officers had clothing both sent to them from England or Scotland and made by tailors or women residing at the post.[6] Servants often purchased large quantities of duffel, cotton cloth, blankets, and so on from post supplies for themselves and their families.

Winter clothing was an example of both adaptation and innovation in material culture. The basic winter dress of an 18th-century employee was largely borrowed from Indian clothing design, but it integrated European materials like flannel and duffel into the costume with the leather and fur the Indians had used.

> The outer garment is an open coat or banian [a loose shirt or jacket] made of moose skin, with cuffs and a cape of beaver or other; but in very cold weather this is not sufficient. It is therefore changed for a beaver toggy [a calf-length great coat of skins] with the fur inwards. It is in the same form as the other. The waistcoat is of cloth with sleeves and lined with flannel. The breeches are made of deer, or elk skin, lined with flannel. The legs are covered with a pair of worsted or yarn stockings without feet; and over them, a pair of cloth stockings Indian fashion, reaching from the ankle to the groin, and tied below the knee with strings or Indian garters. The feet are defended from the cold by three pairs of socks made of duffel, or blanketing, and reaching half way up the leg. The shoes are the same as the natives' with a piece of leather or cloth sewed around the quarters which wrap round the instep and excludes the cold and snow in travelling. In mild weather an otter

skin wig or cap is worn, having a broad piece of the above skin around it, the crown of cloth lined with linen; but when the cold is great or snow drifting much another kind of cap is used, the crown also of cloth but lined with flannel, and has a large flap or cape which comes down over the shoulders, and ties under the chin. The face is defended by a chin-cloth made of beaver, duffel, flannel or blanketing. It comes under the chin, over the cheeks and ties with strings on the crown of the head under the cap; so that little more than the eyes, nose and mouth is exposed to the air.... In warm days we use only large leather mittens lined with duffel or blanketing, and fastened together with a string like the natives. But in sharp weather, beaver mittens with the fur outwards, for defending the face on occasions, these are lined and fastened like the others.[7]

Effective as this clothing was at providing warmth and protection from wind and snow, it changed over time. In the 1780s the beaver toggy was replaced by a leather coat, probably as a result of the declining numbers of beaver and the increased numbers of traders, and after 1800, references can be found to the use of buffalo hides in winter coats.[8] The best-known of all items of fur trade clothing, the capote, was not adopted by company employees until about 1821.[9] The capote, the hooded blanket coat so closely associated with the fur trade and the Hudson's Bay Company, appears to have been taken up by company employees in imitation of the Nor'Westers, who had borrowed it in turn from the fur traders of New France.[10]

Given that many of its characteristic features, like fringing, were adapted from Indian styles, the capote represents an extraordinary example of the transmission of material culture from native peoples to the French- and English-speaking fur traders of Montreal, to Hudson's Bay Company employees, and on to the modern consumer. Not only was the coat warm and durable, but its decorative fringes drew moisture away from the coat body and helped keep it dry. It was also relatively easily made, and when properly cut, left very little waste from a blanket.

The capote also became subject to whims of fashion:

The Grey cloth Capots for sales to Servants have for these last three Seasons, been indented for as "light blue mixed" which is the colour universally asked for throughout the Country, instead of which, at least three fourths of every Supply has consisted of "Dark Grey mixed", — a colour far less popular — and less durable.

The belts used for tying capotes also underwent a change of fashion. Crimson belts became less popular than scarlet ones, and end fringes were lengthened to two feet.[11]

Unlike the toggy or leather coat, the capote was not supplied free of charge by the company to its employees, and it became an important item of trade. After the capote was introduced, all clothing, with the exception of tracking shoes, which were given to tripmen to protect their feet and their own footwear on the York–Norway House route,[12] became the responsibility of the individual employee to supply for himself. After 1841, company employees even had to purchase furs for their own personal use from company stocks at London prices. Some continued, nevertheless, to buy furs to make small items of winter clothing. Otter skins, generally used to make hats or caps, were the most common purchase.[13] Furs were also occasionally purchased as gifts, and the wives of wealthy company officers often acquired large numbers of furs for clothing. Letitia Hargrave described herself as "well skinned" over the winter of 1842-43. James Hargrave had given her "nearly 60 ermine skins a white fox muff [and] a new lynx boa." Her most valuable fur was a marten tippet:

> One of the three skins [of the tippet] is a prodigy. Mr. Sinclair on his way here found an Indian preparing to make a medicine bag of it & made him yield it up. Hargrave could not let it pass, so he bought it & made Wilson [the post master] select the two nearest it in blackness so that it is a good size.[14]

In addition to offering some insight into her wardrobe, her letter reveals something of the prerogatives of rank in the fur trade.

The wives and daughters of company men wore clothing that was often Indian in style, but with European materials integrated into the overall outfit in the form of knitted stockings, cloth leggings, and duffel socks.[15] Even Letitia Hargrave adopted the leggings and moccasins of native women, though she retained at least the external appearance of a well-to-do Victorian woman with her merino gown. Still, this gown had been adapted to suit the cold climate of York by being lined.

> While the stove rages I am clothed in flannel from the neck down to the wrist & ankle, wearing a man's flannel jacket (knitted) drawers to my feet made of bath coating duffle socks & English stockgs under moccasins & a merino gown the body lined with the said bath coating. Mr. Mactaggart wd be worse than when I wore muslin ones if he saw me with a pair of dark blue cloth leggins wch the women here tie around their waists as we used to have our stockgs when little, but I button mine to my drawers wch they dont

wear. Mine are embroidered with crimson pink white [and] black ribbons but theirs have beads wch look much better & dont fade as mine do.[16]

In combining native clothing styles with European clothing materials, company employees and their families made an adequate and effective response to the climatic and work conditions at York. Fur trade clothing was clearly functional, but it also allowed for variation in personal tastes, including a taste for finery. The importance some individuals placed on small luxuries in the area of clothing was recognized by Governor Simpson and the management of the company. Simpson noted that some were prone to become "dissatisfied and troublesome" if the saleshop at York did not include a wide variety of clothing items, and the company willingly tried to ensure all had opportunities to spend their wages on whatever clothing they liked.[17]

The main buildings used to accommodate York's residents changed considerably over time as company employees attempted to adjust building styles and techniques to suit the needs of living in a harsh and difficult environment. In theory, at least, employees lived at York Factory, but in reality many spent much of the year living in hunting, fishing, and woodcutting camps. Somewhat surprisingly this was not viewed as a great hardship by most since accommodations in these camps were in some respects preferable to housing at bayside factories.

Company posts on the shores of Hudson Bay in the 18th century paid little attention to the peculiarities of the environment. Initially posts appear to have been constructed with considerations of defence, not comfort, in mind. York Factory was generally described as cold, damp, and draughty, while the "log tents" used in hunting and wooding camps were not.[18] The "log tent" was adapted from Cree dwellings and it proved to be both a flexible and effective winter residence. It could be varied in size to house different numbers of people, and it was easily constructed using only locally available materials.

Most log tents were built by attaching a pole 14 to 16 feet long to two trees, at a height of about nine or ten feet. Logs were laid up against either side of the cross pole, sloping outwards towards the ground. A space was left for a small doorway on the south side and the ends of the structure were filled with logs just like the sides. The overall shape was like the "eves of a house." Such a tent would accommodate 14 men. Moss was stuffed between logs, and the whole structure was daubed with mud. Shorter logs were used above the doorway, creating a chimney in the centre of the tent, beneath which the men built their hearth. About the hearth large squared logs were

18   A log tent.
[Theodore Swain Drage], *An Account of a Voyage for the Discovery of a North-West Passage....* (London: Printed and sold by Mr. Jolliffe et al., 1748-49), Vol. 1, facing p. 136.

arranged as seats, and the men slept around the outside of the tent with their feet towards the inside and the fire. Beds were laid on piles of pine or, at York, black-spruce boughs that raised the bedding at least a foot off the ground.[19] In later years as hunting and fishing camps became more permanent, small log cabins were built to house hunters and fishermen, but temporary shelters in the Indian style continued to be used on occasion.[20] Tents of leather, canvas, and "Russia duck," a type of linen canvas, were also used sometimes for temporary housing.[21]

The appeal of wintering away from the factory in log or other types of tents was explained by William Hemmings Cook, the officer in charge of York in 1810-11, as "partly owing to the bad quality of the Wood which is green Poplar a species of Fuel which when frozen is no less difficult to cut than reluctant to burn & totally destitute of every property congenial to the Idea of a comfortable fires side."[22] At the time most residences at York were large structures, like that built at Joseph Colen's request in 1792 with

19 In a double Carron stove, made in Scotland, the upper chamber is an oven. This stove has been reconstructed from parts found at York Factory.
Photo by G. Adams.

66 bedplaces.[23] These bedplaces or "cabins" were not heated individually, but by large central fireplaces that consumed enormous quantities of firewood without much effect. According to fur trade writers rime, or frost, usually formed to a depth of several inches on the exterior walls of such residences since most of the heat of the fireplaces simply went up the chimney.[24]

The solution to making housing at York and other bayside posts more comfortable and appropriate to the climate was to build smaller dwellings and to heat them with stoves. The policy of building smaller winter residences is clearly evident after the Hudson's Bay and North West companies merged in 1821: as part of the new construction at York, small winter houses accommodating eight men each made their appearance in 1823.[25] At about the same time, new residences for senior officers and a house for unmarried officers, called Bachelors' Hall, were also built.[26]

The introduction of wood burning stoves as replacements for open fire-places was probably an even more important adaptation in post housing. As early as 1744 it was suggested that stoves like those used in Northern Europe would make the Hudson's Bay Company's posts more comfortable places in winter, but this suggestion was not taken up until the early 19th century.[27] In 1811 Miles Macdonell, leader of the first party of Lord Selkirk's settlers, had stovepipes and elbows made for his use by the blacksmith at York.[28] Three years later, in 1814, the London committee sent iron stoves to its bayside posts, suggesting that a "very important saving [of firewood] would be affected by the adoption of Stoves either of Iron like those of Canada or of Brick or Stone like those of Sweden."[29] Thereafter iron stoves became the normal means of heating residences at York Factory.[30] In the 1840s Governor Simpson decided that Russian-style stoves would be a valuable innovation at York, presumably as a result of his travels in Russia while negotiating with representatives of the Russian-American Fur Company. Simpson sent an employee of the Russian-American Fur Company from Sitka to York to advise in the construction of brick stoves and in the use and preparation of charcoal for blacksmith work. Simpson anticipated that the stoves and charcoal would result in great savings of coal and firewood and thus allow the reduction of York Factory's complement of men.[31] James Hargrave resisted this innovation and would "not let [brick stoves] be built in any of the gentlemens houses."[32] Nor did he feel charcoal could be substituted for blacksmith's coal at York since "pine does not make charcoal & the expense of bringing the proper wood wd be much heavier than the coal from Engd."[33]

Some innovations were better received. Mosquitoes and other biting insects were a great nuisance at York Factory. In the early 1840s Bachelors' Hall was described as at the height of summer "filled with mosquitoes and bull-dog flies, which kept up a perpetual hum night and day."[34] It must have been a welcome relief for the residents of York when, at about the same time, "mosquito frames or blinds" were introduced as summer window attachments.[35]

Thus in slow, incremental fashion, housing at York Factory was adapted to local environmental constraints. Although log tents and other temporary housing were quickly adopted for use at work encampments around the factory, housing at the factory itself changed more slowly than most other features of material culture. At the camps company employees could build the sort of housing they desired without concern for much beyond their own comfort and what was quick and simple to build. At the factory itself other constraints beyond the purely practical prevailed. Concern with defence discouraged the proliferation of outbuildings until the late 18th century and may well have been a factor in the continued construction of large Men's Houses. Even after defence was abandoned as a serious concern though, the main buildings at York Factory employed European-style materials and methods. It required considerable effort, for example, to saw logs into planks and boards for construction at the post, but as a result York Factory did not resemble the sort of ramshackle log post most people associate with the fur trade. Appearances were more important at the factory than at the camps, and as perhaps the most important post in company territories after 1821, practicality sometimes had to give way to notions of what was proper and seemly.

The furnishings of dwellings at York reflect this. No description of the interior appearance of log tents survives other than simple descriptions of their floor plans. Aside from a hearth with log seats around it and bedplaces built from pine or spruce boughs, a log tent probably contained no more than a few personal possessions like clothes and necessary equipment like guns, axes, and cooking utensils. The residences of tradesmen and labourers at the factory itself probably contained little more. However, R.M. Ballantyne described the internal layout and furnishings of Bachelors' Hall in the 1840s in vivid detail, providing a rare view of the interior of a company residence.

[Bachelors' Hall] was only one story high, and the greater part of the interior formed a large hall, from which several doors led into the sleeping apartments of the clerks. The whole was built of wood; and few houses could be found wherein so little attention was paid to ornament or luxury. The walls were originally painted white, but this, from long exposure to the influence of a large stove, had changed to a dirty yellow. No carpet covered the floor; nevertheless, its yellow planks had a cheerful appearance; and gazing at the numerous knots with which it was covered often afforded me a dreamy kind of amusement when I had nothing better to do. A large oblong iron box, on four crooked legs, with a funnel running from it through the roof, stood exactly in the middle of the room; this was a stove, but the empty wood-box in the corner showed that its services were not required at that time. And truly they were not; for it was the height of summer, and the whole room was filled with mosquitoes and bull-dog flies, which kept up a perpetual hum night and day. The only furniture that graced the room consisted of two small unpainted deal tables without table-cloths, five whole wooden chairs, and a broken one — which latter, being light and handy, was occasionally used as a missile by the

young men when they happened to quarrel. Several guns and fish-ing-rods stood in the corners of the hall, but their dirty appearance proclaimed that sporting, at that time, was not the order of the day. The tables were covered with a miscellaneous collection of arti-cles; and from a number of pipes reposing on little odoriferous heaps of cut tobacco, I inferred that my future companions were great smokers. Two or three books, a pair of broken foils, a bat-tered mask, and several surgical instruments, over which a huge mortar and pestle presided, completed the catalogue.

The different sleeping apartments around were not only interest-ing to contemplate, but also extremely characteristic of the pur-suits of their different tenants. The first I entered was very small — just large enough to contain a bed, a table, and a chest, leaving little room for the occupant to move about in; and yet, from the appearance of things, he did move about in it to some purpose, as the table was strewn with a number of saws, files, bits of ivory and wood, and in a corner a small vice held the head of a cane in its iron jaws. These were mixed with a number of Indian account-books and an inkstand, so that I concluded I had stumbled on the bedroom of my friend Mr. Wilson, the postmaster.

The quadrant-case and sea-chest in the next room proved it to be the skipper's, without the additional testimony of the oiled-cloth coat and sou-wester hanging from a peg in the wall.

The doctor's room was filled with dreadful-looking instruments, suggestive of operations, amputations, bleeding wounds, and human agony; while the accountant's was equally characterized by methodical neatness, and the junior clerks' by utter and chaotic confusion. None of these bedrooms were carpeted; none of them boasted of a chair — the trunks and boxes of the persons to whom they belonged answering instead; and none of the beds were graced with curtains. Notwithstanding this emptiness, however, they had a somewhat furnished appearance, from the number of greatcoats, leather capotes, fur caps, worsted sashes, guns, rifles, shot-belts, snow-shoes, and powder-horns with which the walls were profusely decorated. The ceilings of the rooms, moreover, were very low — so much so that by standing on tiptoe I could touch them with my hand; and the window in each was only about three feet high by two and a half broad, so that, upon the whole, the house was rather snug than otherwise.[36]

The residences of senior and married officers were quite different. The officers in charge of York were given separate accommodation in the form of apartments, or in the 19th century, houses. They were granted the prerogative of keeping servants at company expense, and many furnished their homes with an eye to both comfort and a certain elegance. Joseph Colen, for example, left considerable personal property at York after his departure from company service. In addition to a library of 1400 volumes, his personal property included 21 prints, a clock, a looking glass, two barometers, a barrel organ, glassware, cruets with silver tops, and an "Electrifying Mac[hi]ne." (He also owned "3 Goats, 13 Sow Pigs, and 6 Breeding Sows.")[37]

James and Letitia Hargrave lived in a square, single-storey house that included two bedrooms, two sitting or drawing rooms, a large dining room that served as the gentlemen's mess in winter, a kitchen, and servants' quarters.[38] In 1842 a nursery was added to accommodate their children.[39] Not only was their residence more imposing than Bachelors' Hall, it was better furnished. Most of the rooms were painted green as James considered "it good for the sight," but their bedroom was painted pale blue with indigo wainscotting, a colour scheme Letitia found rather gloomy.[40] Their bedroom was well furnished.

> *I have got a French wardrobe painted green with black feet & a broad stripe of palest yellow — This is the uniform of the house. My own & Hs chests of drawers his wardrobe 2 book cases night table the very screen for holding towels & drying cloths with the large tin dishes on the stoves are all green black & palest yellow — Two large mirrors are the last & look Mr. Wilson says, very fine. The most of this is all new — The basin stands & bed are brown but [how] long they will remain so I cant tell.[41]*

The dining room boasted a mahogany dining table and several large engravings in bird's-eye-maple frames.[42] It was lit on special occasions by an oil lamp, though its appointments did not extend to a carpet and the chairs at the mahogany table were "home-made."[43] The main drawing room of the house had a Kidderminster carpet, a Viennese mahogany piano, a mirror, a sofa, and a table. The tables, sofa, and piano were all covered in green cloth, and the beds in the bedrooms had green blankets.[44] The windows of the house had print curtains, and in the main drawing room the curtains were secured with pins "wch look like so many sunflowers magnified."[45] These pins had been intended for someone in Red River when Letitia Hargrave "seized" them, apparently yet another prerogative of rank in fur trade society.

The Hargrave residence had other ornaments and furniture too. For example, they owned both special patented oil lamps and "fine" candle lamps.[46] When Robert Harding, the clerk in charge of Churchill, returned to England he gave Letitia a large piece of cut crystal he had intended to use as a tobacco box.[47] The Hargraves also purchased "a very pretty British plate" in 1840. James apparently considered plate silver sufficient for York, but he promised that when they returned from "out of the world" they would purchase real silver.[48] The overall picture of their residence was one of "solid comfort and a cosy clutter" — the predominant features of middle-class Victorian interiors.[49]

Company housing in the mid-19th century has been described as " 'unpretending' but not 'indecent.' "[50] Certainly some of the less salubrious aspects of post life like emptying chamber pots out of the windows of the Men's House had been abandoned, and some effort was made to keep residences clean if not always tidy.[51] However, for senior officers, housing and furnishings often were more than "unpretending," and the solid comforts of the Hargraves' residence contrasted sharply with the simplicity of the furnishings in Bachelor's Hall.

The public rooms at York Factory were also decorated and furnished to create an atmosphere of refinement. In the officers' summer mess room a large portrait of Admiral Lord Nelson hung on one wall and a companion painting of the Battle of Trafalgar hung on the opposite wall.[52] Cutlery and crockery were also periodically sent out to adorn mess tables. William Hemmings Cook requested a supply of earthenware dishes from Churchill to replace a set that had become something of an embarrassment.

> *The Dishes are only valued for their decent appearance before Strangers for we have pewter ones of every description — tho rather freckled with age & borne down by the delapidations of time Yet these veritable relics of ancient times notwithstanding their unsavory aspect would answer our purpose well enough & we should be always happy to see them full, were we not like the rest of mankind allured by the fascinations of modern refinement & pretty strongly tinctured with the vain ambition of appearing gay in the Eyes of the world—.[53]*

At the same time Cook proposed to replace much of the window glass at the factory as part of a campaign "to brush up the exterior of the Factory & devest it of that [jail]-like appearance it has exhibited for the last 15 years — ."[54] Thereafter some attention appears to have been paid to keeping the exterior of the factory and its outbuildings "brushed up." The surrounding countryside may have lacked charm, but Letitia Hargrave was "much surprized" by her first view of York. She called it a "great swell." The houses and other buildings were painted pale yellow and their windows and "some particular parts" a contrasting white, and although she later revised her opinion, at first she thought it looked "beautiful."[55]

In comparison with the housing most employees probably had enjoyed prior to entering company service, accommodations at York Factory may very well have seemed attractive. York's work force was dominated by Orkneymen, with a significant admixture of persons from the Shetlands, Hebrides, mainland Scotland, England, Lower Canada, and Rupert's Land itself. Residents of Rupert's Land who entered company service probably saw very little change in their accommodation. At most they changed residence from one post community to another. Recruits from Lower Canada came primarily from the parishes along the St. Lawrence between Montreal and Trois-Rivières, which had a tradition of supplying men to the fur trade. Housing in these well-established communities was of a reasonably high standard. Most accounts of life in Lower Canada and New France suggest that the traditional home of the habitant was carefully designed to withstand the rigours of winter, well constructed, and comfortable.[56] It is unlikely that company servants recruited from Lower Canada were better housed at posts like York Factory, but for Orkneymen the housing at York Factory, even at its most spartan, probably seemed relatively luxurious.

The traditional Orcadian home

> *was long and low in proportion, built of drystone with a roof of thatch supported on a frame of imported timber or driftwood.... The house was divided into a 'but' and a 'ben' end by a free-standing fire 'back', against which a peat fire perpetually burned filling the whole house with acrid smoke. There was ... a hole in the roof framed by rough boards, called a lum, which drew out some of the smoke, but the general effect was to fill the house with smoke without either warming or drying it effectively. Roofs were not waterproof, and in heavy rain a mixture of cold water and soot dripped down the necks and into the food of the unwary.[57]*

These cold, damp, draughty houses were usually shared with hens, geese, and calves too young to be out in the byre. There were no windows and furniture was scarce. Box beds partititioned the single rooms as there were usually no internal walls. Most floors were earth, and the cattle byre was built directly onto the "but" end of the house.[58] Company servants recruited in Shetland lived in similar homes, although walls there were built with an outer and an inner skin of stone, the space between being filled with earth.

In most other respects including furnishings, dampness, and smokiness, Orkney houses resembled those of Shetland and the Hebrides too.[59] Most Scottish employees of the late 18th and 19th centuries would have found their accommodations at York Factory no greater a hardship than those they were used to. Indeed, with the improvements in house building and heating of the early 19th century, York's housing was probably less damp and smoky than the traditional homes of Orkney or Shetland, and company servants may well have had greater privacy and space there than in single-room cottages at home.

Company officers of all ranks would not have faced the same sort of bleak housing prospects as labourers in Britain. This was also probably true for the more highly skilled tradesmen, like blacksmiths or masons. In Britain in the late 18th and 19th centuries a clerk or tradesman might aspire to housing that consisted of four or more rooms, which allowed separation of bedrooms from kitchen and kitchen from parlour. Such houses also often included gardens, privies, sculleries, wash houses, and other such badges of respectability and refinement.[60] In comparison, Bachelors' Hall and the tradesmen's residences at York were rather rough and lacking in amenities. Moreover, the residences of married senior officers, which might contain several bedrooms, drawing rooms, separate nurseries, and a clutter of furniture and ornaments, were probably not as grand as their salary levels would command in England or Scotland. Between 1840 and 1860, chief traders averaged £346/4/0 a year in income from the company and chief factors, twice that.[61] Many also had investments and as their food was provided at company posts, their incomes were probably equivalent to wages of at least £450 a year in Britain. That sort of income would have supported a comfortable home in London on a fashionable square or within the inner suburbs and a household of several servants. Outside of London such an income would have supported an even more comfortable and even luxurious way of life.[62] Nevertheless, the gap between middle-class housing in Britain or the Canadas and the residences of commissioned officers like James Hargrave was not so great as to argue any great privation, and most company employees at York were probably at least as well housed as they would have been in Britain.

In the area of diet employees' standards of living were even more attractive. Despite suggestions that hunger was known as "Hudson's Bay sauce" and that the initials HBC stood for the Hungry Belly Company,[63] there is good evidence company servants and officers ate extremely well. Indeed, many employees attained huge sizes. James Hargrave grew so large that

John Ballenden was moved to write: "Cummings and others gave me awful accounts of your increased bulk, but 2 cwt. is terrific."[64]

Company records divide the food consumed at York and other posts into two categories: country provisions and imported provisions. Country provisions included all the foods produced in the North-West whether by hunting, fishing, or gathering around posts, or as the produce of gardening and livestock-rearing operations. Most country provisions were produced and consumed locally, but by the 19th century many were shipped to posts like York Factory from other places in Rupert's Land where food supplies were more plentiful. Imported provisions were sent to York from Britain on the annual supply ships. Their importance in the overall diet at York changed considerably over time because their use was frequently discouraged as economy measures. Despite this they never entirely disappeared from York's tables, and they formed important supplements to supplies of country provisions.

Country provisions formed the bulk of the food consumed at York Factory. Some food was available merely through making the effort of collecting it. Large numbers of berries grew in the area. Gooseberries, black currants, strawberries, raspberries, and cranberries were collected, often for use as antiscorbutics.[65] Cranberries were particularly popular and plentiful. Some were packed in kegs with sugar and shipped back to England as gifts, while those consumed at York were usually made into tarts "two feet long and 8 inches or so broad."[66]

Considerable effort was made to establish gardens at York Factory. Vegetable gardening at company posts began as early as the 17th century, but aside from the James Bay posts, most gardens produced very little.[67] York's garden crops were usually disappointing and considerable ingenuity was expended explaining away these failures. Finally, after "Blight & Cattapillar" were offered as an excuse for a poor crop, someone on the London committee made the blunt comment in the journal margin, "my eye."[68] In fact the soil at York was not really suited to gardening and the growing season there was not long enough for most garden plants, especially those used in Britain. To overcome these shortcomings, attempts were made to improve the quality of the soil in post gardens and to extend the growing season.

On occasion soil was collected and moved to post gardens, and compost made from "Night Soil — Grey Mould & rotten Tobacco" was added. Other types of fertilizer, including livestock manure and lime, were also tried, along with improving drainage. York's gardens were trenched and even built up on beds of willows to try to drain excessive ground water away.[69]

20 York Factory in the 1870s showing its less formal side. From left: married officers' residence; cattle byre; two mens' residences; an unidentified structure, probably a cookhouse; and two tradesmens' workshops.
Hudson's Bay Company Archives, Provincial Archives of Manitoba.

None of these expedients were entirely successful any more than moving the location of gardens, such as the construction of a large garden across the Hayes River at Ten Shilling Creek in 1843.[70]

To overcome the problem of a short and erratic growing season, quickly maturing seed types like "Early Yellow" turnip were tried, and plants were sometimes started indoors in boxes or in hotbeds or greenhouses.[71] Yet even such methods were of limited value when the climate could be so capricious that as late as June gardens might still be covered with several feet of snow.[72] On rare occasions all this effort and ingenuity were rewarded with good crops. In 1838, post gardens produced 135 bushels of turnips, more than could be eaten at the factory, but this was an exceptional year.[73] The following year only 77 bushels of turnips were grown, and turnip crops of 30 bushels or less were more normal.[74]

Turnips were the most important crop at York, but attempts were made to grow a wide variety of other vegetables. At Lord Selkirk's request parsnips were planted in 1814, and in 1816 one lonely parsnip was found growing.[75] Carrots, cabbages, onions, leeks, watercress, mustard, broccoli, kohlrabi,

134

21 Gardens at York Factory in 1878.
National Archives of Canada, PA-123668.

cucumber, cauliflower, spinach, radishes, beets, potatoes, and French beans were all tried at York but yields were low.[76] Letitia Hargrave offered some insight into the importance placed on growing something at York. She tried to cultivate mignonette in boxes in her room, but all that grew was "a huge crop of chick weed." Still, it "flowered & looked green & that of itself was something."[77]

Attempts to raise livestock at York were somewhat more successful than gardening. Domestic animals provided some welcome fresh meat, often as part of the menu for holiday celebrations. In the 1840s geese and turkeys were kept at York, but only geese from the Orkney Islands found conditions to their liking: "The Turkeys became somnolent when the cold set in & had to be brought into the kitchen where they are doing well. The Orkney geese thrive amazingly in the stable & are killed for the Holidays."[78] Sheep and goat rearing were tried at York, but without much success.[79] Pigs were raised more successfully, and as much as 1200 pounds of fresh meat could be added to factory stocks in a year.[80] Company officers valued the pork as an alternative to salt or cured meat, but some employees were not inclined to eat it. Even when fed on pease for some time before being slaughtered, it was seen as "very indifferent pork," and many felt it was "expensive and unprofitable to attempt rearing pigs at a place where potatoes or any kind of grain can not be raised."[81]

Cattle fodder was less of a problem as hay could be cut close to York Factory on Hay Island. Still, haymaking was laborious and returns were sometimes indifferent so on at least one occasion an attempt was made to feed the post cattle on willow tops and pine branches.[82] The post cattle were rarely left alive for long. Calves and adult animals were slaughtered even when in good condition: a policy someone on the London committee in 1813 described as "*Folly.*"[83] As a result the herd at York was not self-sustaining, and providing livestock to the post remained an on-going expense. Nevertheless, cattle did produce "excellent" but "tough" meat,[84] and the oxen were very useful as draught animals.

Overall neither gardening nor stock-rearing produced more than a tiny fraction of the food consumed at York. They did not make much economic sense, requiring considerable labour but producing generally disappointing returns. One can only wonder at the persistence with which these activities were pursued: perhaps like Letitia Hargrave's flower boxes, their value was psychological rather than purely practical.

Country provisions were also shipped to York from other posts. Potatoes and other vegetables were often shipped to York from Oxford House when space was available in boats or canoes.[85] Donald Ross sent James Hargrave onions from Nelson House, and James Sutherland sent vegetables from Red River to John George McTavish:

> *I have sent a Parcel of Kegs for Sugar & Rum, three of the former*
> *I have filled with Potatoes and in a fourth I have Put a Pumpkin &*
> *4 Doz. of Onions merely as a Curiosity and to show you what Red*
> *River produces. Neither is at Maturity or Ripe and am affraid will*
> *not keep, if they should not, Please accept of the intention.*[86]

It was more common to ship meat and fish of various sorts to friends. Gourmands at York received various delicacies: carp tongues and northern pike from Oxford House and muskox from Churchill, as well as arctic char, pickled trout, buffalo bosses, and tongues.[87]

Most of these food shipments were sent to officers at York more, as James Sutherland suggested, as curiosities than as a means of provisioning the post. There were, however, more concerted efforts made to supply York with food from other parts of the North-West. Flour was sent to York from Red River on several occasions, but the quality was not very high. In 1845 James Hargrave complained that Red River flour was frequently damaged by moisture, and mouldy and rotten. Other casks of flour were "hard as lumps of chalk & so sour as to be unfit for food & is refused to be taken as such by the people now at the depot."[88] Salt geese were regularly sent to York from Severn, but again the quality left much to be desired.

> *Your supply of Geese to this Factory last summer ... has turned out very badly, — more than one fourth of them being rotten and unfit for use. — Even of those that are used, many are spongy and rancid — and the whole of them are burnt up with too much saltpetre, insomuch that two of them are required for one ration. The cause of this I consider to be that the Geese are kept too long fresh, either by the Indian hunters or by the Curers, — and also that many of them have been singed by the former which entirely spoils them, and which Indians are apt to do, to save themselves trouble, unless carefully looked after. The use of Saltpetre, at all, in curing meat is not now considered necessary in England, — but if ever used, not more than a moderate Table spoonful should be put in one Cask.*[89]

The main source of country provisions and the source of most of the food consumed at York were the Homeguard Cree and company employees who acted as hunters and fishermen for the post. Fishing was not pursued with much system or success at York Factory before 1821. Unlike Prince of Wales's Fort where arctic char and whitefish figured prominently in the diet, at York less attention was paid to fishing, perhaps because returns were so variable. Trout were caught sometimes near Rock Depot, and hooks were set for "methy," a type of burbot or freshwater cod, and whitefish in the rivers near York.[90] In 1816 a fish pound was built out of willows, but no mention was made of its success.[91]

Returns from fishing were prone to enormous fluctuations from season to season and year to year even in the same fishing spots. Ten Shilling Creek was the best and most productive fishing area around York, but good catches were by no means assured there. For example, one fishing party composed of nine men spent a full day at the creek fishing with nets but only caught nine suckers.[92] Fishing could not be relied upon as a steady source of food until lakes with large stocks of edible fish were located. John George McTavish, after taking command of York in 1821, set out to solve the problem of finding a reliable source of fish. He apparently followed the sensible course of consulting local Cree fishermen, and a fishing party was sent to Rock Lake near Rock Depot. This lake proved to be a consistent and productive source of fish, and a permanent camp of six men and their families was established there in 1826.[93] The Rock Lake fishery produced about 7000 whitefish a year until 1835-36 when quantities of fish caught there showed signs of decline.[94] Most of the fish were caught in the fall and spring and contributed greatly to supplies of country provisions during the winter and spring months at York when scurvy had formerly been a problem. Fish apparently played a major role in helping to control that disease at York by providing a plentiful and nutritious substitute for salt provisions.

When the quantity of fish caught at Rock Lake began to decline, the fishery was moved in 1836, again with Indian advice, to a number of small lakes north of the Nelson River.[95] These new fishing lakes were used until 1844 when they in turn began to produce fewer fish.[96] Several new sites were tried without much success, and in 1848 the fishery was moved back to Rock Lake. Thereafter it moved between the two fishing areas as fish stocks declined and replenished themselves until 1889, when the lake fishery was abandoned.[97] In the 1840s fishing was also carried on at various sites on the Hayes River near York Factory.[98] Yearly lists of country provisions procured often distinguished between "lake" and "river" fish, and by the 1840s the river fishery had become more important than that of Rock Lake or the northern fishing lakes. In 1849-50, for example, 4204 lake whitefish were caught and 15 799 river whitefish.[99]

The fish caught may be divided into two general categories. The larger whitefish were generally used as food for employees and their families, along with trout and the most tempting parts of other fish, like methy livers, which were considered the equal of pâté de foie gras.[100] The smaller whitefish, suckers, carp, and other "fish of sorts" were usually used as food for the dog teams. The way the fish had been preserved also affected their use. Prior to freeze-up, fish were hung by their tails from tall poles or drying racks to be cured by the sun and wind. "Hung fish," as they were called, were not considered as suitable for human consumption as frozen fish, and like "fish of sorts," tended to be used as food for the dog teams.

Hunting provided the residents of York Factory with the largest component of their diet. Native and European hunters exploited most of the available game resources in the area, but not equally. Company employees had distinct game preferences. Rabbits and beaver do not seem to have been used much as food at York, and only periods of great scarcity could induce anyone to eat wolves, foxes, martens, or muskrats.[101] Beluga whales were hunted, but only for oil and dog meat.[102] Geese, ducks, plover, and partridges, as company men persisted in calling ptarmigan, were hunted extensively as food, as were caribou, which were usually called deer in post records.

York Factory was fortunate to be situated in an area rich in waterfowl, particularly during the spring and fall migration seasons. Geese passed in vast numbers most years, and their potential as food was immediately realized. Geese figured prominently as country provisions at all the Hudson's Bay Company's bayside posts throughout the 18th and 19th centuries.

Much of the goose hunting was done by the York Factory Cree. Their advice was sought on locations for the spring and fall hunts and on methods of hunting.[103]

> *As a great part of the Factory provisions consists of geese killed by the Indians, the English supply them with powder and shot for this purpose allowing them the value of a beaver skin for every ten geese they kill; accordingly, after the Indian has got this supply, he sets off from his tent early in the morning into the marshes, where he sets himself down, with a degree of patience difficult to be imitated, and being sheltered by a few willows, waits for the geese. They shoot them flying, and are so very dexterious at this sport, that a good hunter will kill, in times of plenty, fifty or sixty in a day.[104]*

Some European servants acquired goose-hunting skills to rival those of the Indians. In 1792 "Messrs Sutherland and Thomas" killed nearly one half of the 1500 geese taken,[105] but for the most part, goose hunting was the preserve of Indians hired on a temporary basis. Goose hunting required considerable patience and fortitude, and many company men were quite content to leave to others the work of sitting motionless for hours in a freezing marsh.[106]

The two goose hunts produced varied results, and generally more geese were killed in the spring than in the fall. Annual returns ranged from slightly more than 1000 geese in a poor year to more than 4500 in a good one.[107] Still, even a poor hunt produced a lot of food; as more geese were killed than could be consumed fresh, most were salted and packed in kegs to be eaten during the winter. Salting had to be done carefully to ensure that the geese were palatable later, and many were spoiled or left too long in their kegs. Despite considerable wastage, large quantities of geese were consumed, and between 14 and 20 per cent of the rations served at York in the 1840s consisted of fresh and salt geese.[108]

Ducks, too, were hunted intensively at York, though duck hunting is not specifically mentioned in post journals until 1823.[109] Like geese, ducks were killed by the thousands at the factory in the 1840s. They do not figure very prominently in ration lists, however, ranging from 11 days' rations in 1843-44 to only half a day's in 1844-45 despite the fact that 2066 were killed that year.[110] Plover, too, were killed by the thousands, but ration lists rarely indicate that they were served as food.[111] Several explanations of these apparent anomalies are possible. Plover and duck may have been killed and preserved as a kind of insurance against the failure of other food sources. It is more likely, however, that ration lists do not detail all food served, and that they are primarily a description of food supplied to trades-men's and labourers' messes. Ducks and plover were described as "luxury" foods and particularly good eating by Samuel Hearne and most, if not all, were probably consumed by company officers.[112]

Another bird, the ptarmigan or "partridge," figured prominently in menues at York Factory. Prior to the development of reliable fall and winter fisheries, partridges formed the most important source of fresh food in winter. In good years, when they were killed and eaten by the thousands, scurvy was usually kept at bay, but when they were scarce and could only be served one day a week or so, scurvy soon appeared.[113] The success of partridge hunting varied enormously. In 1793 only about 140 were pro-cured, yet 6778 were killed in 1842.[114] Given the capriciousness of the supply of birds and the number needed to feed a man — four per day if possible[115] — considerable effort and ingenuity went into hunting them. Unlike geese, partridges were usually hunted by company employees, usu-ally officers, who were sent out to winter hunting camps. These camps were distributed over a wide area so that hunting zones did not overlap, and even if the hunters produced few surpluses, it was hoped that they would at least feed themselves. Most partridges were hunted with guns and birdshot, but this was a relatively expensive way to kill small birds. Sometimes nets were set up and the birds were driven into them. Netting birds seems to have been something of an all-or-nothing proposition. When successful, 150 or more partridges could be caught, but all too often the birds simply refused to be driven into the net and none were caught.[116]

Given the wide variation in the success of partridge hunting, the numbers of partridges consumed at York also fluctuated widely. Up until the 1820s, partridges were probably the single most important type of country provi-sions in the winter diet of fur traders, but their importance declined as fish become increasingly available. Nevertheless, partridges continued to pro-vide a significant, if highly variable, fraction of food rations served at York. Lists of rations served in the 1840s indicate partridges formed as much as ten per cent of all food supplied some years and less than one per cent in others.[117]

Deer, moose, and other large mammals were hunted, but most of the venison or "deer" meat eaten at York almost certainly came from caribou.

(1) The trees the snares are tied to (2) the Hedge (3) the Snare (4) Snare Slack tied to the hedge (5) stakes to Keep the Deer from going under.

22 Deer hedges.
James Isham, *Observations on Hudson's Bay, 1743....*, ed. and intro. E.E. Rich, with A.M. Johnson (Toronto: Champlain Society, 1949), p. 153.

In the late 18th century David Thompson described two immense herds of "rein deer," perhaps three and a half million in number, that took two days to pass by the factory. He also described how these animals were hunted.

> *At York Factory, in the early part of the open season, the Rein Deer are sometimes numerous; when they are so, commencing about four miles above the Factory, strong hedges of small pine trees, clear of their branches, are made, near to, and running parallel with, the bank of the River; at intervals of about fifteen yards door ways are made in which is placed a snare of strong line, in which, the Deer in attempting to pass, entangles itself; when thus caught, it is sometimes strangled, but more frequently found alive; and ready to defend itself; the men, who every morning visit the hedge, are each armed with a spear of ten to twelve feet; and must take care that the deer is at the length of his line and carefully avoid the stroke of his fore feet, with which he is very active, and defends itself.[118]*

Despite the great amount of work that went into constructing and maintaining these deer hedges, they were not infallible and the caribou were wary of them. Some traders suspected that they smelled "the tarry Rope from whence the snars are made, also the lashings of the Rails,"[119] so caribou were hunted with guns as well, especially during the winter between migrations.

In the 18th century the venison was preserved either by drying[120] or by pickling in salt. In 1805-06 an icehouse was built at York and it became possible to preserve venison killed in the late fall, winter, and spring without recourse to salt.[121] Often a ton or more of venison was stored on huge blocks of ice cut from the river. The blocks of ice, three feet square and two feet deep, were large enough to keep venison, fish, and fowl frozen over the summer.[122] Frozen food probably retained more of its nutrient value than salted or dried provisions, though one writer complained that the frozen venison he was served at York was tasteless albeit tender.[123]

It is difficult to determine what proportion of the diet at York was composed of venison. In the 1840s fresh venison was served out as rations between four and 15 times per annum; however, this may underrate the importance of venison.[124] Ration lists also include entries for dried meat and pemmican, and most of the former was in all likelihood caribou meat. That would mean venison made up between about 9 and 16 per cent of the food dispensed at York.[125]

The other major category of food consumed at York Factory was imported provisions. Over the years the London committee and economizing administrators like Governor Simpson strove to limit consumption of imported foodstuffs by residents of the company's posts. Simpson even combed indents for unnecessary luxuries. In 1843, for example, he took James Hargrave to task for requesting "Sauces & Pickles on public account":

> I never used fish sauce in the country, and never saw anyone use it or pickles either. From the quantity of Mustard indented for one would suppose it is now issued as an article of trade with the Indians.[126]

Simpson's irritation over the size of mustard imports was only an extreme form of a long-standing concern. Whenever plans were made to cut costs and reorganize the trade, the expense of imported provisions was raised as an issue. Increasingly, imported provisions were seen only as emergency supplies of food and as supplements to country provisions that filled dietary gaps between what could be produced locally and what was needed for working and providing some dietary variety.

York Factory was in more need of imported food supplies than many other posts since gardening and livestock rearing were not particularly successful there. As a result, salt pork, salt beef, and bacon were all used in large quantities. Consumption of these foods declined after 1821, but even so pork and beef made up between 14 and 22 per cent of rations served in the 1840s.[127] Unfortunately provision records do not distinguish between salt pork and salt beef and the fresh pork and beef that came from animals kept at the factory. As a result the actual reliance on imported provisions was somewhat lower than these figures would suggest. Flour, dried peas, oatmeal, rice, barley, biscuit, and cornmeal were also imported in varying quantities. Together they formed between 16 and 24 per cent of the rations at York in the 1840s and early 1850s.[128]

The London committee paid close attention to the diets of its employees and encouraged the use of new products and cooking techniques. The expanding trade in food in the late 18th and 19th centuries made new products like Dutch cheese and rice available for shipment to York. Technological innovations improved methods of food preservation, and the London committee sent supplies of " 'Edward's' preserved potato" to York in 1845 as an experiment. These dried potatoes were well received, and James Hargrave remarked that they were "a great acquisition to the Officers on this Coast who for eight months each year have no vegetable food of any Description except Flour."[129] Encouraged by the success of preserved potatoes, preserved vegetables were given a trial at York in 1856. They, too, were well-received and were often used in soups.[130]

On other occasions the London committee's enthusiasm for new products and processes was misplaced. In 1799 it urged the use of a new cooking device.

We have sent you and our other Factories & their Dependent Settlements a Pot or Kettle call'd a Digester both simple in its construction & in its use but of the utmost Utility. — Scarcely will there be a Family here Rich or Poor but will soon be in posession of one. They are calculated entirely for making Soup as you will perceive by the printed Instructions which accompany each other [sic]. It is needless to dwell on its usefulness, common sense will immediately point it out to everyone who see it and we trust you will not fail to make constant use of it. The digesters after first boiling are to be put on a slow Fire or in the Oven & there to simmer for any length of time which may be thought necessary. Cakes of this Portable Soup when cold may be taken Inland, but it should be diluted with water discretionally before eaten.[131]

Despite the glowing testimonial, use of digesters does not seem to have been eagerly taken up at York. That fall the committee was informed that its digesters had been received and some had been sent inland, where they would be "of the greatest Utility."[132] Thereafter they are not mentioned again in York Factory records.

Diligent as the London committee was in seeking out new products and inventions, the quality of the food exported to York Factory was the subject of frequent complaint. There was a great deal of food that was found to be "unfit for use." For example, the entire supply of bacon in 1809 was as "Yellow as marigolds" and rancid on inspection, and the flour shipped from

England in 1847 had "a sour musty smell" and produced loaves that were "solid masses, heavy, and of a very disagreeable taste."[133] However, neither bad flour nor rancid meat were unique to the fur trade. Such problems were common at a time when the means of preserving foods were limited, and consumers in Britain, just like company employees at York, had to accept that at least a portion of the food they ate would not be, in Letitia Hargrave's words, "exactly 1st chop."[134] Moreover, complaints about food quality rarely were directed at more than a small portion of total food imports, and it should be remembered that company employees were more likely to comment on problems with their food supplies than on imports that arrived in good condition.

York Factory records include lists of country provisions collected and rations of food served for several years between 1835 and 1851. Although records are not complete for every year during the period, they are full enough to give a picture of the range of food eaten at York and some indication of consumption levels. Lists of rations served seem to underestimate consumption of certain foods like plovers, ducks, and perhaps venison that were collected in vast quantities but that are not indicated as being consumed in equivalent amounts. Nor do they include the seven pounds of flour company employees were given per week with which they baked bread and which was sometimes used in other cooking. Nevertheless, they suggest that about one-third of the food consumed at York was imported from Britain and two-thirds was produced locally as country provisions. They also indicate that the diet was overwhelmingly based on consumption of meat and fish that together made up over 80 per cent of daily food rations.

These dietary records set out in Tables 6 and 7 do not, however, indicate the quantities of food that formed a days' ration. A company circular written in 1858 does detail the normal size of food rations for most items consumed at York:

Barley	2 lb.
Oatmeal	2 lb.
Peas	1 quart
Beef (fresh or salt)	2 lb.
Salt Pork	1-1/4 lb.
Pemmican	2 lb.
Dried Meat	2 lb.
Geese (salt or fresh)	1
Ducks (salt or fresh)	2 to 3
Plover (salt or fresh)	6
Fresh Lake Fish	2 or 3 at 3 to 5 lb. each
Fresh River Fish	8

Fresh Venison	*4 lb.*
Rabbits	*4*
Partridges	*4*[135]

Food rations listed in Table 7 suggest that company employees at York consumed the following quantities of food over the course of a year:

365 lb. of flour

47.2 lb. of oatmeal

29.8 lb. of barley

11.6 quarts of peas

61 lb. of salt pork

24.4 lb. of salt and fresh beef

79-119 lake whitefish weighing 3 to 5 lb. each

263 river whitefish

7-10 ducks

53-59 geese

37 plover

43.6 lb. of fresh venison

31 lb. of dried meat

103.2 lb. of pemmican

106 partridges

This list takes no account of the short rations occasionally issued, nor does it question the accuracy of what company officials claimed were normal daily rations. Nevertheless, other evidence suggests that the quantities of daily rations were reasonably well established and did not differ greatly from those listed above.[136]

These supplies of food were supplemented by undetermined quantities of cornmeal, rice, biscuit, and whatever fish and rabbits men caught for themselves. Company officers could consume even greater quantities of food if they wished, for in the officers' mess geese, ducks, whitefish, and other meats appeared on the table at the same time.[137] Some company employees also received gifts of food, usually small luxuries, from friends and family members either in their home communities or stationed elsewhere in the North-West.

It is difficult to assess the nutritional value of such a diet. It clearly lacked the fresh vegetables and fruit now usually recommended in a balanced and healthy diet, though some vegetables and berries were eaten but not recorded in these lists of country provisions procured. Moreover an all-meat or almost entirely meat diet is not necessarily nutritionally deficient. Historically many peoples have survived on such a diet, and experiments have shown even those who are unused to an all-meat diet can adjust to it without any great health risk.[138] Fresh meat and fish contain enough vitamin C to

Table 6
Country Provisions Acquired at York

	1834-35	1839-40	1840-41	1841-42	1842-43
Methy [Burbot] or Freshwater Cod	38				
Trout	420	498	341	258	
Lake White fish	5352	6722 *	5161	9480	10380
River Whitefish	11994	8605 **	11704	7924	11419
Jack [Northern pike]		36	205	357	
Fish "of sorts"	2715	5276	3203	1680	2725
Fresh Venison, lbs.	7725	7403	5793	1782	2926
Dried Venison, lbs.	125	174	58	42	23
Deer [Caribou] Heads	15				
Deer [Caribou] Tongues	35	35	35	6	8
Ducks	4298	3943	6377	4467	2901
Geese	4274	3378	2300	1124	1243
Plovers	3359	3122	5059	1117	3068
Partridges [Ptarmigan]	4663	4646	5952	6778	4458
Rabbits	816	108	17	140	279
Beaver		1	4		
Porcupines		1			
White Whales [Beluga]					
Cranberries, gal.	307				

* Listed as "large whitefish."
** Listed as "small river white fish."

Source: HBCA, B.239/a/148, 152, 154, 155, 157, 159, 161, 168, 171, 173, 176.

Table 6
(continued)

1843-44	1844-45	1847-48	1848-49	1849-50	1850-51	Average Amount
						3.5
380	205	430	330		38	263.6
7650	1183	6211	2941	4204	7781	6096.8
14647	15981	23472	19267	15799	24414	15020.5
	371	87	28	589		152.0
2112	535	2512	4689	3675	1813	2812.2
6042	6566	6534	5037	4301	4172	5299
60	99	40	80	71	20	72.0
10						2.2
20	43		9	18	12	20.0
2100	2066	2979	2820	4635	1774	3487.2
4621	4398	2230	1826	1815	2736	2722.2
2134	4311	3361	2793	919	4116	3032.6
7072	5951	7382	1626	1010	4078	4874.1
	451	116	249	213	113	227.4
		5				1.0
						.1
		16	26	33	43	10.7
137-1/2		67		80	12-1/4	65.4

Table 7
Number of Days on Which Rations were Served at York Factory*

	1840-41	1841-42	1842-43	1843-44	1844-45
Oatmeal	27	25	28-1/2	20	30
Dried Peas	16	19	9-1/2	17	29
Biscuit			4		
Rice				1	
Cornmeal					
Barley					9**
Pork, Salt and Fresh	32	36	54	61	54
Beef, Salt and Fresh	27	15	28	17	5
Lake Whitefish	44	54	55-1/2	63	4
River Whitefish	23-1/2	26	21	25-1/2	30-1/2
Ducks, Fresh			8-1/2	2	1/2
Ducks, Salt	3-1/2		1	9	
Geese, Fresh	6	2		7-1/2	10
Geese, Salt	63	59	[56]+	58	60
Venison, Fresh	15	12	4	11	12
Dried Meat	47	25	24	4	7
Pemmican	24	48	36	36	68
Plover	9	4	5-1/2		9
Partridges [Ptarmigan]	28	40	29-1/2	34	36
Rabbit					1

*   Ration lists were not included in post journals for 1834-35 and 1839-40.
** Listed as barley and rice.
+   The number of geese consumed is omitted in the journal entry.
++ Listed as salt geese and ducks.
+* Listed as salt geese and ducks.

Source: HBCA, B.239/a/148, 152, 154, 155, 157, 159, 161, 168, 171, 173, and 176.

Table 7
(continued)

1847-48	1848-49	1849-50	1850-51	Average No. of Days	% of Year
11	22-1/2	26-1/2	21-1/2	23.6	6.5
10		2-1/2	1-1/2	11.6	3.1
				.4	–
				.1	–
9	20	25	21	8.3	2.3
35	42-1/2	31	17	14.9	4.1
38	52	52	53	48	13.2
7	10		1	12.2	3.3
46	16	28	47	39.7	10.9
49	43	37	41	32.9	9.0
3	1/2	3		1.9	.5
				1.5	.4
2	2	1	3	3.7	1.0
45	53[++]	53-1/2[+*]	52	[55.4]	[15.2]
12	11-1/2	12-1/2	8	10.9	3.0
14	4	10-1/2	4	15.5	4.2
42	72-1/2	75	63	51.6	14.1
4	7	5	12	6.2	1.7
39	8-1/2	2-1/2	20	26.4	7.2
				.1	–

prevent scurvy, and even dried or salt provisions have to be consumed for a period of six weeks or more before symptoms of scurvy begin to appear.[139] The main dietary deficiency at York Factory was probably not vitamins but calcium, and traders may well have suffered from bad teeth and brittle bones. Cheese, however, was imported as a food supply and some milk would have been available from the small herd of cows kept at York. The high incidence of digestive disorders at York indicates that the diet may have been short on roughage and that methods of preserving meat and fish were not perfect.

After fish began to be caught in large numbers the winter diet at York seems to have been satisfactory nutritionally even without many vegetables. It also compares well with what is known about the food consumption of English agricultural labourers, semi-skilled workers, and skilled tradesmen. In 1810 a highly paid London typesetter could afford weekly purchases of 20 pounds of bread and flour, 14 pounds of meat, two pounds of butter, one pound of cheese, and two pounds of sugar, as well as beer, milk, tea, some vegetables, and condiments like salt, pepper, and vinegar for himself, his wife, and two children. A Lancashire cotton spinner earning better than average wages and with a wife and five children purchased weekly one and half pounds of butter, one and half ounces of tea, four quarts of oatmeal, one and a half pounds of bacon, 40 pounds of potatoes, seven quarts of milk, one pound of meat for Sunday, one and half pounds of sugar, and small quantities of salt, pepper, and mustard. The family also baked its own bread in unspecified quantities. The less well-to-do subsisted almost entirely on bread and potatoes. A semi-skilled worker, his wife, and three children in 1841 ate 20 pounds of bread, five pounds of meat, 40 pounds of potatoes, one pound of butter, one pound of sugar, and three ounces of tea, while he supplemented this meagre diet with seven pints of porter.[140]

These and other available household budgets indicate that few vegetables other than potatoes were eaten by English workingmen and their families. Nor was this just a feature of urban diets. Agricultural labourers also ate few vegetables other than potatoes, and in general ate less and lower quality food than almost any other group in England. The absence of vegetables from the diets of York's residents was probably not perceived as a hardship since few were used to eating many vegetables anyway. In addition, although company employees consumed similar quantities of flour, bread, oatmeal, dried peas, and barley to workingmen in England, they ate much more meat and fish. The Englishman's diet in the early 19th century has been described as "at best stodgy and monotonous, at worst hopelessly deficient in quantity and nutrient,"[141] yet for all that it was the diet of a resident of the wealthiest nation in the world.

The average inhabitant of the Orkneys or Shetland or the Hebrides was by all accounts even less likely to enjoy a varied and ample diet than English workingmen. In the 1750s one company officer dismissed complaints from Orkney servants about their food with the comment that few had ever eaten anything other than "Pease or Barley Bread with Salt Sellocks [cod or coal-fish fry] and Kale" until they joined company service.[142] Orkney diets in the 19th century did not change much, and have been characterized as "monotonous" though not "inadequate."[143] Most Orkneymen subsisted primarily on oatmeal and barley-meal porridges, barley bread, and a few vegetables like cabbage, kale, turnips, and potatoes. Meat and fish were available, but the former at least was usually reserved for special occasions.

Shetland Islanders' diets were very similar, though sheep were raised there in large numbers and lamb and mutton were not unusual items of food. Nevertheless one crofter, or small farmer, described his diet in 1804 as coalfish for breakfast, coalfish and cabbage for lunch, and coalfish for dinner.[144] On Lewis in the Hebrides, fish, oatmeal, and potatoes were the mainstays of islanders' diets, and in 1811 it was estimated that most Hebridean islanders ate a half to a quarter as much as the average Englishman.[145] If this is correct, much of the appeal of company service for Scottish islanders may well have been the variety and quantity of food they could consume.

Company servants were recruited in Lower Canada primarily from the Montreal area and a few parishes along the St. Lawrence. In the "voyageur" parishes, agricultural productivity was usually low and in some areas like Sorel, subsistence crops like oats, corn, beans, and potatoes had replaced wheat as the main crop.[146] The Hudson's Bay Company recruited its Lower Canadian employees in those areas of Lower Canada where standards of living, including diet, were lowest.

On the whole, company employees were well fed by the standards of the day though supplies of food were not always plentiful. Returns from hunting and fishing were subject to capricious fluctuations and short rations were sometimes necessary, especially before 1821. In 1797, for example, supplies of country provisions ran short and allowances of dried peas and flour were cut to one quarter of a pint per person per day. Joseph Colen wrote in some anguish of his distress "to hear the Crys of Children for food."[147] Fortunately such bleak times were rare, and if one type of food ran short, others in more plentiful supply could be substituted. In 1813, for example, stocks of flour and oatmeal were low, and rations of these items were cut.

To prevent dissatisfaction and hardship, biscuit was distributed and extra rations of venison, fish, and partridges were offered.[148] Privations and worries about food supplies were not unknown at York, but they were surprisingly rare. Indeed, Andrew Graham suggested that in the 1780s and 1790s company employees usually could not eat all the food they were given and gave some of it to the Homeguard Cree. He also remarked that Orkney servants saved the flour they could not eat and shipped it home to their families on the supply ship.[149]

Cooking at York usually followed British patterns, which in the 18th and 19th centuries meant "plain" cooking for the most part: roasts, meat pies, stews, soups, boiled vegetables, and porridge or gruel. In Britain it was only the very wealthy who were attracted to French or continental styles of cuisine, and most avoided "impertinent and miserable attempts at foreign cooking" in which dishes "appeared upon the table under false pretenses."[150] Similarly at York food was usually plentiful but neither imaginatively nor skilfully prepared for the most part. Mess cooks were not highly esteemed and few seem to have had many qualifications for the post. The cook assigned to the officers' mess in 1843 was reputed to have had a repertoire of dishes limited to boiled potatoes and fish.[151]

In fact, officers' meals were more varied than this and were usually marked by some formality and abundance. Visitors to the post, like Dr. Helmcken, were often surprised by the dining habits of their hosts.

> The first time I dined at the mess, Hargrave at the head and Mactavish at the foot of the table, Hargrave descanted on the beauties and benefits of a 'white fish' of which some small ones were on the table — caught I suspect in the river. However, ducks came on — and asked whether I would take duck or goose — duck — so a whole one was put on my plate! Not [a?] very large one to be sure, but I did not know how to begin eating it, but before I had begun my neighbour sent for another! 'Oh,' said he, 'if you were here in the winter, you would see us eat two or three geese each!'[152]

Letitia Hargrave described a meal she shared with three other women from the post as including "a roast of venison at the top [of the table] 3 geese at the foot, 4 ducks on one side 6 plover on the other, a large Red River ham (whole leg) & potatoes & mashed turnips or boiled lettuce."[153] She does not suggest that the quantity of food served was unusual, but she did remark on another occasion that her dining companions had "good swallows," which they would have needed to do justice to such meals.[154]

23 Refreshments.

Officers and their families patterned their dining habits on those of well-to-do Britons who could afford food in quantity but who preferred not to see it appear upon the table under exotic sauces. Even so, the officers aspired to a certain fashionableness and formality at mealtimes. At York the officer in charge sat at the head of the table and his deputy at the foot, and other officers and guests arranged themselves around the table. Certain officers and guests, either through promotion from the ranks or long service in remote regions, found their manners or conversation lacking. Some were baffled, for example, by the process of eating fish without using a knife — scarcely an important skill for a fur trader but one that officers at York took seriously.[155]

Tradesmen's and labourers' meals were almost certainly simpler and little attention would have been paid to whether or not anyone used a knife on their fish course. Like officers, however, they probably preferred to eat their food prepared in familiar ways as soups, stews, roasts, and pies. York's residents were willing to eat caribou and ptarmigan and other foods they would not have encountered before, but they were generally unwilling to adopt new cooking methods. Few were willing to try, as Samuel Hearne did, the half-raw fish, caribou stomachs, and embryonic animals eaten by the Chipewyan and other Indians as delicacies. Hearne, however, suggested that anyone who overcame their prejudices against such foods was liable to become fond of them for "whoever wishes to know what is good, must live with the Indians."[156] In spite of Hearne's adventurous approach to dining, most fur traders' dietary preferences were highly conservative, and Letitia Hargrave confessed that despite the whole geese, roasts of venison, and plates of ducks and plovers she encountered on her table, she pined for someone who would bake "scones and cakes."[157]

Still, if company employees thought wistfully about sones or sellocks or sheep's pluck and onions from time to time, they did not have to look solely to wages to find a reason to work in the fur trade. Conditions of material life at posts like York Factory were neither as primitive nor as fraught with hardship as they are often depicted.

"The Most Respectable Place in the Territory"

York Factory was an unusual fur trade post in many respects, and as a result it cannot be assumed that the experiences of its residents exactly paralleled those of other fur traders. Nevertheless, a close and critical examination of York Factory records suggests that many widely held perceptions of life in the fur trade need to be reconsidered.

A career in the fur trade might bring to mind notions of an exciting and adventurous life, but the reality of work at York was more prosaic. The men stationed there were employed for the most part at copying out invoices, making axes, cutting firewood, and doing other familiar and largely mundane tasks. There was little romance involved in packing furs or keeping ledgers, and the work of a clerk or blacksmith or labourer at York resembled nothing quite so much as the work of a clerk or blacksmith or labourer in Britain or Canada. Even senior commissioned officers at York were hired more as accountants and managers from the late 18th century on than for more esoteric skills like bartering with the Homeguard or a knowledge of Indian languages.

The courage and fortitude of company employees are unquestioned, but there is little evidence in York Factory records to support the contention in one recent popular history that traders had "to exist near the limits of human endurance."[1] Hours of work at York were not particularly onerous for the period, and company employees enjoyed a surprising amount of leisure time. Wage rates were generally quite attractive, and because the company

155

provided its employees with room and board at no charge, most almost certainly had greater disposable income than individuals employed in similar jobs in either Britain or Canada could command.

Nor were material conditions at York as harsh or as primitive as they are sometimes assumed to have been. Through a judicious blending of native and European materials and techniques, company employees learned to clothe and house themselves, if not always in comfort, at least in an effective and sensible manner given environmental conditions at York. Their diet was probably monotonous, but it was not normally inadequate, and indeed the diet at York compares favourably in many respects with the diets of tradesmen and labourers in 18th- and 19th-century Britain. While scurvy was a problem at York, especially in the period between about 1790 and 1821, the effective exploitation of fish stocks in the area after 1821 largely controlled the disease. Company employees at York did not suffer undue nutritional hardships for the most part, and in fact they consumed great quantities of some foodstuffs, like meat and wildfowl, that were considered luxuries in Britain.

Although residents of York Factory were subject to a variety of diseases and accidents were by no means uncommon, the general standard of health there — at least for company employees — was reasonably high. The fur trade was not a particularly risky career, and the mortality rate at York in the 18th century was comparable to that of similar colonial communities. While post surgeons were not always possessed of high skills, their knowledge and surgical expertise was sufficient to deal with most of the diseases and injuries they had to treat, and from the late 18th century on, the company instituted a number of practical reforms in the areas of diet, cleanliness, and exercise that helped to improve community health standards.

Perhaps the best indication that company employees did not exist at the limits of human endurance was the fact that the company successfully recruited employees year after year in areas like the Orkneys and Lower Canada where conditions in the North-West were no secret. Indeed as early as the mid-18th century even critics of the company were forced to admit, albeit with some incredulity, that many employees enjoyed their time in company service and sought to remain in it.[2]

York Factory records reveal some surprising and hitherto largely unexamined features of fur trade life. Post residents enjoyed a lively and varied recreational life and considerable leisure. Pastimes consisted of much more than brandy and brawls, the importance of which may well have been overstated. The drinking habits of company men in particular need to be put into a broader context. The hard-drinking traditions of the fur trade were part of a larger tendency in 18th- and 19th-century Britain and elsewhere to condone drunkenness. As a result, company men were often binge drinkers, but their overall levels of alcohol consumption do not seem to have been unusual for the period. Moreover, available figures suggest that alcoholism was not a major cause of death at York Factory despite widely held suspicions to the contrary. In fact recreational practices at York had a surprisingly intellectual side. The post library served many avid readers, while other men pursued their own literary aspirations and scientific interests. As might be expected, hunting, fishing, and trapping were seen as both work and leisure activities, but company employees also found time to play football, chess, checkers, and cards.

Another unexpected feature of fur trade life that has all too often been ignored was the ability of tradesmen and labourers to control their own labour and to press, individually and collectively, for higher wages, better work and living conditions, and redress of some grievances. Company employees were far from powerless in their dealings with their superiors. They employed a variety of tactics ranging from the threat of mass resignations to attempts to interfere with recruitment of new employees in their home communities to force the company and its officers to meet their demands at least on occasion.

Company employees were subject to a range of disciplinary measures including fines and physical punishments; however, there is little evidence that these disciplinary powers were viewed as draconian or openly resented. Most employees appear to have accepted that the company and its officers had the right to discipline them and that this was no more than the way of the world. Similarly the hierarchical structure of post society at York was not directly questioned except in a handful of instances. York Factory, however, was a small community — even including the Homeguard Cree of the immediate area and the wives and children of company employees it was probably composed of no more than two or three hundred persons in the mid-19th century — and distinctions of wealth and power were enormous. Between 1840 and 1860, for example, the average annual value of a chief trader's share from company profits was nearly £350, while chief factors received twice this amount.[3] Thus a chief trader or chief factor, by virtue of his commission, earned between three and a half and seven times the income of senior clerks. The comparison between commissioned officers' incomes and tradesmen's and labourers' wages was even more stark. During the same period the average wage for tradesmen and labourers in company service ranged between about £20 and £25 per annum; considerably less than ten per cent even of chief traders' incomes.[4] Housing, food, and even leisure time were allocated, like income, on the basis of rank in a complex system of differential privilege. Some social mobility was possible at York Factory in the late 18th and 19th centuries, but only a handful of individuals through ability or long service managed to pass from servant to officer status. They were the exceptions that proved the societal rule in the fur trade that life dictated firm distinctions in status, and few questioned that notion.

Jennifer Brown, a noted fur trade historian, has called the fur trade in the North-West a partial or semi-autonomous society, a kind of hybrid society that drew on both its native and European roots. Too often history has overlooked fur traders' cultural borrowings from native peoples, though the impact of contact on Indian cultures has often been studied. Cultural transfer in the fur trade was not just a one-way street, and contemporary observers often felt that the adoption of many native ways was one of the distinguishing features of fur trade life. The Reverend David Jones, an Anglican missionary at Red River, wrote:

> I have been often astonished at the amazing degeneracy which [fur traders] have shown by falling by degrees into the habits of the Indian. The Trader found the Indians with fishing nets peculiar to themselves both in structure and mode of setting — this he has adopted: — he found the Indian in his small Birch-rind canoe — he gets into it and performs voyages of hundreds of miles in it: — he found the Indian preparing his food in a way peculiar to himself that of making it into Pemican — this is now the food of the labouring class throughout the country — in short the European follows the same track that the Indians did — lives by the Chase — travels in Winter in the Indian Carioles drawn by Indian Dogs — adopts the Indian dress — with many other things that may be enumerated.[5]

Jones's view that this was a symptom of degeneracy seems misplaced, and this cultural transfer now appears symptomatic of the vigour of fur trade communities and the adaptive skills of the traders themselves.

At York Factory a similar pattern of cultural exchange was also present, but at York the European or British roots of the fur trade were particularly strong. York's work force was overwhelmingly British in origin, and the community they built there resembled pre-industrial Britain in its work patterns and techniques and social structure. It was a colonial settlement largely dependent on Britain in economic and cultural terms. Perhaps that was why Letitia Hargrave found it, at least initially, to be less alien than she had feared and "the most respectable place in the Territory."

Suggestions for Further Reading

The most authoritative general history of western Canada up to 1870 remains A.S. Morton's *A History of the Canadian West to 1870-71* (Toronto: University of Toronto Press, 1973), 2nd edition edited by Lewis G. Thomas. Gerald Friesen's *The Canadian Prairies: A History* (Toronto: University of Toronto Press, 1984) covers a much longer time period and focusses less on the pre-1870 period than Morton's book; however, it pays much more attention to native history and integrates most of the major revisionist findings of recent scholarly work into a lively and readable overview. The relationship between the fur trade and the early history of western Canada is ably explored in E.E. Rich's *The Fur Trade and the Northwest to 1857* (Toronto: McClelland and Stewart, 1976).

Company histories are well represented. E.E. Rich has prepared a lengthy and scholarly history of the Hudson's Bay Company, *The History of the Hudson's Bay Company, 1670-1870* (London: Hudson's Bay Record Society, 1958-59). A much shorter but nevertheless sound overview of company history may be found in Glyndwr Williams's "Highlights in the History of the First Two Hundred Years of the Hudson's Bay Company," *The Beaver*, Outfit 301, No. 2 (Autumn 1970), pp. 4-63. The best popular history of the company is Douglas MacKay's *The Honourable Company* (Toronto: McClelland and Stewart, 1966). Peter C. Newman's *Company of Adventurers* (Toronto: Viking-Penguin Books, 1985) is a vivid and phenomenally successfully popular history, but it has been widely criticized by fur trade scholars for being overly sensational in some of its conclusions.

The best general history of the French fur trade in the West is W.J. Eccles' *The Canadian Frontier, 1534-1760* (New York: Holt, Rinehart and Winston, 1969). Corporate histories of the North-West Company are fewer in number than those of the Hudson's Bay Company. One of the best remains *Documents Relating to the North West Company*, edited by W.S. Wallace (Toronto: Champlain Society, 1934). A more popular but still very useful

159

study of the Nor-Westers can be found in Marjorie Wilkins Campbell's *The North West Company* (Toronto: MacMillan, 1957).

After long years of neglect the role of women in the fur trade and the importance of family and kinship ties are explored in two excellent social histories: Sylvia Van Kirk's *"Many Tender Ties": Women in Fur-Trade Society in Western Canada, 1670-1870* (Winnipeg: Watson and Dwyer, 1980), and Jennifer S. Brown's *Strangers in Blood: Fur Trade Company Families in Indian Country* (Vancouver: University of British Columbia Press, 1980). A full study of the Homeguard Cree at York Factory still awaits an author. A valuable study of relations between fur traders and another Cree group, the Cree of eastern James Bay, may be found in Daniel Francis and Toby Morantz's *Partners in Furs: A History of the Fur Trade in Eastern James Bay, 1600-1870* (Montreal and Kingston: McGill-Queen's University Press, 1983). Arthur Ray and Donald Freeman's *"Give Us Good Measure": An Economic Analysis of Relations between the Indians and the Hudson's Bay Company before 1763* (Toronto: University of Toronto Press, 1978) covers an earlier period than this study, but is an insightful and method-ologically interesting contribution to native history. Arthur Ray's earlier study, *Indians in the Fur Trade: Their Role as Trappers, Hunters and Middlemen in the Lands Southwest of Hudson Bay, 1660-1870* (Toronto: University of Toronto Press, 1974), covers a much longer time period and includes much information of interest on trade and trade relations at York Factory.

The Canadian Parks Service has produced a number of valuable studies on York Factory including structural, land-use, and archaeological reports. Interested researchers should contact Research Publications, Canadian Parks Service, Environment Canada, 1600 Liverpool Court, Ottawa, Ontario K1A 0H3, for information on available manuscript and microfiche reports.

A number of first-hand accounts of life at York Factory have been pub-lished, and anyone interested in the social history of the fur trade could do worse than begin with what the fur traders themselves found interesting about their lives. For the period between 1789 and 1870 the best of these are R.M. Ballantyne's *Hudson Bay, or, Everyday Life in the Wilds of North America During Six Years' Residence in the Territories of the Hon. Hudson Bay Company* (most recently published by Hurtig, 1972); David Thompson's *Narrative, 1784-1812* (Toronto: Champlain Society, 1962), edited by Richard Glover; Letitia Hargrave's *The Letters of Letitia Hargrave* (Toronto: Champlain Society, 1947), edited by Margaret Arnett MacLeod; and James Hargrave's *The Hargrave Correspondence, 1821-1843* (Toronto: Champlain Society, 1938), edited by G.P. de T. Glazebrook.

Finally, most readers will find much to interest them on the history of York Factory and other posts in the pages of *The Beaver*. Articles written in a popular and accessible style frequently represent some of the best new research on fur trade subjects. Both the *Dictionary of Canadian Biography* (Toronto: University of Toronto Press, 1966-) and *The Canadian Encyclopedia* (Edmonton: Hurtig, 1985) include informative entries on individuals and events associated with the history of York Factory.

Endnotes

Introduction

1   Eric Ross, *Beyond the River and the Bay....* (Toronto: Univ. of Toronto Press, 1970), p. 32.

A Short History of York Factory to 1870

1   *See,* for example, Paul Clifford Thistle, *Indian-European Trade Relations in the Lower Saskatchewan River Region to 1840* (Winnipeg: Univ. of Manitoba Press, 1986), p. 3; Victor P. Lytwyn, "York Factory Native Ethnohistory: A Literature Review and Assessment of Source Material," Microfiche Report Series, No. 162, Parks Canada, Ottawa, 1984, pp. 14-19.

2   Daniel Francis and Toby Morantz, *Partners in Furs: A History of the Fur Trade in Eastern James Bay, 1600-1870* (Montreal and Kingston: McGill-Queen's Univ. Press, 1983) (hereafter cited as Francis and Morantz, *Partners in Furs),* pp. 16-17.

3   The name York Factory seems to date from the early 18th century. The terms "fort" and "factory" were often used interchangeably and it is unclear what distinction, if any, the company implied in the use of these terms. In the 18th century, "factory" did not necessarily imply a manufacturing institution but was used to describe the overseas stations of merchant trading companies. In the Hudson's Bay Company's service it became convention to refer to its two main bayside posts — Moose and York — as factories rather than posts, perhaps as an indication of their greater trade and administrative importance.

4   William Lewis Morton, *Manitoba, A History* (Toronto: Univ. of Toronto Press, 1961), p. 12.

5   Several accounts of this confusing period exist. A short summary of the main events may be found in Douglas MacKay, *The Honourable Company: A History of the Hudson's Bay Company* (Toronto: McClelland and Stewart, 1966), pp. 47-56. A more detailed account of who built what and where, and then who captured it and how, is included in Joseph Burr Tyrrell, ed., *Documents Relating to the Early History of Hudson Bay* (Toronto: Champlain Society, 1931), pp. 1-34.

6   *See* Arthur J. Ray and Donald B. Freeman, *"Give Us Good Measure": An Economic Analysis of Relations between the Indians and the Hudson's Bay Company before 1763* (Toronto: Univ. of Toronto Press, 1978), p. 34, Fig. 4.

7   *See* Arthur J. Ray, *Indians in the Fur trade: Their Role as Trappers, Hunters, and Middlemen in the Lands Southwest of Hudson Bay, 1660-1870* (Toronto: Univ. of Toronto Press, 1974), p. 52, Fig. 16.

8   Joseph Robson, *An Account of Six Years Residence in Hudson's-Bay, from 1733 to 1736 and 1744 to 1747*, reprint of 1752 ed. (New York: Johnson Reprint Corp., 1965), p. 6.

9   These adjustments and the problems they created are discussed in Richard Gilchrist Glover, "The Difficulties of the Hudson's Bay Company's Penetration of the West," *Canadian Historical Review*, Vol. 29, No. 3 (Sept. 1948), pp. 240-54.

10   Construction at York Factory between 1789 and 1821 is described in detail in Bruce F. Donaldson, "York Factory: A Land-Use History," Manuscript Report Series, No. 444, Parks Canada, Ottawa, 1981 (hereafter cited as Donaldson, "Land-Use"), pp. 17-42.

11   Ibid., p. 33.

12   Construction at York between 1821 and 1870 is covered in ibid., pp. 43-75.

13   The importance of American railroads and steamboats in ending the comparative isolation of the Canadian West is discussed in greater detail in Alvin Charles Gluek, *Minnesota and the Manifest Destiny of the Canadian Northwest: A Study in Canadian-American Relations* (Toronto: Univ. of Toronto Press, 1965).

14   Eric Ross, *Beyond the River and the Bay....* (Toronto: Univ. of Toronto Press, 1970), p. 96.

15   Peter Cecil Bailey, *Leisure and Class in Victorian England: Rational Recreation and the Contest for Control, 1830-1885* (London: Routledge and Kegan Paul, 1978) (hereafter cited as Peter C. Bailey, *Leisure and Class*), p. 1.

Social Structure and Social Relations

1   *See*, for example, Andrew Graham, *Observations on Hudson's Bay, 1767-91*, ed. Glyndwr Williams (London: Hudson's Bay Record Society, 1969) (hereafter cited as Graham, *Observations*), pp. 242-330; Joseph Robson, *An Account of Six Years Residence in Hudson's-Bay, from 1733 to 1736 and 1744 to 1747*, reprint of 1752 ed. (New York: Johnson Reprint Corp., 1965), pp. 9-84; Edward Umfreville, *The Present State of Hudson's Bay....*, ed. and intro. W. Stewart Wallace (Toronto: Ryerson Press, 1954) (hereafter cited as Umfreville, *Present State*), pp. 6-15, 33-65. All of the above discuss life at Hudson's Bay Company posts. Other fur trade companies have their own equivalent authors.

2   The writings of Jennifer Brown, Sylvia Van Kirk, Frits Pannekoek, and John Foster dominate this approach. The idea of "fur trade society" has received a certain amount of criticism from other scholars. The debate is not so much about whether or not the fur trade was a "socio-cultural" as well as commercial undertaking — there is little argument about that — as about the definition of what is meant by fur trade society. It has been pointed out that there were many fur trades carried on by different companies, from different countries, with different native groups, in different regions. Unfortunately, most of the work done to date concentrates on Hudson's Bay Company and, to a lesser extent, North West Company sources. In turn, these sources reflect almost exclusively the concerns and insights of the officers of those companies, and thus the picture they paint of fur trade society may be elitist and narrow. *See* Francis and Morantz, *Partners in Furs*, esp. p. 167; and Adrian Tanner, "The End of Fur Trade History," *Queen's Quarterly*, Vol. 90, No. 1 (Spring 1983), pp. 176-91.

     The debate over what is properly meant by "fur trade society" may be passed over quickly for the purposes of this study. The term is used occasionally to avoid more cumbersome terminology, but does not imply that there are not important differences between the fur trade in separate locations even within the operations of a single company. Life at York was not exactly analogous to life at Lac La Pluie. What this study suggests about the main features of society at York should not be assumed to be always true for other fur trade communities, even other Hudson's Bay Company posts.

3   Of the sort of society envisioned by the officers and London committee of the Hudson's Bay Company at any rate. Some authors, notably Jennifer Brown in *Strangers in Blood: Fur Trade Company Families in Indian Country* (Vancouver: Univ. of British Columbia Press, 1980) (hereafter cited as Brown, *Strangers in Blood*), have pointed out that Nor'Westers and Hudson's Bay Company men had different notions about social organization that reflected in part the differing recruitment patterns and personnel of the two companies.

4   Letitia (Mactavish) Hargrave, *The Letters of Letitia Hargrave*, ed. and intro. Margaret Arnett MacLeod (Toronto: Champlain Society, 1947) (hereafter cited as L. Hargrave, *Letters*), p. 246, Letitia Hargrave to Mrs. Dugald Mactavish Sr., 30 Oct. 1849.

5   Some authors have felt that the facts that social distinctions were preserved and even given formal encouragement in fur trade communities and that a system of ranks prevailed in posts need explanation. The levelling influence some have detected in frontier society seems to have been weakly expressed in the fur trade. Philip Goldring, in "Papers on the Labour System of the Hudson's Bay Company, 1821-1900: Volume II," Manuscript Report Series, No. 412, Parks Canada, Ottawa, 1980 (hereafter cited as Goldring, "Papers: Vol. II"), p. 37, argues that these fur trade communities were "far enough *beyond* the frontier to escape its democratizing influence." Sylvia Van Kirk in turn suggests that the frontier in Canada differed from the American frontier in terms of the importance of hierarchy and "class," basing her argument on W.J. Eccles, *The Canadian Frontier, 1534-1760* (New York: Holt, Rinehart and Winston, 1969). *See* Sylvia Van Kirk, *"Many Tender Ties": Women in Fur-Trade Society in Western Canada* (Winnipeg: Watson and Dwyer, 1980) (hereafter cited as Van Kirk, *Many Tender Ties*), pp. 9, 256. It may be, though, that no special explanation of the hierarchical nature of post communities is necessary. William McNeill has argued that frontiers do not necessarily have a levelling effect. He suggests instead that as "most human beings prefer the safe and familiar," fundamental social change in frontier settlements occurs only when "inherited institutions ... cease to work well." *See* William H. McNeill, *The Great Frontier: Freedom and Hierarchy in Modern Times* (Princeton: Princeton Univ. Press, 1983), esp. pp. 9-10.

6   The use of these terms is discussed in some detail in Goldring, "Papers: Vol. II," pp. 37-39.

7   The study of who dined with whom at posts like York is probably worthy of an academic paper on its own. In 1822, guides and interpreters were excluded from the officers' mess at York by a specific rule of the Northern Council. In turn, their superior status to ordinary servants was recognized by granting them their own mess. Canada. National Archives. Manuscript Division, MG20, Hudson's Bay Company Archives (hereafter cited as HBCA), B.239/k/1, fol. 17d, minutes of council 1822, item 104. When someone not entitled to the privilege was by accident or oversight admitted to the officers' mess, care was taken to see that the error was not repeated.

> *Neil McDonald who is engaged to Capn [Franklin] in the capacity of a Steersman has been admitted to the Table at this place [York] from our not exactly understanding the footing he was upon when he first came ashore, but you can easily*

> *evade ushering him to your table, to which, I conceive he has not the smallest tittle of right to be admitted....*

HBCA, B.239/b/88b, p. 12, John George McTavish to James Leith, 1 Sept. 1824. Inclusion in the officers' mess and one's treatment there appear to have been used less than subtly to put some visitors and new employees in their social place. John MacLeod, an apprentice clerk with Miles Macdonell's party bound for Red River in 1811, reported that they received a "Cold & haughty reception" and had to dine with the cooks on scraps from the governor's table. Manitoba. Provincial Archives (hereafter cited as PAM), MG1, D5, John MacLeod Diary, pp. 1-2. A few years later Lieutenant Chappell of the Royal Navy was greeted with a guard of honour playing bagpipes and an enormous meal of buffalo tongues and venison. Edward Chappell, *Narrative of a Voyage to Hudson's Bay in His Majesty's Ship Rosamond Containing Some Account of the North-Eastern Coast of America and of the Tribes Inhabiting that Remote Region*, reprint of 1817 ed. (Toronto: Coles Publishing, 1970), p. 184.

8   The powers and prerogatives of commissioned officers are described in greater detail in Goldring, "Papers: Vol. II," pp. 39-41.

9   L. Hargrave, *Letters*, p. 205, Letitia Hargrave to Mrs. Dugald Mactavish Sr., 5 Sept. 1845.

10   In the 1840s Robert Wilson was the butt of most of the jokes in the officers' mess at York, and he was viewed more as a comic figure than anything else because of his background as a tradesman. Ibid., pp. 86-87, Letitia Hargrave to Mrs. Dugald Mactavish, 1 Dec. 1840.

11   "Middlemen" was the title given to employees who paddled or rowed from a middle position in the canoe or boat. Unlike bowsmen or steersmen, they had few responsibilities except to pull when told to.

12   As for all other employees of the Hudson's Bay Company, except perhaps commissioned officers, wages for labourers and midmen rose over the course of the 19th century. Their wages are discussed in some detail in Goldring, "Papers: Vol. II," pp. 174-75.

13   Ibid., p. 169.

14   The Northern Council resolution in 1822 to exclude guides and interpreters from the officers' mess at York makes no sense unless up until that time they had messed on occasion with the officers.

15   Goldring, "Papers: Vol. II," p. 235.

16   In 1829-30, after George Simpson's reorganization of York Factory's functions and in keeping with his attempts to make York a centre of artisanal production, they made up nearly 47% of the total population of servants, but this was an extreme case.

17   *See* Goldring, "Papers: Vol. II," pp. 186-215.

18   Peter Laslett, *The World We Have Lost: England Before the Industrial Age* (New York: Charles Scribner's Sons, 1971), p. 23.

19   Goldring, "Papers: Vol. II," p. 37.

20   Company use of the terms "officers" and "men" as well as the near-military chain of command at fur trade posts led many historians to compare company service to military service. While "military monasticism" may have been the ideal of the London committee, the "semi-autonomous" nature of fur trade life meant that neither monasticism nor military discipline could be effectively enforced. Brown, *Strangers in Blood*, pp. 11-18. Some historians have argued that over the course of the 18th century, company service became less and less military in character and came more to resemble the large-scale "household" that Peter Laslett suggests was the basic social and economic unit of pre-industrial England. Ibid., pp. 20-22, and Sylvia Van Kirk, "Fur Trade Social History: Some Recent

Trends," in Carol Judd and Arthur Ray, eds., *Old Trails and New Directions: Papers of the Third North American Fur Trade Conference* (Toronto: Univ. of Toronto Press, 1980), pp. 161-62. It would be stretching the case somewhat to suggest that a British regiment and Laslett's "household" are competing paradigms of fur trade society as neither has been used in much more than a descriptive sense by fur trade historians. Nevertheless, they represent the two most commonly invoked models of how fur trade society was structured.

Neither seems entirely suitable as a description of York Factory. York was not a single "household" even by the broadest definition of what Laslett meant by the term. Chief factors may have had quasi-paternal functions like Laslett's master baker, but only with the apprentice clerks and junior officers they messed with. For an apprentice tinsmith at York Factory, his household patriarch was the tinsmith, if anyone, and his household the other apprentices and tradesmen he associated with. A post like York resembled the English villages Laslett describes as communities of separate households a great deal more than the London bakery he uses to illustrate his idea of the pre-industrial household. Moreover, fur trade society provided a series of ranks that individuals filled for varying lengths of time, unlike the lengthy commitments to group and community Laslett found in pre-industrial England. Peter Laslett, *The World We Have Lost: England Before the Industrial Age* (New York: Charles Scribner's Sons, 1971), pp. 1-22.

In that respect at least, fur trade communities bore a close resemblance to military institutions. What both models do illustrate is that fur trade society was not so much a society of classes as a society of ranks or status — pre-industrial in character and endlessly complex in distinctions.

21 Van Kirk, *Many Tender Ties*, pp. 201-30; Frits Pannekoek, "The Rev. James Evans and the Social Antagonisms of Fur Trade Society, 1840-1846," in *Religion and Society in the Prairie West*, ed. Richard Allen, Canadian Plains Research Center, Univ. of Regina, Regina, 1974, p. 11; John McLean, *John McLean's Notes of a Twenty-Five Year's Service in the Hudson's Bay Territory*, ed. W.S. Wallace (Toronto: Champlain Society, 1932), pp. 383-90.

22 A recent article adopting this approach is Carol Judd, " 'Mixt Bands of Many Nations': 1821-70" in Carol M. Judd and Arthur J. Ray, eds., *Old Trails and New Directions: Papers of the Third North American Fur Trade Conference*, Univ. of Toronto Press, Toronto, 1980, pp. 127-46. Such analyses of company servants by place of origin are often interesting historical detective work, but they appear to rest on an assumption that has yet to be demonstrated — that place of origin did in fact shape behaviour. That George Simpson and other officers thought Orkneymen to be frugal does not mean that they were so. Indeed, in most other historical writing, "national character" arguments are now rarely invoked as so many of them have been shown to be false. Canadians may well have been hardy and Orkneymen docile, but such statements ought to be made cautiously until more research is done.

23 Quoted in Goldring, "Papers: Vol. II," p. 37.

24 HBCA, A.11/117, fol. 52, William Walker to London committee, 25 July 1790; ibid., B.239/a/90, fols. 27-28, 4 March 1790. Accounts of this sort of hostility between employees of different backgrounds are not uncommon in fur trade records. Perhaps the most spectacular of these at York was the brutal assault on some Orkneymen by a group of Irishmen in Miles Macdonell's party on New Year's Day 1811. Canada, National

Archives. Manuscript Division (hereafter cited as NA), MG19, E1, Thomas Douglas, Lord Selkirk, Vol. 1, pp. 260, 267-68.

25 Quoted in John Nicks, "Orkneymen in the HBC, 1780-1821," in Carol M. Judd and Arthur J. Ray, eds., *Old Trails and New Directions: Papers of the Third North American Fur Trade Conference*, Univ. of Toronto Press, Toronto, 1980, p. 102.

26 *See*, for example, HBCA, B.239/a/89 fol. 35, 18 July 1789. That English servants should have shown a greater tendency to demand what they considered their rights than Orkneymen or others would not have surprised contemporaneous observers of English society. Over the course of the 18th century the English labouring classes had acquired a not undeserved reputation for political awareness as well as a taste for political and social dissent. With an incredible lack of foresight, one French witness to the Gordon Riots of 1780 remarked that such "terrors and alarms" would be inconceivable in Paris, as it was so well policed in comparison to London. The long tradition of radicalism amongst tradesmen and labourers in England is discussed in numerous sources, notably George F. Rudé, *Paris and London in the 18th Century; Studies in Popular Protest* (London: Fontana/Collins, 1974), and Edward Palmer Thompson, *The Making of the English Working Class* (Harmondsworth, Eng.: Penguin, 1968), especially Parts 1 and 3.

27 As previously mentioned, this was the general impression company officers had of Orkneymen as a group. Individuals were often neither sober, frugal, nor docile, and this general image of Orkneymen in Hudson's Bay Company service may need closer examination.

28 Carol Judd, " 'Mixt Bands of Many Nations': 1821-70" in Carol M. Judd and Arthur J. Ray, eds., *Old Trails and New Directions: Papers of the Third North American Fur Trade Conference*, Univ. of Toronto Press, Toronto, 1980, p. 135.

29 Ibid., p. 131. As the chapter "Work" indicates, however, leagues and cabals were formed, and not always along the lines of ethnic background. Company employees were able on occasion to extract concessions from the company and to defend their rights.

30 HBCA, B.239/a/123, fols. 17d, 18, 6 and 7 March 1816; ibid., fol. 22d, 17 and 20 April 1816; ibid., fol. 27, 22 May 1816.

31 HBCA, B.239/a/97, fol. 27d, 3 July 1795; ibid., fol. 34, 31 Aug. 1795; B.239/a/99, fol. 14d, 31 May 1796; ibid., fol. 16, 16 June 1796; ibid., fol. 21d, 17 July 1796; B.239/a/100, fol. 35d, 11 Sept. 1797.

32 Aside from James Knight in the early 18th century and later Duncan Finlayson and Donald A. Smith, company officers had no chance of joining the real elite of the Hudson's Bay Company — the London committee. Unlike North West Company officers who could aspire to partnerships, commissioned officers in the Hudson's Bay Company, however vast the territory they managed in Rupert's Land, were no more than prosperous employees from the vantage point of London. This set of social relationships is illustrated in Brown, *Strangers in Blood*, p. 46.

33 HBCA, B.239/b/83, fols. 5d-6, Miles Macdonell to William Auld, 4 Dec. 1812. Auld was not a commissioned officer — the rank was only created after 1821 — but his position was analogous to a chief factor.

34 Dr. John Sebastian Helmcken, *The Reminiscences of Doctor John Sebastian Helmcken*, ed. Dorothy Blakey Smith, intro. W. Kaye Lamb (Vancouver: Univ. of British Columbia Press, 1975) (hereafter cited as Helmcken, *Reminiscences*), p. 95.

35 Goldring, "Papers: Vol. II," p. 47.

36   George Simpson McTavish, *Behind the Palisades: An Autobiography* (Sidney, B.C.: E. Gurd, [1963]) (hereafter cited as McTavish, *Behind the Palisades*), p. 30.

37   HBCA, B.239/a/90, fols. 38d-39.

38   This is not to say that the only way to manage men is by threatening or punching and kicking one's subordinates. It was, however, assumed that this was one of the prerogatives of rank in fur trade communities and that it served a necessary function.

39   HBCA, B.239/a/126, fols. 27-27d, 22 May 1819. *See also* "Work" below.

40   L. Hargrave, *Letters*, p. 132, Letitia Hargrave to Mrs. Dugald Mactavish Sr., 2 Dec. 1842.

 It is with much regret I gather from your last letter that some acts of assault and personal violence have arisen between you and Donald McLean — one of your servants.—Such occurences [sic] *it is my duty to acquaint you are highly censured by the Honble Coy. who have repeatedly issued instructions for their prevention. —Indeed I should scarcely consider such as being necessary to enforce discipline, under almost any circumstances; as neglect of duty or a mutinous refusal of it is already provided with exemplary and most proper punishment by fine agreeably to the terms of the contract which the offending servant has signed.*

 HBCA, B.239/a/96, fol. 33, James Hargrave to William McKay [Trout Lake], 4 March 1845.

41   R.M. Ballantyne was to become a best-selling author of boy's novels, but his competence as a clerk was often questioned during his stay at York. L. Hargrave, *Letters*, p. 162, Letitia Hargrave to Florence Mactavish, 10 Sept. 1843.

42   Ibid., p. 94, Letitia Hargrave to Mrs. Dugald Mactavish Sr., 20 Feb. 1841.

43   HBCA, B.239/a/100, fols. 16d-17, 27 March 1797. Punishments for crimes may well have been less physical at posts like York than on brigades or in more remote regions like New Caledonia where whipping or some equivalent probably survived into the 19th century.

44   HBCA, B.239/k/1, fols. 81-81d, minutes of council 1825, item no. 135.

45   Given that this punishment was in response to disobeying orders, probably as a result of an argument, a few hours in handcuffs in the launch house may well have worked wonders at cooling at least one of the parties down. Few were ever locked up for long, and often the punishment lasted no more than hours. *See*, for example, HBCA, B.239/a/120 fol. 17d, 8 April 1813, or ibid., fol. 27, 21 July 1813.

46   HBCA, B.239/b/82, fols. 36d-37, W.H. Cook to J. Swain, 20 July 1812.

47   *See*, for example, HBCA, B.239/b/77, fol. 18, William Auld to J. McNab, 25 July 1809, or B.239/b/93, fol. 15, James Hargrave to Robert Harding, 9 July 1838.

48   HBCA, A.11/117, fol. 160, London committee to William Tomison and council, 25 May 1792.

49   HBCA, B.239/b/78, fol. 30d, annual letter to York Factory, 28 May 1800.

50   *See*, for example, HBCA, B.239/b/78, fol. 36, annual letter to York Factory, 20 May 1801.

51   HBCA, A.6/18, p. 84, London committee to Auld and Thomas, 30 May 1812.

52   For example, Chief Trader John Spencer was fined £20 in 1826 for the unnecessary expenditure of 20 bags of pemmican. HBCA, B.239/k/1, fols. 103d-104, minutes of council 1826.

53   HBCA, A.6/18, pp. 253-54, governor and committee to Thomas Thomas, 4 Jan. 1815.

54   Genuinely disruptive individuals or those who were incompetent might be sent home early on the rare occasions where keeping them on was felt to be more expensive than dismissing them. The tinsmith Robert Beith was sent home a year early because he was a "brute" and

a "miserable tradesman" and because it saved £35 per annum on his wages. L. Hargrave, *Letters*, p. 152, Letitia Hargrave to Dugald Mactavish Sr., 9 Sept. 1843.

55 HBCA, A.6/20, fols. 53d-54, London committee to William Williams, George Simpson, and Andrew Bulger, 1 June 1822.

56 HBCA, B.239/k/3, pp. 94-5, minutes of council 1854, resolve no. 7.

57 *See* HBCA, B.239/b/78, fols. 440-44d, annual letter to York Factory, May 1803.

58 HBCA, B.239/a/99, fols. 8d-9, 22 Feb. 1796.

59 Ibid., fol. 16d, 19 June 1796; ibid., fol. 19, 7 July 1796; ibid., fol. 19d, 7 July 1796.

60 L. Hargrave, *Letters*, p. 176, Letitia Hargrave to Mrs. Dugald Mactavish Sr., 14 Sept. 1843. The Abishabis cult is described in greater detail in Francis and Morantz, *Partners in Furs*, pp. 165-66, and Jennifer S.H. Brown, "The Track to Heaven: The Hudson Bay Cree Religious Movement of 1843," in Algonquian Conference (13th: 1981: Ontario Institute for Studies in Education), *Papers of the Thirteenth Algonquian Conference*, ed. William Cowan, Carleton Univ. Press, Ottawa, 1982, pp. 56-63.

61 *See* HBCA, B.239/b/105, fol. 77d, James Hargrave to George Simpson, 27 Feb. 1858; ibid., fol. 79, James Hargrave to John Cromartie, 8 March 1858; ibid., fol. 103d, James Clare to George Simpson, 16 Aug. 1858.

62 Atasawapoh's imprisonment at York may be traced through regular journal entries in HBCA, B.239/a/154 and B.239/a/155.

63 HBCA, B.239/b/94, fol. 50, James Hargrave to Alexander Christie, 23 July 1842.

64 HBCA, B.239/a/92, fols. 3-3d, 5 Oct. 1791.

65 *See*, for example, HBCA, B.239/b/107, fol. 38, James Clare to Thomas Fraser, 17 Sept. 1859.

66 HBCA, B.239/b/78, fol. 36d-37, annual letter to York Factory, 20 May 1801.

67 NA, MG19, D23, "Unfinished Journal of a Clerk [James Hargrave]," p. 8, 6 Nov. 1828.

68 Wage rates for individuals working at different occupations for the Hudson's Bay Company have been discussed in some detail in Goldring, "Papers: Vol. II."

69 L. Hargrave, *Letters*, p. 130, Letitia Hargrave to Mrs. Dugald Mactavish Sr., 2 Dec. 1842.

70 John Nicks, "Orkneymen in the HBC, 1780-1821," in Carol M. Judd and Arthur J. Ray, eds., *Old Trails and New Directions: Papers of the Third North American Fur Trade Conference*, Univ. of Toronto Press, Toronto, 1980, pp. 121-22.

71 Ibid.; Philip Goldring, "Lewis and the Hudson's Bay Company in the Nineteenth Century," *Scottish Studies*, Vol. 24 (1980), p. 32; Allan Greer, "Fur Trade Labour and Lower Canadian Agrarian Structures," [Canadian Historical Association] *Historical Papers/Communications historiques* (1981), pp. 197-214.

72 Philip Goldring, "Papers on the Labour System of the Hudson's Bay Company, 1821-1900: Volume I," Manuscript Report Series, No. 362, Parks Canada, Ottawa, 1979 (hereafter cited as Goldring, "Papers: Vol. I"), pp. 73-75. Mean experience varied between a low of 6.5 years in 1865 and a high of 10.53 years in 1830.

73 In Goldring's sample years the median length of service was always less than the mean, an indication that a few individuals of extremely long service raised the average.

74 After 1821 the company revised its record-keeping system, and personnel records for posts like York Factory were kept on a more consistent basis. No attempt has been made to use employee records for the pre-1821 period for several reasons. Records are incomplete and often do not contain information on servants' home parishes or lengths of service. It is also difficult to establish who was resident at York Factory. Many personnel lists from

the 1780s and 1790s include all employees of the York Factory district including sub-posts and not just the factory itself.

75 The close correspondence between the sizes of the work force at York and of the company's total work force may be traced by comparing Figures 10 and 11 with Goldring's Tables 2.1 and 3.2.1 in "Papers: Vol. I," pp. 33 and 71.

76 Ibid., pp. 65, 85, Figs. 3.1.1 and 4.1.1.

Work

1 Wind and water mills were built in the North-West at Red River and some missionary settlements, but they did not have much to do with the fur trade. On the plains, horses could be used for transport, but at York only dogs and oxen were used with any success as an alternative to human muscle. The most successful application of steam to fur trade tasks was its use by boatbuilders and carpenters for bending wood. *See*, for example, HBCA, B.239/a/109, fol. 6, 14 Nov. 1803.

2 HBCA, B.239/c/3, fol. 329, Robert Gill to James Hargrave, 1 Feb. 1844.

3 For example, the output of the woodcutters was normally calculated at the end of the entire winter cutting season. There were so many variables affecting output, ranging from weather conditions to how far away timber had to be cut, that no clear way existed to judge the effort of the men sent out to the wooders' tents. All the officers could do was hope output would be sufficient for the following year's requirements for lumber and firewood.

4 According to E.P. Thompson, this pattern of idleness followed by intensive effort is found "wherever men were in control of their own working lives." Thompson suggests that it is probably the "natural" human work-rhythm. *See* Edward Palmer Thompson, "Time, Work-Discipline, and Industrial Capitalism," in M.W. Flinn and T.C. Smout, eds., *Essays in Social History* (Oxford: Clarendon Press, 1974) (hereafter cited as E.P. Thompson, "Time, Work-Discipline"), p. 50.

5 HBCA, B.239/a/92, fol. 27d, 25 April 1792.

6 Ibid., fol. 23, 21 March 1792.

7 HBCA, B.239/a/89, fol. 21, 2 March 1789; fol. 33d, 15 June 1789; fol. 36, 29 June 1789.

8 Goldring, "Papers: Vol. II," pp. 12-25.

9 David Thompson, *Narrative, 1784-1812*, ed. and intro. Richard Glover (Toronto: Champlain Society, 1962) (hereafter cited as David Thompson, *Narrative*), p. 56. In spite of his approach to his duties as clerk and accountant, Joseph Colen declared Thompson to be the ideal type of servant, particularly in terms of behaviour and morality. HBCA, A.11/117, fol. 113d, Joseph Colen to London committee, 24 Sept. 1791.

10 HBCA, B.239/a/154, fol. 4d, 12 Sept. 1840.

11 Donaldson, "Land-Use," p. 59.

12 One example of the kind of scrutiny employees could expect will suffice. Over the winter of 1789-90 the boatbuilder at York, Robert Farrar, was set the task of constructing one of the first York boats. By November Colen was commenting that Farrar was a "very slow Workman" and "much at a loss in executing the duties he engaged to perform." HBCA, B.239/a/90, fol. 11d, 13 Nov. 1789. The boat was not completed until July 1790. Colen had made up his mind that Farrar was incompetent, and Farrar was sent home in September. HBCA, B.239/a/90, fol. 68d, 6 Sept. 1790. Farrar confessed that he had told the company agent in the Orkneys he had no qualifications as a boatbuilder, but that he had been sent out and paid as such anyhow. Interestingly, despite an early premonition

that Farrar was out of his depth, Colen did nothing until the boat was completed. It was only with the unsatisfactory completion of the task that he was moved to act.

13 *See* NA, MG19, A21, Hargrave Family, reel C81, James Hargrave Letter Book No. 15, 26 July 1839–18 May 1840.

14 E.P. Thompson, "Time, Work-Discipline," pp. 49-50. For many workers, industrialization meant less variety in their work and greater specialization of trades. At York, carpentry, joinery, and boatbuilding were all to some extent interchangeable trades, but this was becoming less common in 19th-century Britain. Greater specialization and distinctiveness in trade skills were sought as a means of restricting entry to the occupation and thus maintaining higher wage rates. *See,* for example, Eric J. Hobsbawm, "The Labour Aristocracy in 19th-Century Britain," in Eric Hobsbawm, *Labouring Men; Studies in the History of Labour* (London: Weidenfeld and Nicolson, 1964), pp. 290-91.

15 HBCA, A.11/118, fol. 142, James Hargrave to Archibald Barclay, secretary, London committee, 28 Sept. 1847.

16 HBCA, B.239/a/126, fol. 32, 10 July 1819; ibid., B.239/a/148, fol. 42, 17 March 1835; ibid., B.239/a/154, fol. 15, 3 Nov. 1840; ibid., B.239/a/149, fol. 12, 2 Nov. 1835. The hours of work described here correspond closely with those listed by Andrew Graham as normal in the 1770s. It would appear that hours of work in the fur trade by the late 18th century, if not earlier, were set by custom, but there are not enough references to hours of work to be certain all chief factors and all posts maintained the same official workday. *See* Graham, *Observations,* p. 244.

17 The distinction between "clock" and "natural" time is drawn in E.P. Thompson, "Time, Work-Discipline," pp. 39-44. The company kept careful records of watches sent back to Britain for repair, and examination of watch repair records, like HBCA, A.63/10, Watch Repair Book, 1804-1826, suggests that watches were usually owned by officers and tradesmen, who may well have seen ownership of a watch as an important symbol of status.

18 For example, a map dated ca. 1743 of Prince of Wales's Fort drawn by James Isham shows a belfry in the centre of the courtyard there. HBCA, G.2/26.

19 NA, MG17, B2, Church Missionary Society (hereafter cited as CMS), reel A94, William Mason Journal 1856, 13 Oct. 1856.

20 McTavish, *Behind the Palisades,* p. 51.

21 HBCA, A.11/117, fol. 56d, William Tomison to London committee, 31 Aug. 1790.

22 HBCA, B.239/b/78, fol. 52d, annual letter to York Factory, 31 May 1805.

23 Ibid., fol. 55, annual letter to York Factory, 31 May 1806.

24 HBCA, A.11/117, fol. 116d, Joseph Colen to London committee, 24 Sept. 1791.

25 HBCA, A.6/14, fols. 38-38d, annual letter to York Factory, 16 May 1788.

26 HBCA, A.11/117, fol. 31, Joseph Colen to London committee, 7 Sept. 1789.

27 Ibid., fols. 31-31d.

28 Ibid., fol. 31d.

29 HBCA, B.239/a/91, fol. 28, 7 July 1791.

30 Ibid., fol. 31d, 23 July 1791.

31 HBCA, B.239/a/92, fol. 41, 26 July 1792.

32 Ibid., fols. 42-43, 27 July 1792.

33 HBCA, A.6/15, fol. 63, annual letter to York Factory, 30 May 1793.

34 HBCA, B.239/a/95, fols. 49-49d, 31 Aug. 1793. Such open resentment of officers' prerogatives was unusual.

35 Ibid., fols. 31d-31B, 29 May 1793.

36 HBCA, B.239/a/100, fol. 26, 17 July 1797.

37 Use of the York boat was gradually extended further inland with profound consequences for the rivalry between the Hudson's Bay Company and its Canadian competitors. It has been argued that the use of the York boat tipped the balance in the competition for furs in favour of the Hudson's Bay Company, allowing it to take advantage of the shorter routes to the interior it commanded. *See* Harold Adams Innis, *The Fur Trade in Canada....*, rev. ed. (Toronto: Univ. of Toronto Press, 1956), pp. 158-60. The canoe never disappeared from use, and whenever speed was at a premium over carrying capacity, as in the transport of correspondence packets, the canoe remained dominant. Thus skilled canoemen continued to find employment with the Hudson's Bay Company though in much reduced numbers.

38 HBCA, B.239/b/78, fols. 2-2d, annual letter to York Factory, 29 May 1794.

39 HBCA, B.239/a/96, fols. 37d-38, 27 June 1794.

40 Goldring, "Papers: Vol. II," pp. 168-85.

41 For example, HBCA, B.239/a/100, fol. 26d, 17 July 1797.

42 HBCA, B.239/b/105, fol. 103, James Clare to George Simpson, 16 Aug. 1858.

43 The incident is discussed in some detail in HBCA, B.239/b/105, fols. 111-111d, James Clare to George Simpson, 27 Aug. 1858; ibid., B.239/b/107, fol. 37, James Clare to Thomas Fraser, secretary, London committee, 17 Sept. 1859.

44 These problems are discussed in HBCA, A.11/118, fols. 451-63, and in Goldring, "Papers: Vol. II," pp. 159-61.

45 HBCA, A.11/118, fol. 437d, James Clare to Thomas Fraser, secretary, London committee, 13 Sept. 1863.

46 Ibid., fols. 505-06d, J.W. Wilson to Thomas Fraser, 23 Sept. 1865.

47 Ibid., fol. 600, J.W. Wilson to William Smith, secretary, London committee, 14 Sept. 1867.

48 HBCA, B.239/a/101, fol. 66d-67d, 30 Dec. 1798–2 Jan. 1799. This story does not appear in the recopied journal for the year, B.239/a/103, suggesting that from time to time officers may have edited out incidents that reflected poorly on their powers of command or the behaviour of other officers.

49 *See*, for example, HBCA, B.239/a/90, fols. 27-28, 14 March 1790, and B.239/a/92, fol. 15, 21 Jan. 1792.

50 HBCA, B.239/b/105, fol. 91, James Hargrave to George Simpson, 26 May 1858; ibid., fol. 102, James Clare to George Simpson, 16 Aug. 1858.

51 HBCA, B.239/a/92, fol. 16d, 24 Jan. 1792.

52 Career persistence for the Northern Department as a whole is discussed in some detail in Goldring, "Papers: Vol. I," pp. 73-77. Persistence of employees at York Factory is discussed in "Social Structure and Social Relations" above. In both cases average lengths of service were greater than the period of one European contract, although the largest single group of employees was always those working on their first contracts.

53 *See* Jennifer S.H. Brown, " 'A Colony of Very Useful Hands,' " *The Beaver*, Outfit 307, No. 4 (Spring 1977), pp. 39-45.

54 *See*, for example, HBCA, B.239/a/157, fol. 7, 8 Oct. 1842; B.239/b/78, fol. 43d, annual letter to York Factory, May 1803; B.239/b/79, fols. 40d-41, annual letter from York Factory, Sept. 1802; B.239/d/919, fol. 13.

55 HBCA, B.239/b/79, fol. 41, annual letter from York Factory, Sept. 1802. For example, in 1850 James Hargrave rejected Joseph Sabiston's request for permission to marry on the grounds that at both York Factory and Oxford House no additional families could be allowed until a "vacancy" occurred in their numbers. HBCA, B.239/b/101, fol. 16, James Hargrave to Laurence Robertson, 18 March 1850.

56 Detailed accounts of payments to the York Factory Indians for casual labour may be found in account books like B.239/d/796, York Factory Indian Services, Outfit 1850.

57 A more detailed discussion of the development of the Hayes River brigades may be found in Goldring, "Papers: Vol. II," pp. 134-41.

Leisure

1 *The Canadian Encyclopedia* (Edmonton: Hurtig Publishers, 1985), Vol. 3, p. 1744, s.v. "Sport History."

2 HBCA, B.42/a/32, fol. 34d, 13 June 1749.

3 NA, MG19, D23, "Unfinished Journal of a Clerk [James Hargrave]," p. 10, 1 March 1829; Robert Michael Ballantyne, *Hudson Bay, or, Everyday Life in the Wilds of North America....* (London: Thomas Nelson, 1902) (hereafter cited as Ballantyne, *Hudson Bay*), p. 99; NA, MG19, B2, CMS, William Mason Journal 1855, 14 Nov. 1855.

4 NA, MG19, D23, "Unfinished Journal of a Clerk [James Hargrave]," p. 6, 10 Oct. 1828.

5 Stanley Parker, *The Sociology of Leisure* (London: Allen and Unwin, 1976) p. 24; Michael Robert Marrus, comp., *The Emergence of Leisure* (New York: Harper and Row, 1974), p. 5.

6 Peter Cecil Bailey, "Rational Recreation: The Social Control of Leisure and Popular Culture in Victorian England, 1830-1885," PhD thesis, Univ. of British Columbia, Vancouver, 1975, p. 14.

7 Tony Mason, *Association Football and English Society, 1863-1915* (Brighton: Harvester Press, 1980), pp. 2-3.

8 John McDougall, *Forest, Lake and Prairie. Twenty Years of Frontier Life in Western Canada, 1842-62* (Toronto: William Briggs, 1895), pp. 83-84.

9 HBCA, B.42/a/14, fol. 17d, 1 Jan. 1734. This was probably the first game of football played in Canada.

10 HBCA, B.239/a/74, fol. 13d, 30 Dec. 1776.

11 HBCA, B.239/a/106, fol. 12d, 26 Dec. 1801; B.239/a/109, fol. 7d, 26 Dec. 1803–1 Jan. 1804; B.239/a/131, fol. 9, 25 Dec. 1822, and fol. 9d, 1 Jan. 1823; B.239/a/132, fol. 11, 25 Dec. 1823, and fol. 11d, 1 Jan. 1824; B.239/a/141, fol. 34, 25 Dec. 1829; B.239/a/151, fol. 19d, 1 Jan. 1839; B.239/a/163, fol. 133d, 30 Dec. 1845.

12 HBCA, B.239/a/132, fol. 11, 25 Dec. 1823.

13 HBCA, B.235/c/1, fol. 3, George Barnston to J. Hargrave, 1 Feb. 1823.

14 HBCA, B.239/a/163, fol. 133d, 30 Dec. 1845.

15 Quoted in Peter C. Bailey, *Leisure and Class*, p.8.

16 Daniel Gorrie, *Summers and Winters in The Orkneys* (London: 1868), pp. 82-84, quoted in Hudson's Bay Company, *Saskatchewan Journals and Correspondence....*, ed. and intro. Alice M. Johnson (London: Hudson's Bay Record Society, 1967) (hereafter cited as HBC, *Saskatchewan Journals*), pp. 78n-79n.

17 The role of popular recreations like football in relieving social tensions, playing out hostilities, and insulting authority with impunity is discussed in R.W. Malcolmson,

Popular Recreations in English Society, 1700-1850 (Cambridge: Cambridge Univ. Press, 1973), pp. 81-85.

18 HBCA, B.239/a/133, fol. 27d, 9 Aug. 1825; McTavish, *Behind the Palisades*, p. 69. Similarly, in 1840 the officers at York acquired a small pleasure boat or gig to use in the autumn after shiptime. HBCA, B.239/a/152, fols. 25-25d, 31 March 1840.

19 HBCA, B.42/a/110, fol. 20d, 23 April 1788.

20 Morris Kenneth Mott, "Manly Sports and Manitobans, Settlement Days to World War One," PhD thesis, Queen's Univ., Kingston, 1980, pp. 43-44; John E. Foster, "Paulet Paul: Métis or 'House Indian' Folk Hero?," *Manitoba History*, No. 9 (Spring 1985), p. 3.

21 Helmcken, *Reminiscences*, pp. 94-95; L. Hargrave, *Letters*, p. 90, Letitia Hargrave to Mrs. Dugald Mactavish, 1 Dec. 1840.

22 James Hargrave, *The Hargrave Correspondence, 1821-1843*, ed. and intro. G.P. de T. Glazebrook (Toronto: Champlain Society, 1938) (hereafter cited as J. Hargrave, *Correspondence*), p. 252, Donald Ross to James Hargrave, 30 Dec. 1836.

23 Henry M. Robinson, *The Great Fur Land: or, Sketches of Life in the Hudson's Bay Territory*, reprint of 1879 ed. (Toronto: Coles Publishing, 1972), p. 102.

24 "They will stake one, two, three, even ten beaver skins at a time; and it frequently happens that he who in the morning was possessed of furs sufficient ... for a twelvemonth, shall in a few hours be destitute of the means to barter a knife or an awl." Graham, *Observations*, p. 168.

25 HBCA, B.239/a/121, fols. 4-4d, 12 Oct. 1814.

26 HBCA, B.239/b/92, fol. 44d, J. Hargrave to Edward Smith, 18 May 1836.

27 NA, MG19, A21, Hargrave Family, reel C84, Letitia Hargrave to Mrs. Dugald Mactavish Sr., 1 April 1848.

28 HBCA, B.239/k/1, fol. 71d, minutes of council, resolve no. 88, 1825.

29 *See* Edmund Henry Oliver, ed., *The Canadian North-West: Its Early Development and Legislative Records....* (Ottawa: Government Printing Bureau, 1914-15), Vol. 2, p. 827, minutes of council 1841, resolve no. 71.

30 McTavish, *Behind the Palisades*, p. 60.

31 L. Hargrave, *Letters*, p. 180, Letitia Hargrave to Mrs. Dugald Mactavish, 30 March 1844.

32 NA, MG17, B2, CMS, A94, William Mason Journal 1855, 14 Nov. 1855.

33 An officer at Churchill, for example, went out with a party of Inuit hunters to watch how they killed seals. He found the process "too labourious to make amusement of it, its no fun to be crawling in cold ice Water for an hour at a stretch." HBCA, B.42/a/183, fol. 50, 3 May 1846. Goose and whale hunting and snaring rabbits and caribou all suffered from the same problem: the discomforts outweighed the sport, and these were all activities left to the Cree, women, or company servants.

34 William Mactavish, for example, was a well-equipped fisherman. In 1842 he wrote to his father asking for "a good strong Hickory fishing Rod 18 feet long in four pieces to screw together, with Reel, Line, & two spare top pieces also a fly Book and a good assortment of flies some trout small flies, sea trout flies with tinsel on the bodies and a few Salmon flies." NA, MG19, A21, Hargrave Family, reel C83, p. 287, William Mactavish to Dugald Mactavish Sr., 31 Aug. 1842.

35 McTavish, *Behind the Palisades*, p. 95.

36 Robert Michael Ballantyne, *The Young Fur Traders: A Tale of the Far North* (London: Ward, Lock and Co., 1901) (hereafter cited as Ballantyne, *The Young Fur Traders*), pp. 212-19; ibid., *Hudson Bay*, pp. 94-97.

37 HBCA, B.239/a/135, fol. 7, 28 Dec. 1826.
38 Provincial Archives of Manitoba, MG1, D11, William Lane Correspondence, James Clare to William Lane, 15 Feb. 1847.
39 HBCA, B.239/a/101, fol. 98, 25 July 1799.
40 HBCA, B.239/a/128, fol. 25, 27 July 1821.
41 John Henry Lefroy, for example, was startled to find a copy of Loudon's *Cyclopedia of Villa and Farm Architecture* at Fort Simpson in 1844, as well he might have been, given Fort Simpson's distance from anywhere a villa might be found. Sir John Henry Lefroy, *In Search of the Magnetic North....*, ed. George F. Stanley (Toronto: Macmillan, 1955), pp. 107-08.
42 David Thompson, *Narrative*, p. 8.
43 L. Hargrave, *Letters*, p. lxiiin.
44 C.E. L'Ami, "Priceless Books from Old Fur Trade Libraries," *The Beaver*, Outfit 266, No. 3 (Dec. 1935), p. 27.
45 NA, MG17, B2, CMS, A87, J.P. Gardiner Journal 1861-62, 14 Oct. 1861.
46 J. Hargrave, *Correspondence*, p. 101, Donald Ross to James Hargrave, 30 Dec. 1832.
47 L. Hargrave, *Letters*, p. 298, James Hargrave to Donald Ross, 10 Nov. 1850.
48 HBCA, B.239/c/1, fol. 66, George Simpson to J.G. Mactavish, 1 Jan. 1822.
49 For examples *see* HBCA, B.239/b/83, fol. 4d, Miles Macdonell to William Auld, 4 Dec. 1812; B.239/b/68, fol. 7d, William Auld to John McNab, 28 Dec. 1802; J. Hargrave, *Correspondence*, p. 101, Donald Ross to James Hargrave, 30 Dec. 1832.
50 J. Hargrave, *Correspondence*, p. 223, John Bell to James Hargrave, 1 Feb. 1836.
51 NA, MG19, D23, "Unfinished Journal of a Clerk [James Hargrave]," pp. 6-7, 10 Oct. 1828.
52 HBCA, B.239/aa/1, fol. 41, 1821 inventory; B.239/b/78, fol. 5, general letter of 1794, 29 May 1794.
53 HBC, *Saskatchewan Journals*, p. xcviii.
54 HBCA, A.11/117, fols. 149-149d, Joseph Colen to London committee, 26 Sept. 1791.
55 HBC, *Saskatchewan Journals*, p. xcviii.
56 L. Hargrave, *Letters*, p. lxiiin.
57 J. Hargrave, *Correspondence*, p. 129, Donald Ross to James Hargrave, 28 Dec. 1833.
58 Ibid., pp. 129-30.
59 NA, MG17, B2, CMS, A87, J.P. Gardiner Journal 1859-60, 27 Sept. 1859.
60 HBCA, B.239/a/92, fol. 16d, 24 Jan. 1792.
61 HBCA, B.239/b/92, fol. 9d, James Hargrave to William Smith, 9 Sept. 1834.
62 Michael Payne and Gregory Thomas, "Literacy, Literature and Libraries in the Fur Trade," *The Beaver*, Outfit 313, No. 4 (Spring 1983), p. 47.
63 Ibid.
64 NA, MG17, B2, CMS, A94, William Mason Journal 1855-56, 18 Feb. 1856.
65 Ibid.
66 Ibid., William Mason Journal 1856, 1 Nov. 1856.
67 Ibid., 29 Oct. 1856.
68 McTavish, *Behind the Palisades*, p. 60.
69 Ibid.
70 Ibid., pp. 60-61.

71   *See* Ralph Parsons, "Catalogue of the Fur Trade Library," manuscript on file, Hudson's Bay House, Winnipeg, 1931, and NA, MG19, A21, Hargrave Family, reel C83, pp. 386-91, 463-64, 703-08.

72   Michael Payne and Gregory Thomas, "Literacy, Literature and Libraries in the Fur Trade," *The Beaver*, Outfit 313, No. 4 (Spring 1983), p. 48.

73   [William Smellie], *The Sea; Sketches of a Voyage to Hudson's Bay; and Other Poems. By The Scald* [pseud.] (London: Hope and Co., 1855), "Landing at York," pp. 92-94.

74   Ibid., pp. v, vii.

75   L. Hargrave, *Letters*, p. lxin.

76   Ibid.

77   Ibid., p. 118, Letitia Hargrave to Dugald Mactavish Sr., 8 Sept. 1842.

78   Ballantyne, *Hudson Bay*, pp. 201-02.

79   HBCA, B.239/a/92, fol. 13d, 8 Jan. 1792.

80   HBCA, B.239/a/149, fol. 21d, 19 Jan. 1836.

81   Ibid., fols. 12-12d, 2 Nov. 1835.

82   HBCA, B.239/aa/1, fols. 39, 45.

83   For examples, HBCA, B.239/a/90, fol. 10, 2 Nov. 1789; B.239/a/130, fol. 41, 21 Feb. 1822.

84   HBCA, B.239/a/90, fol. 10, 2 Nov. 1789.

85   HBCA, B.239/a/130, fol. 41, 21 Feb. 1822.

86   HBCA, B.239/a/149, fols. 8d-9, 10 Oct. 1835.

87   HBCA, B.239/a/104, fol. 24, 17 Feb. 1800; ibid., fol. 33d, 15 April 1800.

88   L. Hargrave, *Letters*, p. 169, Letitia Hargrave to Mary Mactavish, 12 Sept. 1843; ibid., pp. 79, 179; HBCA, B.239/c/3, fol. 363.

89   HBCA, A.6/18, fol. 116, governor and committee to William Auld and Thomas Thomas, 31 May 1811. *See also* D.W. Moodie and Barry Kaye, "Taming and Domesticating the Native Animals of Rupert's Land," *The Beaver*, Outfit 307, No. 3 (Winter 1976), pp. 10-19.

90   HBCA, B.239/b/107, fol. 23d, James Clare to George Simpson, 26 Aug. 1859.

91   HBCA, B.239/a/161, fol. 55d, 6 Sept. 1844.

92   L. Hargrave, *Letters*, p. 169, Letitia Hargrave to Mary Mactavish, 12 Sept. 1843.

93   Relations between company officers and representatives of the Smithsonian Institution are described in Gregory Thomas, "The Smithsonian and the Hudson's Bay Company," *Prairie Forum: The Journal of the Canadian Plains Research Center*, Vol. 10, No. 2 (Fall 1985), pp. 283-305.

94   HBCA, A.64/33, fols. 2-2Ad, Miscellaneous Notebooks 1850.

95   HBCA, B.239/b/78, fol. 59d, Alexander Lean to John McNab and council, 3 June 1806; B.239/b/100, fol. 65, James Hargrave to W.G. Smith, 23 Aug. 1849; B.239/b/105, fol. 36, James Hargrave to Andrew Murray, 7 Aug. 1857.

96   Meteorological records have proved particularly useful. *See*, for example, Timothy Francis Ball, "Hudson's Bay Company Journals as a Source of Information for the Reconstruction of Climate," in North American Fur Trade Conference (4th: 1981: Grand Portage, Man., and Thunder Bay, Ont.), *Rendezvous: Selected Papers of the Fourth North American Fur Trade Conference, 1981*, ed. Thomas Cotter Buckley, St. Paul, 1984, pp. 43-50.

97   *See*, for examples, HBCA, B.239/a/95, fol. 42d; B.239/a/123, fol. 20, 29 March 1816; B.239/c/1, fol. 3, George Barnston to James Hargrave, 1 Feb. 1823.

98 NA, MG17, B2, CMS, A87, J.P. Gardiner Journal 1861-62, 20 Oct. 1861.

99 *See*, for examples, HBCA, B.239/b/81, fols. 8d-9d, William Hemmings Cook to Mr. Sinclair, 8 June 1811; B.239/b/50, fols. 18d-19, John Thomas to Joseph Colen, 6 July 1789.

100 William B. Ewart, MD, "Causes of Mortality in a Subarctic Settlement (York Factory, Man.), 1714-1946," *Canadian Medical Association Journal*, Vol. 129, No. 6 (15 Sept. 1983) (hereafter cited as Ewart, "Causes of Mortality"), p. 572.

101 Frits Pannekoek, " 'Corruption' at Moose," *The Beaver*, Outfit 309, No. 4 (Spring 1979) (hereafter cited as Pannekoek, "Corruption"), p. 5.

102 L. Hargrave, *Letters*, p. 158, Letitia Hargrave to Mrs. Dugald Mactavish, 10 Sept. 1843.

103 HBCA, A.64/2, Miscellaneous Notebook 1791.

104 HBCA, B.239/a/135, fol. 17, 15 June 1827.

105 HBCA, B.239/a/105, fol. 8, 25 Oct. 1800.

106 HBCA, B.239/k/1, fol. 16d, minutes of council 1822, resolve no. 97.

107 HBCA, B.239/k/2, fol. 120, minutes of council 1841, resolve no. 94.

108 Ibid., fol. 156d, Standing Rules and Regulations 1844, resolve no. 59.

109 HBCA, B.239/b/104b fols. 32d-33, William Mactavish to George Simpson, 9 Sept. 1853.

110 HBCA, B.239/a/148, fol. 30d, 1 Jan. 1835; B.239/a/151, fol. 18d, 25 Dec. 1838.

111 HBCA, B.239/a/154, fol. 25, 1 Jan. 1841.

112 HBCA, B.239/a/155, fol. 20, 1 Jan. 1842.

113 NA, MG17, B2, CMS, A87, J.P. Gardiner Journal 1860-1, 29 Dec. 1860.

114 Ibid., Journal 1861-62, 1 Jan. 1862. Gardiner listed the alcohol consumed that Christmas season by approximately 50 men:

Sold to Officers and Servants	Brandy	*16-3/8 galls.*
"	Wiskey	17 "
"	Port Wine	5-3/8 "
"	Rum	33-7/8 "
Regales for Servants	Rum	10-1/4 "
For the Company's Ball	Rum	3 "
"	Shrub	1 "
"	Port Wine	1 "
"	Brandy	1 "
"	Whiskey	2 "
Given for Visiting New	Shrub	4-1/2 "
Years day	Brandy	2-1/2 "
"	Port Wine	3 "
		104-7/8 "

As well, eight to ten gallons of alcohol were given to Indians.

115 Quoted in Roy Porter, *English Society in the Eighteenth Century* (Harmondsworth, Eng.: Penguin Books, 1982), p. 34.

116 George Macaulay Trevelyan, *Illustrated English Social History* (London: Longman's, Green and Company for Readers' Union, 1958), Vol. 4, The Nineteenth Century, p. 111. Per capita alcohol consumption continued to rise from 18th-century levels through the 19th century until it peaked in the mid-1870s. Thereafter consumption levels declined slightly. Peter C. Bailey, *Leisure and Class*, p. 88.

117 Peter C. Newman, *Company of Adventurers* (Markham, Ont.: Viking-Penguin Books, 1985) (hereafter cited as Newman, *Company of Adventurers*), p. 161.

118 According to current figures, Canadians drink 12 litres of absolute alcohol per adult per year. Most spirits are about 40 per cent alcohol by volume, meaning that adult Canadians consume the equivalent of about 30 litres — nearly eight gallons — of rum, gin, or brandy. *See The Canadian Encyclopedia* (Edmonton: Hurtig Publishers, 1985), Vol. 1, p. 44, s.v. "Alcoholism."

119 Graham, *Observations*, p. 307.

120 HBCA, B.239/a/99, fol. 3d, 5 Nov. 1795.

121 HBCA, B.239/a/100, fol. 18d, 24 April 1797.

122 HBCA, B.239/a/168, fol. 31d, 22 April 1848.

123 HBCA, B.239/a/141, fol. 31, 30 Nov. 1829; B.239/a/148, fol. 24d, 29 Nov. 1834; B.239/a/151, fol. 14, 30 Nov. 1838.

124 NA, MG19, D23, "Unfinished Journal of a Clerk [James Hargrave]," p. 6, 20 Sept. 1828.

125 NA, MG17, B2, CMS, A87, J.P. Gardiner Journal 1859-60, 30 Sept. 1859; ibid., Journal 1860-61, 20 Sept. 1860; ibid., Journal 1861-62, 14 Sept. 1861.

126 HBCA, B.239/a/132, fol. 30, 14 Aug. 1824.

127 L. Hargrave, *Letters*, p. 182, Letitia Hargrave to Mrs. Dugald Mactavish, 30 March 1844.

128 Ballantyne's description of Christmas at York Factory is much quoted and accords well with other sources' accounts of what occurred at York at Christmastime. *Hudson Bay*, pp. 100-06.

129 HBCA, B.239/a/141, fol. 34, 24 Dec. 1829.

130 Ballantyne, *Hudson Bay*, p. 102.

131 Ibid., pp. 104-05.

132 L. Hargrave, *Letters*, pp. 94-95, Letitia Hargrave to Mrs. Dugald Mactavish, 20 Feb. 1841.

133 NA, MG17, B2, CMS, A87, J.P. Gardiner Journal 1858-59, 31 Dec. 1858, 29 Jan. 1859.

134 Ibid., Journal 1860-61, 31 Dec. 1860.

135 Ibid., Journal 1861-62, 1 Jan. 1862.

136 Ibid.

137 Joseph Strutt, *The Sports and Pastimes of the People of England; including the Rural and Domestic Recreations, May Games, Mummeries, Shows, Processions, Pageants, & Pompous Spectacles from the Earliest Period to the Present Time*, new ed. by William Hone (London: William Reeves, 1830), pp. xvii-xviii.

Accidents, Disease, and Medical Care

1 HBCA, B.42/a/94, fol. 24, Samuel Hearne to Humphrey Marten, 20 March 1777.

2 J. Hargrave, *Correspondence*, p. 252, John Bell to James Hargrave, 30 Jan. 1837.

3 Ewart, "Causes of Mortality," pp. 572-73.

4 *See* David Victor Glass, "Population and Population Movements in England and Wales, 1700 to 1850," in D.V. Glass and D.E.C. Eversley, eds., *Population in History: Essays in Historical Demography*, Edward Arnold, London, 1965, p. 241.

5 Ewart, "Causes of Mortality," p. 572. *See also* HBCA, B.239/a/115, fol. 28, 12 Aug. 1809; B.239/a/128, fol. 25, 27 July 1821; B.239/a/157, fol. 53d, 16 Aug. 1843; B.239/a/173, fol. 8d, 15 Oct. 1849, for examples of drowning accidents.

6 HBCA, B.239/a/92, fols. 20d-21, 26 Feb. 1792.

7 Ballantyne, *The Young Fur-Traders*, p. 218.

8 HBCA, B.239/b/84, fol. 3d; B.239/a/120, fol. 6d, 28 Nov. 1812.

9   HBCA, B.239/b/105, fol. 135, James Clare to W.G. Smith, 1 Dec. 1858. McDonald died the following year. *See* HBCA, B.239/g/38, p. 23.
10 HBCA, B.239/a/148, fol. 29, 28 Dec. 1834.
11 HBCA, B.239/a/106, fol. 34d, 30 June 1802.
12 Ibid., fol. 40, 9 Aug. 1802.
13 HBCA, B.239/a/130, fol. 37, 2 Feb. 1822.
14 L. Hargrave, *Letters*, p. 143, Letitia Hargrave to Mrs. Dugald Mactavish, 10 April 1843. Hargrave established the following regulations to try to ensure that fires were prevented at York:

> *The Stove funnels of all the winter houses to be cleaned and their perfect security ascertained by the Blacksmith on the first Saturday of every month*
> *No fire to be carried from one house to another or to any place in the open air unless in a covered fire shovel. —*
> *The Blowholes of the stoves in the workshops to be carefully shut on going to meals and the fires to be thoroughly extinguished with water or snow each evening on leaving off work for the day. —*
> *All shavings or any other substance liable to catch fire easily to be carefully kept at a distance from the stoves*
> *All the workshops to be swept out in the afternoon of each Saturday*
> *All candles taken into the workshops, Ration room or other place after dark to be kept shut up in a lantern and not to be taken out of it while lighted for any purpose whatever*
> *No smoking permitted in any of the Companys Stores Retail Shops, Trading room or Ration Room.*

HBCA, B.239/a/161, fols. 11-11d, 9 Nov. 1844.
15 HBCA, B.239/a/105, fol. 36d, 31 March 1801.
16 HBCA, B.239/a/154, fol. 21, 11 Dec. 1840.
17 HBCA, B.239/b/104b, fol. 3, William Mactavish to Archibald Barclay, 6 Sept. 1852.
18 PAM, MG1, D20, Donald Ross Correspondence, file 121, William Mactavish to Donald Ross, 23 May 1851, postscript dated 4 June.
19 L. Hargrave, *Letters*, p. 179, Letitia Hargrave to Mrs. Dugald Mactavish, 29 Nov. 1843.
20 HBCA, B.239/a/173, fol. 35d, 25 March 1850.
21 Michael Payne, "Prince of Wales' Fort: A Social History, 1717-1782," Manuscript Report Series, No. 371, Parks Canada, Ottawa, 1979 (hereafter cited as Payne, "Prince of Wales' Fort") pp. 76-78.
22 HBCA, A.6/15, fol. 63d, York Factory annual letter, 30 May 1793. Restraint continued to be used with violent individuals well into the 19th century. *See* HBCA, B.239/b/107, fol. 11d, James Clare to George Simpson, 20 May 1859.
23 HBCA, B.239/a/101, fol. 60, 19 Nov. 1798.
24 Ibid., fols. 70d-71, 18 and 19 Jan. 1799.
25 HBCA, B.239/a/103, fol. 28, 10 Feb. 1799.
26 Ibid., fol. 28d, 10 Feb. 1799.
27 Ibid., fols. 43d-44, 28 May 1799.
28 Ibid., fol. 47d, 30 May 1799.
29 HBCA, B.239/a/101, fol. 99d, 4 Aug. 1799; B.239/a/103, fol. 101d, 18 Aug. 1799.
30 HBCA, B.239/a/104, fol. 1, 15 Sept. 1799.
31 HBCA, B.239/a/155, fol. 13d, 15 Nov. 1841.

32   Ibid., fols. 13d-14, 22 Nov. 1841.

33   Ibid., fol. 15, 29 Nov. 1841.

34   Pannekoek, "Corruption," pp. 4, 6-7. Similar views are expressed in Newman, *Company of Adventurers*, especially p. 163.

35   Ewart, "Causes of Mortality," p. 572. Of 52 deaths at York for which causes were clearly indicated, only four were attributed to murder, suicide, or alcoholism.

36   HBCA, A.5/15, p. 66, Archibald Barclay to J. Clouston, 14 Oct. 1846.

37   NA, MG17, B2, CMS, A94, William Mason Journal 1856, 16, 19, and 30 Nov. 1856; HBCA, B.239/b/105, fols. 10d-11, James Hargrave to William Smith, 1 Dec. 1856.

38   HBCA, A.11/118, fol. 106, James Hargrave to A. Barclay, 6 Aug. 1846.

39   HBCA, B.239/b/97a, fol. 10d, James Hargrave to George Simpson, 10 Aug. 1845.

40   HBCA, A.11/118, fol. 478d, W. Wilson to Thomas Fraser, 19 Nov. 1864; B.239/a/148, fol. 37, 4 Feb. 1835.

41   HBCA, A.11/118, fol. 82, James Hargrave to Archibald Barclay, 20 Sept. 1843; ibid., fols. 435-35d, James Clare to Thomas Fraser, 13 Sept. 1863.

42   HBCA, B.239/a/157, fol. 47, 18 July 1843.

43   HBCA, A.11/118, fols. 435-35d, James Clare to Thomas Fraser, 13 Sept. 1863.

44   Ibid., fols. 446d-47, James Clare to Thomas Fraser, 1 Dec. 1863.

45   HBCA, B.239/b/92, fol. 45d, James Hargrave to John Charles, 28 May 1836; ibid., fols. 60d-61, John Charles to Captain Graves, 27 Sept. 1836.

46   HBCA, B.239/z/26, fols. 143-44.

47   Ewart, "Causes of Mortality," p. 572.

48   HBCA, A.11/118, fol. 167, James Hargrave to Archibald Barclay, 6 Sept. 1848; ibid., fol. 177d, James Hargrave to Archibald Barclay, 8 Sept. 1849.

49   Payne, "Prince of Wales' Fort," p. 84.

50   HBCA, B.239/a/89, fols. 25-25d, 22 April 1789.

51   Wyndham E.B. Lloyd, *A Hundred Years of Medicine*, 2nd ed. (London: Gerald Duckworth, 1968), p. 172.

52   HBCA, B.239/a/95, fol. 18, 13 Feb. 1793.

53   HBCA, B.239/a/90, fol. 21, 1 Feb. 1790; ibid., fol. 39d, 29 April 1790.

54   HBCA, B.239/a/95, fols. 18d-19, 18 Feb. 1793.

55   Ibid., fol. 19d, 19 Feb. 1793.

56   HBCA, A.6/15, fol. 108d, annual letter to York Factory, 29 May 1794.

57   HBCA, B.239/a/118, fol. 1d, 9 Oct. 1811; A.6/21, fol. 35, London committee to George Simpson, 11 March 1825.

58   HBCA, B.239/a/89, fol. 20, 23 and 23d, 21 Feb., 28 March, and 4 April 1789.

59   HBCA, A.6/15, fol. 26, annual letter to York Factory, 25 May 1792.

60   HBCA, B.239/b/78, fols. 15d, 16d-17, annual letter to York Factory, 31 May 1797.

61   HBCA, A.11/117, fol. 117, annual letter from York Factory, 26 Sept. 1791.

62   HBCA, A.6/14, fol. 134, annual letter to York Factory, May 1791.

63   HBCA, B.239/b/78, fols. 2d-3, annual letter to York Factory, 29 May 1794.

64   HBCA, B.239/a/96, fols. 4-4d, 3 Oct. 1793; B.239/a/90, fol. 37, 21 April 1793.

65   HBCA, B.239/a/96, fols. 4-4d, 3 Oct. 1793.

66   HBCA, B.239/a/92, fol. 31, 28 May 1792; B.239/a/97, fol. 20, 17 April 1795.

67   Pannekoek, "Corruption," p. 9.

68   HBCA, B.239/b/78, fol. 62, annual letter to York Factory, 31 May 1807.

69   L. Hargrave, *Letters*, p. 244n, George Simpson to James Hargrave, 20 June 1848.

70 The main exception to this pattern was William Todd, who began his career with the company as a surgeon at York. He showed enough ability as both trader and surgeon that he rose to the position of a chief trader and was in charge of the Swan River District from 1832 to 1842.

71 L. Hargrave, *Letters*, p. 244n, George Simpson to James Hargrave, 20 June 1848.

72 Arthur J. Ray, "Smallpox: The Epidemic of 1837-38," *The Beaver*, Outfit 306, No. 2 (Autumn 1975), pp. 8-13.

73 HBCA, B.239/a/151, fol. 16, 8 Dec. 1838.

74 HBCA, B.239/a/166, York Factory Medical Journal 1846-47. Smellie recorded 136 individual cases though some patients were treated more than once.

75 Smellie treated 16 Indians from York Factory, Severn, Oxford House, and Norway House, and 32 boatmen, guides, and other seasonal visitors to the post.

76 Ballantyne, *The Young Fur-Traders*, p. 55.

Education and Religion

1 Some of the best of these are Keith Wilson, "The Development of Education in Manitoba," PhD thesis, Michigan State Univ., East Lansing, 1967); Robert Walter Gustafson, "The Education of Canada's Indian Peoples: An Experience in Colonialism," MEd thesis, Univ. of Manitoba, Winnipeg, 1978; John W. Chalmers, "Education and the Honourable Company," *Alberta Historical Review*, Vol. 13, No. 3 (Summer 1965), pp. 25-28; Thomas Bredin, "The Red River Academy," *The Beaver*, Outfit 305, No. 3 (Winter 1974), pp. 10-17, and "The Reverend David Jones: Missionary at Red River 1823-38," *The Beaver*, Outfit 312, No. 2 (Autumn 1981), pp. 47-52.

2 Notably D. Bruce Sealey, "Education of the Manitoba Métis: An Historical Sketch," paper presented at the Métis Historical Conference, Brandon University, Brandon, Manitoba, 6 and 7 May 1977, p. 2.

3 Douglas MacKay, *The Honourable Company: A History of the Hudson's Bay Company* (Toronto: McClelland and Stewart, 1966), pp. 64-65.

4 Van Kirk, *Many Tender Ties*, p. 97.

5 For example, J.H. Plumb, "The New World of Children in Eighteenth-Century England," *Past and Present: A Journal of Historical Studies*, No. 67 (1975) pp. 64-95.

6 HBCA, B.239/b/78, fol. 5, annual letter to York Factory, 29 May 1794.

7 Jennifer S.H. Brown, " 'A Colony of Very Useful Hands,' " *The Beaver*, Outfit 307, No. 4 (Spring 1977), p. 39.

8 HBCA, B.239/b/78, fol. 36, annual letter to York Factory, 20 May 1801.

9 HBCA, B.239/b/78, fol. 57d, annual letter to York Factory, 31 May 1806.

10 HBCA, B.239/b/79, fols. 50d-51, annual letter from York Factory, 30 Aug. 1806.

11 HBCA, B.239/b/78, fol. 62, annual letter to York Factory, 31 May 1807.

12 Ibid.

13 HBCA, B.239/a/114, fol. 2d, 14 Oct. 1807.

14 Ibid., fol. 6d, 7-13 March 1808.

15 HBCA, B.239/b/79, fols. 53d-54, annual letter from York Factory, 28 Sept. 1807. The sentiments expressed in this letter suggest that little attention was paid to the wishes of the children's mothers in these plans for a school. It is reasonable to assume that they were less convinced that their children needed to be estranged from their influence.

16 HBCA, B.239/b/78, fol. 73, annual letter to York Factory, 20 May 1809.

17 HBCA, B.239/a/115, fol. 2, 9 Sept. 1808; ibid., fol. 17d, 2 June 1809; B.239/a/116, fol. 23d, 28 Aug. 1809.

18 For example, HBCA, B.239/a/115, fol. 5, 30 Sept. 1808; B.239/a/116, fol. 9, 3 Jan. 1810.

19 HBCA, B.239/b/79, fol. 59d, annual letter from York Factory, 14 Sept. 1809.

20 HBCA, B.239/a/116, fol. 1d, 18 Sept. 1809; ibid., fol. 3, 3 Oct. 1809.

21 *See* HBCA, A.30/12, Lists of Servants, 1813.

22 John West, *The Substance of a Journal During a Residence at the Red River Colony....*, reprint of 1824 ed. (New York: Johnson Reprint Corp., 1966), pp. 12-13.

23 Ibid., p. 12. West gave the boy the name "John Hope." A second Indian pupil, named Henry Budd, from Norway House later became the first native ordained by the Anglican Church in North America. *See* Henry Budd, *The Diary of the Reverend Henry Budd, 1870-1875*, ed. Katherine Pettipas (Winnipeg: Manitoba Record Society, 1974).

24 Thomas Bredin, "The Red River Academy," *The Beaver*, Outfit 305, No. 3 (Winter 1974), p. 11.

25 The Hargraves, for example, despite Letitia Hargrave's initial opposition to the idea, eventually sent Joseph James off to school in Scotland. *See* L. Hargrave, *Letters*, pp. 144-45, 293-94, 299-300. *See also* Jennifer S.H. Brown, "Ultimate Respectability: Fur-Trade Children in the 'Civilized World,' " [Pt. 1], *The Beaver*, Outfit 308, No. 3 (Winter 1977), pp. 4-10, and [Pt. 2], *The Beaver*, Outfit 308, No. 4 (Spring 1978), pp. 48-55.

26 HBCA, B.239/a/148, fol. 22d, 10 Nov. 1834.

27 HBCA, B.239/a/154, fols. 12d-13, 21 Oct. 1840.

28 HBCA, B.239/a/161, fol. 30, 25 March 1845.

29 NA, MG17, B2, CMS, A87, J.P. Gardiner Journal 1858-59, 25 Oct. 1858.

30 Ibid., A94, William Mason Journal 1855, 2 July 1855; ibid., William Mason to secretary of CMS, 24 May 1856.

31 Ibid., A87, J.P. Gardiner Journal 1860-61, 11 June 1861 (Gardiner lists enrollment as 24 boys and 32 girls on average); ibid., Journal 1858-59, 2 Dec. 1858, and Journal 1860-61, 15 Nov. 1860. The reported subject of the conversational class was "ought the conduct of a man to be influenced by public opinion?"; needless to say, most opted for the negative.

32 Ibid., A94, William Mason to secretary of CMS, 1 Dec. 1857. William Mason, with the aid of his wife, Sophia, a daughter of Chief Factor Thomas Thomas, became something of an expert in the use of Cree syllabics and is credited with translating the Gospel of St. John and the Epistles from Ephesians to 1 John. He and his wife were also involved in the publication of the Bible in Cree syllabics in 1861. Mrs. Mason translated the Lord's Prayer, Apostles' Creed, and the Ten Commandments. *See* Thomas Charles Boucher Boon, *Use of Catechisms and Syllabics by the Early Missionaries of Rupert's Land, 1820-1880* (Toronto: Canadian Church Historical Society, 1960), unpaginated.

33 HBCA, B.239/k/1, fol. 152, minutes of council 1830, resolve no. 87.

34 *See* Goldring, "Papers: Vol. I," p. 81, and Figure 11 above.

35 HBCA, B.239/b/100, p. 60, James Hargrave to George Simpson, 15 Aug. 1849.

36 Quoted in Arthur Silver Morton, *A History of the Canadian West to 1870-71....*, 2nd ed., ed. Lewis G. Thomas (Toronto: Univ. of Toronto Press, 1973), p. 81.

37 For example, Samuel Hearne was a deist, John McLoughlin was a devout convert to Catholicism, and Moses Morton lived "in open defiance of every law, human and divine," according to Samuel Hearne.

38 NA, MG19, E1, Thomas Douglas, Lord Selkirk, Vol. 1, pp. 376-77.

39 *See* William Brooks, "Methodism in the Canadian West in the Nineteenth Century," PhD thesis, Univ. of Manitoba, Winnipeg, 1972.

40 HBCA, B.239/b/94, fols. 7-7d, James Hargrave to Robert Harding, 19 July 1841.

41 Deciphering the attitude of the Hudson's Bay Company towards missionary activity is no easy matter. Much depends on whose opinions one considers held sway in the company: George Simpson, who initially opposed allowing missionaries into the North-West and who showed few evidences of any religious sentiment in his own life, or Nicholas Garry, who was a great supporter of the Church Missionary Society and other evangelical organizations and who organized an Auxiliary Bible Society at York in 1821. *See* John West, *The Substance of a Journal During a Residence at the Red River Colony....,* reprint of 1824 ed. (New York: Johnson Reprint Corp., 1966), p. 66, and John S. Galbraith, *The Little Emperor: Governor Simpson of the Hudson's Bay Company* (Toronto: Macmillan, 1976), pp. 64-65. Biographers of individual missionaries, particularly of James Evans, have often emphasized the missionaries' difficulties with the company, but a strong case can be made for arguing that mutual reliance, not conflict, was the main feature of relations between the company and the missionaries, especially Roman Catholic and Anglican missionaries who were more amenable to centralized control. *See* Norma Jaye Goosen, "The Relationship of the Church Missionary Society and the Hudson's Bay Company in Rupert's Land, 1821 to 1861, with a Case Study of Stanley Mission under the Direction of the Rev. Robert Hunt," MA thesis, Univ. of Manitoba, Winnipeg, 1975, pp. 148-49. In recent years a number of studies have emphasized the social tensions that missionaries introduced into fur trade society. Some have suggested that the difficulties missionaries faced were a product as much of these tensions and of fur trade politics as of any conflict between the civilizing urges of the missionaries and the economic demands of the fur trade. Van Kirk, *Many Tender Ties,* p. 145 et passim; Brown, *Strangers in Blood,* pp. 201-02, 211-14; Frits Pannekoek, "The Rev. James Evans and the Social Antagonisms of Fur Trade Society, 1840-1846," in *Religion and Society in the Prairie West,* ed. Richard Allen, Canadian Plains Research Center, Univ. of Regina, 1974, pp. 1-16.

42 NA, MG17, B2, CMS, A77, "Extracts from the Minutes of Council held at York Factory July 5/1823," pp. 67-70.

43 They were sometimes omitted to give the men an extra day of exercise for their health, for example. *See* "Leisure" above.

44 NA, MG17, B1, Society for the Propagation of the Gospel in Foreign Parts (hereafter cited as SPG), North West Mission, David [Anderson, Bishop of] Rupert's Land to the Reverend Mr. Hawkins, secretary, SPGFP, 27 Sept. 1850, p. 603.

45 Ibid., "Petition from the Christian Indians at York for a Minister," p. 629.

46 Ibid., David, Rupert's Land, to Hawkins, 4 Aug. 1851, p. 627.

47 Ibid., p. 628.

48 Ibid., David, Rupert's Land, to Hawkins, 22 Nov. 1852, p. 632.

49 Ibid., David, Rupert's Land, to Hawkins, 24 Nov. 1852, p. 635.

50 Charles Frederick Pascoe, comp., *Classified Digest of the Records of the Society for the Propagation of the Gospel in Foreign Parts, 1701-1892,* 6th ed. (London: Society for the Propagation of the Gospel in Foreign Parts, 1898), p. 179.

51 NA, MG17, B1, SPG, North West Mission, David, Rupert's Land, to Hawkins, 25 Jan. 1854, p. 657. McDonald was sent instead to Islington Mission, where he worked for nine years. Transferred to Fort Simpson in the Mackenzie District, he later became archdeacon of Mackenzie River. He also translated the scriptures into the Tukudh language. Eugene

Stock, *History of the Church Missionary Society, Its Environment, Its Men and Its Work* (London: Church Missionary Society, 1899), Vol. 2, p. 325.

52 NA, MG17, B2, CMS, A94, p. 6, William Mason to secretary, CMS, 12 Sept. 1854.

53 HBCA, B.239/b/104b, fol. 74d, William Mactavish to George Simpson, 30 Nov. 1854.

54 HBCA, B.239/b/104b, fol. 128, William Mactavish to George Simpson, Sept. 1856; NA, MG17, B2, CMS, A94, William Mason to secretary, CMS, 16 Sept. 1856.

55 NA, MG17, B2, CMS, A87, J.P. Gardiner Journal 1860-61, 23 Sept. 1860.

56 Ibid., A94, William Mason Journal 1855-56, 2 July 1856.

57 Ibid., A87, J.P. Gardiner Journal 1860-61, 13 June 1861; ibid., Affidavit of Henry Beddome Surgeon at York Factory, 11 Sept. 1863.

58 Ibid., J.P. Gardiner Journal 1859-60, 6 Oct. 1859.

59 Ibid., A94, William Mason Journal 1855, 22 July 1855.

60 PAM, MG1, D16, Roderick Macfarlane Papers, W.W. Kirby to Roderick Macfarlane, 28 Nov. 1870.

Standard of Living

1 Graham, *Observations*, p. 298.

2 David Thompson, *Narrative*, p. 40; HBCA, B.239/b/93, fol. 64d, James Hargrave to George Simpson, 5 Sept. 1840.

3 For example, *see* HBCA, B.239/b/105, fol. 127d, James Clare to W.G. Smith [secretary, London committee], 9 Sept. 1858.

4 HBCA, B.239/c/1, fol. 350, John Clowes to James Hargrave, 27 May 1828.

5 David Thompson, *Narrative*, pp. 51-52.

6 *See* Van Kirk, *Many Tender Ties*, pp. 54-55, or HBCA, B.239/a/120, fol. 4d, 28 Oct. 1812.

7 Graham, *Observations*, pp. 297-98.

8 David Thompson, *Narrative*, p. 38; HBCA, B.239/a/120, fol. 4, 20 Oct. 1812.

9 HBCA, B.239/a/130, fol. 39, 11 Feb. 1821.

10 The pattern for a late-19th-century version of this coat may be found in Dorothy Burnham, *Cut My Cote* (Toronto: Royal Ontario Museum, 1973), p. 21.

11 HBCA, B.239/b/92, fols. 16 and 18d, Report upon the Shipment of Merchandise.

12 HBCA, B.239/b/107, fol. 141d, James Clare to William Mactavish, 14 Aug. 1862.

13 L. Hargrave, *Letters*, p. 129, Letitia Hargrave to Mrs. Dugald Mactavish, 2 Dec. 1842; HBCA, B.239/z/28, fol. 127.

14 L. Hargrave, *Letters*, p. 129, Letitia Hargrave to Mrs. Dugald Mactavish, 2 Dec. 1842.

15 Ibid., p. 165, Letitia Hargrave to Mary Mactavish, 12 Sept. 1843.

16 Ibid., pp. 89-90, Letitia Hargrave to Mrs. Dugald Mactavish, 1 Dec. 1840.

17 HBCA, B.239/c/2, fol. 37, George Simpson to Alexander Christie, 18 Dec. 1830.

18 James Isham, *Observations on Hudson's Bay, 1743....*, ed. and intro. E.E. Rich and A.M. Johnson (Toronto: Champlain Society, 1949), pp. 172-73, 172n; Graham, *Observations*, pp. 293-94.

19 Graham, *Observations*, p. 293; James Isham, *Observations on Hudson's Bay, 1743....*, ed. and intro. E.E. Rich and A.M. Johnson (Toronto: Champlain Society, 1949), p. 91; [Theodore Swain Drage], *An Account of a Voyage for the Discovery of a North-West Passage ... Performed in the Years 1746 and 1747, in the Ship California ... By the Clerk of the California* (London: Printed and sold by Mr. Jolliffe et al., 1748-49), Vol. 1, pp. 135-37.

20 Ballantyne, *The Young Fur-Traders*, pp. 233-34.

21 *See*, for example, HBCA, B.239/a/89, fol. 22, 13 March 1789, or B.239/a/90, fol. 4, 24 Sept. 1789.

22 HBCA, B.239/a/117, fols. 2d-3, 26 Sept. 1810.

23 HBCA, B.239/a/92, fol. 26, 21 April 1792.

24 Ibid.; Payne, "Prince of Wales' Fort," pp. 65-66.

25 HBCA, B.239/a/132, fol. 7d, 1 Nov. 1823; Donaldson, "Land-Use."

26 Donaldson, "Land-Use," p. 53.

27 Arthur Dobbs, *An Account of the Countries adjoining to Hudson's Bay in the North-West Part of America*, reprint of 1744 ed. (New York: Johnson Reprint Corp., 1967), p. 2.

28 HBCA, B.239/b/82, fols. 4d-5, W.H. Cook to Miles Macdonell, 3 Nov. 1811.

29 HBCA, A.6/18, fol. 196, governor and committee to Thomas Thomas, April 1814.

30 The use of Carron stoves at York Factory is discussed in some detail in Gordon Moat, "Canada Stoves in Rupert's Land," *The Beaver*, Outfit 310, No. 3 (Winter 1979), pp. 54-57.

31 L. Hargrave, *Letters*, p. 147n, George Simpson to James Hargrave, 1 Dec. 1842.

32 Ibid., p. 147, Letitia Hargrave to Mrs. Dugald Mactavish, 1 April 1843.

33 Ibid.

34 Ballantyne, *Hudson Bay*, p. 92.

35 The earliest reference to mosquito blinds in the York post journals is HBCA, B.239/a/173, fol. 9d, 19 Oct. 1849. Letitia Hargrave indicates that they graced some windows at least as early as 1840. L. Hargrave, *Letters*, p. 62, Letitia Hargrave to Mrs. Dugald Mactavish, Sept. 1840.

36 Ballantyne, *Hudson Bay*, pp. 92-93.

37 HBCA, A.5/4, fol. 51d, London committee to John Ballenden, 31 May 1799.

38 L. Hargrave, *Letters*, p. xlii.

39 Ibid., p. 122, Letitia Hargrave to Mrs. Dugald Mactavish, 8 Sept. 1842.

40 Ibid., p. 74, Letitia Hargrave to Mary Mactavish, 1 Sept. 1840.

41 Ibid., p. 88, Letitia Hargrave to Mrs. Dugald Mactavish, 1 Dec. 1840.

42 Ibid. p. xlii; *see also* Ballantyne, *Hudson Bay*, pp. 101-02.

43 L. Hargrave, *Letters*, p. xlii.

44 Ibid., pp. lxii and 89, Letitia Hargrave to Mrs. Dugald Mactavish, 1 Dec. 1840.

45 Ibid., p. 72, Letitia Hargrave to Mary Mactavish, 1 Sept. 1840, and p. 88, Letitia Hargrave to Mrs. Dugald Mactavish, 1 Dec. 1840.

46 HBCA, B.239/b/97a, fol. 24d, James Hargrave to Archibald Barclay, 1 Dec. 1845; A.11/118, fol. 142d, James Hargrave to Archibald Barclay, 28 Sept. 1847.

47 L. Hargrave, *Letters*, p. 198, Letitia Hargrave to Dugald Mactavish Sr., 1 Sept. 1845.

48 Ibid., p. 17, Letitia Hargrave to Mrs. Dugald Mactavish, 5 May 1840.

49 John Burnett, *A Social History of Housing, 1815-1970* (Newton Abbot, Eng.: David and Charles, 1978) (hereafter cited as Burnett, *Social History of Housing*), p. 110.

50 John A. Hussey, " 'Unpretending' But Not 'Indecent': Living Quarters at Mid-19th Century HBC Posts," *The Beaver*, Outfit 305, No. 4 (Spring 1975), pp. 12-17.

51 HBCA, B.239/a/66, fol. 17d, 16 Dec. 1771.

52 L. Hargrave, *Letters*, p. 236, Letitia Hargrave to Florence Mactavish, 8 Sept. 1848.

53 HBCA, B.239/b/84, fols. 61d-62, W.H. Cook to Mr. Charles, 20 March 1814. Not everyone agreed with Cook that residents of York sought the appearance of refinement. In 1838 a shipment of earthenware to Red River was left at York Factory. It consisted of ewers and basins that "will never be disposed of at this Place [York], while Buckets and

Pails can be Obtained, or at least till we become a little more Polished than we are at present." HBCA, B.239/b/93, fol. 9d, J. Charles to Alexander Christie, 16 Feb. 1838.

54 HBCA, B.239/b/84, fols. 61d-62, W.H. Cook to Mr. Charles, 20 March 1814.

55 L. Hargrave, *Letters*, p. 62, Letitia Hargrave to Mrs. Dugald Mactavish, Sept. 1840.

56 Lower Canadian housing is discussed at some length in Robert-Lionel Séguin, *La Civilisation traditionnelle de l' "habitant" aux 17e et 18e siècles; fonds matériel* (Montreal: Fides, 1967), pp. 307-60. *See also* Raymond Douville and Jacques Casanova, *Daily Life in Early Canada from Champlain to Montcalm*, trans. Carola Congreve (London: Allen and Unwin, 1968), pp. 45-49.

57 Patrick Bailey, *Orkney* (Newton Abbot, Eng.: David and Charles, 1971), p. 105.

58 Ibid.

59 James R. Nicolson, *Traditional Life in Shetland* (London: Robert Hale, 1978), pp. 71-78; John Mercer, *Hebridean Islands: Colonsay, Gigha, Jura* (Glasgow: Blackie, 1974), pp. 192-95.

60 Burnett, *Social History of Housing*, pp. 77-78, 108-15.

61 Goldring, "Papers: Vol. II," p. 40.

62 Burnett, *Social History of Housing*, pp. 98-103.

63 McTavish, *Behind the Palisades*, pp. 50, 58; *A Dictionary of Canadianisms on Historical Principles* (Toronto: W.J. Gage, 1967), s.v. "H.B.C. jocular."

64 L. Hargrave, *Letters*, p. 197n, John Ballenden to James Hargrave, 2 May 1845.

65 Umfreville, *Present State*, p. 14.

66 HBCA, B.239/c/1, fol. 62d, George Simpson to John George McTavish, 20 Dec. 1821; Helmcken, *Reminiscences*, p. 97.

67 Some of the interior posts after 1774 were more successful as agriculture centres; *see* HBCA, B.239/z/23, p. 445. According to Umfreville, the gardens at Moose and Albany produced potatoes, turnips, and most kitchen garden vegetables. Umfreville, *Present State*, p. 14.

68 HBCA, B.239/e/1, fol. 5, York Factory District Report 1815.

69 Ibid.; B.239/a/101, fol. 88d, 17 May 1799; B.239/a/126, fol. 11, 30 Oct. 1818; B.239/a/126, fol. 5, Standing Orders for York Factory, item no. 5; B.239/a/106, fol. 3, 29 Sept. 1801; L. Hargrave, *Letters*, p. 76, Letitia Hargrave to Dugald Mactavish Sr., 2 Sept. 1840; McTavish, *Behind the Palisades*, pp. 25-26.

70 HBCA, B.239/a/159, fol. 4d, 29 Sept. 1843; L. Hargrave, *Letters*, p. 201, Letitia Hargrave to Dugald Mactavish Sr., 1 Sept. 1845.

71 HBCA, B.239/a/157, fol. 7, 8 Oct. 1842; L. Hargrave, *Letters*, p. 107, Letitia Hargrave to Mrs. Dugald Mactavish, 14 May 1842; HBCA, B.239/a/126, fol. 26d, 15 May 1819. Dr. Helmcken mentioned that in 1847 there was a shed covered with glass at York in which radishes, turnips, and other vegetables were planted. According to Helmcken, these vegetables grew to the size of marbles. Helmcken, *Reminiscences*, p. 97.

72 HBCA, B.239/a/91, fol. 23d, 4 June 1791.

73 HBCA, B.239/a/151, fol. 4d, 26 Sept. 1838.

74 HBCA, B.239/a/152, fol. 4d, 20 Sept. 1839; B.239/a/157, fol. 7, 8 Oct. 1842; B.239/a/168, fol. 3, 24 Sept. 1847; B.239/a/173, fol. 5, 21 Sept. 1849.

75 HBCA, B.239/a/121, fol. 31d, 14 June 1815; B.239/a/123, fols. 28d-29, 5 June 1816.

76 HBCA, B.239/a/155, fol. 46d, 11 June 1842; B.239/a/141, p. 10, 25 Sept. 1829; B.239/a/121, fol. 5, 19 Oct. 1814; B.239/a/157, fol. 41d, 16 June 1843; B.239/a/161, fol. 41d, 10 June 1845.

77 L. Hargrave, *Letters*, pp. 183-84, Letitia Hargrave to Mrs. Dugald Mactavish, 30 March 1844. The following lists the seed in stock at York Factory in 1833, with which gardeners could try to get something "green" to grow.

3		*Lb.*	*Red Beet Seed*
2		*"*	*Dwarf Cabbage Do*
1		*"*	*Red Cabbage Do*
4		*"*	*Early York Cabbage Do*
	1/4	*"*	*Cauliflower Do*
2		*"*	*Carrot Do*
1		*Lb.*	*Solid Celery Seed*
1		*"*	*Water Cresses Do*
	1/4	*"*	*Cucumber Do*
11		*"*	*Red Clover Grass Do*
3		*"*	*White Clover Grass Do*
	1/4	*Bush.*	*Cocksfoot Grass Do*
	1/4	*"*	*Cyno: Crestal: Grass Do*
	1/4	*"*	*Festucal Avina Grass Do*
	1/4	*"*	*Mead: fescue Grass Do*
3- 1/2		*Lb.*	*Pod pratensic Grass Do*
40		*"*	*Timothy Grass Do*
1		*Bush.*	*Rye Do*
1		*Lb.*	*Curled Kale Do*
1		*"*	*Leeks Do*
1		*"*	*Green cos Lettuce Do*
1		*"*	*Hammersmith Lettuce Do*
1		*"*	*Marseilles Lettuce Do*
1		*Lb.*	*Mustard Do*
4		*"*	*Deptford Onion Do*
2		*"*	*Strasburg Onion Do*
1		*"*	*Welch Onion Do*
	1/2	*"*	*Curled Parsley Do*
2		*Quarts*	*Early Pease Do*
3		*Lb.*	*Salmon Radish Do*
1		*"*	*black Spanish Radish Do*
1		*"*	*White Turnip Radish Do*
1		*"*	*Dwarf Savoy Radish Do*
1		*"*	*Prickly Spinage Do*
1		*"*	*Round Spinage Do*
2		*"*	*Dutch Turnip Do*
5		*"*	*Early White Turnip Do*
5		*"*	*Early Yello Turnip Do*
4		*"*	*Swedish Turnip Do*

HBCA, B.239/aa/14, pp. 21-22, York Factory inventory 1833. The amount of seed stocked indicates what was grown most successfully; however, the amount of grass seed is unexpected.

78 HBCA, B.239/a/154, fol. 47d, 8 May 1841; L. Hargrave, *Letters*, p. 135, Letitia Hargrave to Mrs. Dugald Mactavish, 2 Dec. 1842.

79 HBCA, B.239/a/104, fol. 12d, 29 Nov. 1799; B.239/a/154, fol. 11d, 15 Oct. 1840.
80 HBCA, B.239/a/114, fol. 4, 30 Nov.–6 Dec. 1807.
81 HBCA, B.239/a/152, fol. 10, 12 Nov. 1839.
82 HBCA, B.239/a/123, fol. 20d, 3 April 1816.
83 HBCA, B.239/a/120, fol. 18, 9 April 1813.
84 HBCA, B.239/a/116, fol. 4d, 26 Oct. 1809.
85 For examples, *see* HBCA, B.239/a/152, fol. 33, 17 June 1840; B.239/a/154, fol. 7d, 27 Sept. 1840; B.239/a/159, fol. 4d, 29 Sept. 1843; B.239/a/148, fol. 17d, 7 Oct. 1843. The last represents the largest of these shipments: 40 bushels of potatoes and 4 bushels of turnips.
86 J. Hargrave, *Correspondence*, p. 172, Donald Ross to James Hargrave, 23 Dec. 1834; HBCA, B.239/c/2, fol. 18, James Sutherland to John George McTavish, 16 Aug. 1829.
87 J. Hargrave, *Correspondence*, p. 335, Richard Grant to James Hargrave, 1 Feb. 1841; HBCA, B.239/a/154, fol. 28, 16 Jan. 1841; L. Hargrave, *Letters*, p. 259, Letitia Hargrave to James Hargrave, 12 Aug. 1851; HBCA, B.239/a/152, fol. 33, 17 June 1840; J. Hargrave, *Correspondence*, p. 172, Donald Ross to James Hargrave, 23 Dec. 1834.
88 HBCA, B.239/b/97a, fol. 8d, James Hargrave to Donald Ross, 23 July 1845.
89 HBCA, B.239/b/93, fol. 84, James Hargrave to John Cromartie [the officer in charge of Severn], 19 April 1841.
90 NA, MG19, A46, Henry Hulse Berens Journal, p. 40, 1 Sept. 1832; HBCA, B.239/a/121, fol. 24, 4 April 1815.
91 HBCA, B.239/a/123, fol. 27, 23 May 1816.
92 HBCA, B.239/a/121, fol. 2d, 5 Oct. 1814.
93 HBCA, B.239/a/137, York Factory Fishing Camp Journal.
94 The following is a list of fish production at the Rock Lake camp from 29 Sept. 1829 to 9 Feb. 1830

	whitefish	fish of sorts (suckers, pike etc.)
September	260	–
October	4370	156
November	1300	187
December	829	192
January	286	120
February	45	21
Totals	7090	676

From these figures it was concluded that "it is a waste of time for the fishermen to be employed later than Xmas." HBCA, B.239/a/141, pp. 41-42, 18 Feb. 1830.
95 HBCA. B/239/a/499, fols. 25-25d, 12 Feb. 1836.
96 HBCA, B.239/a/161, fol. 16d, 20 Dec. 1844.
97 Donaldson, "Land-Use," p. 192.
98 One favoured location was "Saunder's House" near Six Mile Island. HBCA. B.239/a/171, fol. 8, 11 Oct. 1848.
99 HBCA, B.239/a/173, fol. 47d, 31 May 1850.

100 McTavish, *Behind the Palisades*, p. 58.

101 HBCA, B.239/a/100, fol. 15, 16 Feb. 1797.

102 HBCA, B.239/a/173, fol. 47d, 31 May 1850.

103 *See*, for example, HBCA, B.239/a/141, p. 11, 27 Sept. 1829. Stoney Creek was suggested as the best location for the fall hunt, whereas Sam's Creek was preferred for the spring hunt.

104 Umfreville, *Present State*, pp. 20-21.

105 HBCA, B.239/b/52, fols. 13-13d, Joseph Colen to John Ballenden, 11 June 1792.

106 Umfreville, *Present State*, pp. 20-21; Graham, *Observations*, p. 42.

107 HBCA, B.239/a/155, fol. 44d, 31 May 1842. The total from the hunt was just 1124 fresh and cured geese. HBCA, B.239/a/159, fol. 39, 31 May 1844. This year's hunt produced 4621 geese, another 1727 being sent from Severn.

108 Records from the 1840s give the following range of goose consumption: 70 days' rations in 1844-45, consisting of 10 days of fresh geese and 60 days of salt geese, down to 47 days in 1847-48, consisting of two days of fresh geese and 45 of salt geese. In some years geese and ducks are listed together, which may indicate a lower consumption of geese, and in 1842-43, a year in which the hunt was poor, geese are not listed as being served; however, this seems unlikely. *See* HBCA, B.239/a/157, fol. 39, 31 May 1843; B.239/a/168, fols. 37-37d, 31 May 1848; B.239/a/161, fol. 40, 31 May 1845.

109 HBCA, B.239/a/131, fol. 18d, 20 May 1823.

110 HBCA, B.239/a/161, fol. 40, 31 May 1845; B.239/a/159, fol. 39, 31 May 1844.

111 If anything, they were more frequently eaten than ducks. In 1850-51, for example, salt plover was served on 12 days whereas ducks are not mentioned. HBCA, B.239/a/176, fol. 41, 31 May 1851.

112 Samuel Hearne, *A Journey from Prince of Wales's Fort in Hudson's Bay to the Northern Ocean....*, ed. and intro. Richard G. Glover (Toronto: Macmillan, 1958), p. 275.

113 *See*, for example, HBCA, B.239/b/65, fols. 12-12d, John Ballenden to Mr. Stayner, 6 April 1801.

114 HBCA, B.239/b/54, fol. 4, Joseph Colen to John Ballenden, 5 Jan. 1793; B.239/a/155, fol. 44d, 31 May 1842.

115 HBCA, B.239/a/154, fol. 45, 21 April 1841.

116 HBCA, B.239/a/121, fol. 14, 10 Jan. 1815; ibid., fol. 15, 17 Jan. 1815. Other ingenious 18th-century methods of hunting ptarmigan are described in Payne, "Prince of Wales' Fort," p. 51.

117 The range is from 40 days' rations in 1841-42 to 2-1/2 days' in 1849-50. HBCA, B.239/a/155, fol. 44d, 31 May 1842; B.239/a/173, fol. 47d, 31 May 1850.

118 David Thompson, *Narrative*, pp. 86-87.

119 HBCA, B.239/a/106, fol. 25d, 30 April 1802.

120 HBCA, B.239/a/90, fols. 17-17d, 31 Dec. 1789.

121 Donaldson, "Land-Use," p. 189.

122 HBCA, B.239/a/159, fol. 27, 7 March 1844.

123 Helmcken, *Reminiscences*, p. 100.

124 HBCA, B.239/a/154, fol. 53d, 31 May 1841; B.239/a/157, fol. 39, 31 May 1843.

125 Ibid. Recently it has been argued that by 1880, caribou had abandoned the York Factory area in winter and summer, with the implication that the numbers of caribou killed by post hunters declined, making it more difficult to feed its residents. Arthur J. Ray, "York Factory: The Crises of Transition, 1870-1880," *The Beaver*, Outfit 313, No. 2 (Autumn

1982), p. 29. Evidence from company records other than Joseph Fortescue's discussion of the problems facing York in 1880 undermines this contention. Provision records from the 1840s indicate that caribou kills ranged from 20, producing 1782 pounds of venison, in 1842 to 78, producing 6534 pounds, in 1848. HBCA, B.239/a/155, fol. 44d, 31 May 1842; B.239/a/168, fol. 37, 31 May 1848. This suggests that each caribou produced about 90 pounds of venison. Buried amidst the miscellaneous papers from York Factory is a list of the numbers of deer killed from 1867 to 1878.

	1867	1868	1869	1870	1871	1872*	1873*	1874	1875	1876	1877	1878
October					4	3			25			
November	12	38	60	40	46		4	7	126	82	28	3
December	45	54	42	81	58	3	14	82	51	19	26	8
January	35	66	12	37	41	38	11	26	29		23	
February	74	91	50	19	41	51	13	100	40	52	15	97
March	116	108	93	142	130	52	32	67	70		151	114
April	44	83	73	102	62	126	112	58	83	26	72	129
May	7		1	4	3	1						
to shanties	11	23	30	31	20	26			17		18	17
Total	344	463	361	456	405	300	188	340	441	179	333	368

*These years there were thousands of partridges.

HBCA, B.239/z/32, p. 501. Even in the least productive year, 1876, the caribou kill was more than double that of the most productive year in the 1840s and would have produced more than eight tons of venison. Exploitation of caribou as a food resource seems to have increased in the 1860s and 1870s.

126 L. Hargrave, *Letters*, p. 159n, George Simpson to James Hargrave, 3 March 1843.

127 In 1843-44, 78 days of pork and beef rations were served out whereas in 1847-48, only 45 days' worth were served. HBCA, B.239/a/159, fol. 39, 31 May 1844; B.239/a/168, fol. 37, 31 May 1848.

128 Grain rations were listed as being from 61 days to 85 days. HBCA, B.239/a/176, fol. 41, 31 May 1851; B.239/a/171, fol. 43, 31 May 1849.

129 HBCA, A.6/26, fols. 169d-170, London committee to James Hargrave, 14 June 1845; B.239/b/97a, fols. 18d-19, James Hargrave to Archibald Barclay, 8 Sept. 1845. George Simpson McTavish mentions that Edwards's dessicated potatoes were a great standby as an antiscorbutic in the 1880s. McTavish, *Behind the Palisades*, p. 57.

130 HBCA, A.6/32, fol. 58, William Smith to William Mactavish, 21 June 1856; B.239/b/104b, fols. 127-127d, William Mactavish to William Smith, 16 Sept. 1856; McTavish, *Behind the Palisades*, p. 57.

131 HBCA, B.239/b/78, fol. 27, annual letter to York Factory, 31 May 1799.

132 Ibid., fol. 28d, annual letter from York Factory, Sept. 1799.

133 HBCA, B.239/a/115, fol. 14d, 10 May 1809; B.239/a/100, p. 100, James Hargrave to George Simpson, 30 Aug. 1849.

134 L. Hargrave, *Letters*, p. 259, Letitia Hargrave to James Hargrave, 12 Aug. 1851.

135 NA, MG19, A21, Hargrave Family, C83, p. 635, printed circular — Thomas Fraser to Hudson's Bay Company agents, 22 Nov. 1858.
136 *See* L. Hargrave, *Letters*, p. 115, Letitia Hargrave to Dugald Mactavish Sr., 27 May 1842; HBCA, B.239/a/154, fol. 45, 21 April 1841; HBCA, B.239/c/3, fol. 98, Thomas Spence to James Hargrave, 2 March 1835.
137 *See*, for example, Helmcken, *Reminiscences*, p. 97.
138 *See* Vilhjalmur Stefansson, *Arctic Manual* (New York: Macmillan, 1944), pp. 219-40.
139 Ibid., p. 224.
140 These sample budgets may be found in John Burnett, *A History of the Cost of Living* (Harmondsworth, Eng.: Penguin, 1969), pp. 259-63. Those interested in greater detail on working-class consumption patterns may consult his *Plenty and Want: A Social History of Diet in England from 1815 to the Present Day* (London: Thomas Nelson, 1966) (hereafter cited as Burnett, *Plenty and Want*), pp. 14-50.
141 Burnett, *Plenty and Want*, p. 50.
142 HBCA, B.42/a/50, fol. 10. Kale is a variety of cabbage usually with curly leaves and without the compact head common to most cabbages.
143 Patrick Bailey, Orkney (Newton Abbot, Eng.: David & Charles, 1971), pp. 106-07.
144 James R. Nicolson, *Traditional Life in Shetland* (London: Robert Hale, 1978), pp. 79-83.
145 John Mercer, *Hebridean Islands: Colonsay, Gigha, Jura* (Glasgow: Blackie, 1974), p. 195.
146 Allan Greer, "Fur Trade Labour and Lower Canadian Agrarian Structures," [Canadian Historical Assocation] *Historical Papers/Communications historiques* (1981), pp. 197-214; Fernand Ouellet, *Le Bas Canada, 1791-1840: changements structuraux et crise* (Ottawa: Editions de l'université d'Ottawa, 1976), pp. 492-97.
147 HBCA, B.239/a/100, fols. 14-14d, 8 Feb. 1797.
148 HBCA, B.239/b/84, fol. 51d, William Auld to William Hemmings Cook, 5 Nov. 1813.
149 Graham, *Observations*, pp. 296-97.
150 Burnett, *Plenty and Want*, p. 57.
151 L. Hargrave, *Letters*, p. 159, Letitia Hargrave to Mrs. Dugald Mactavish, 10 Sept. 1843.
152 Helmcken, *Reminiscences*, p. 97.
153 L. Hargrave, *Letters*, p. 61, Letitia Hargrave to Mrs. Dugald Mactavish, Sept. 1840.
154 Ibid., p. 100, Letitia Hargrave to Mary Mactavish, 9 Sept. 1841.
155 Ibid., p. 77, Letitia Hargrave to Dugald Mactavish Sr., 2 Sept. 1840.
156 Samuel Hearne, *A Journey from Prince of Wales's Fort in Hudson's Bay to the Northern Ocean....*, ed. and intro. Richard G. Glover (Toronto: Macmillan, 1958), pp. 203-5.
157 L. Hargrave, *Letters*, p. 108, Letitia Hargrave to Mrs. Dugald Mactavish, 14 May 1842.

"The Most Respectable Place in the Territory"

1 Newman, *Company of Adventurers*, p. 8.
2 *See*, for example, Henry Ellis, *A Voyage to Hudson's Bay, by the Dobbs Galley and California, in the years 1746 and 1747*, reprint of 1748 ed. (New York: Johnson Reprint Corp., 1967), p. 181.
3 Goldring, "Papers: Vol. II," p. 40.
4 Ibid., "Papers: Vol. I," p. 60.
5 NA, MG17, B2, CMS, reel A77, p. 91, David Jones Journal, 6 Nov. 1823.

References Cited

Bailey, Patrick
Orkney. David and Charles, Newton Abbott, Eng., 1971.

Bailey, Peter Cecil
Leisure and Class in Victorian England: Rational Recreation and the Contest for Control, 1830-1885. Routledge and Kegan Paul, London, 1978.
"Rational Recreation: The Social Control of Leisure and Popular Culture in Victorian England, 1830-1885." PhD thesis, University of British Columbia, Vancouver, 1975.

Ball, Timothy Francis
"Hudson's Bay Company Journals as a Source of Information for the Reconstruction of Climate." In North American Fur Trade Conference (4th: 1981: Grand Portage, Minn., and Thunder Bay, Ont.), *Rendezvous: Selected Papers of the Fourth North American Fur Trade Conference, 1981,* ed. Thomas Cotter Buckley, St. Paul, 1984, pp. 43-50.

Ballantyne, Robert Michael
Hudson Bay; or, Everyday Life in the Wilds of North America During Six Years' Residence in the Territories of the Hon. Hudson Bay Company. Thomas Nelson, London, 1902.
The Young Fur-Traders: A Tale of the Far North. Ward, Lock and Co., London, 1901.

Boon, Thomas Charles Boucher
Use of Catechisms and Syllabics by the Early Missionaries of Rupert's Land, 1820-1880. Canadian Church Historical Society, Toronto, 1960.

Bredin, Thomas F.
"The Red River Academy." *The Beaver*, Outfit 305, No. 3 (Winter 1974), pp. 10-17. Winnipeg.
"The Reverend David Jones: Missionary at Red River 1823-38." *The Beaver*, Outfit 312, No. 2 (Autumn 1981), pp. 47-52. Winnipeg.

Brooks, William
"Methodism in the Canadian West in the Nineteenth Century." PhD thesis, University of Manitoba, Winnipeg, 1972.

Brown, Jennifer S.H.
" 'A Colony of Very Useful Hands.' " *The Beaver*, Outfit 307, No. 4 (Spring 1977), pp. 39-45. Winnipeg.
Strangers in Blood: Fur Trade Company Families in Indian Country. University of British Columbia Press, Vancouver, 1980.
"The Track to Heaven: The Hudson Bay Cree Religious Movement of 1843." In Algonquian Conference (13th: 1981: Ontario Institute for Studies in Education), *Papers of the Thirteenth Algonguian Conference*, ed. William Cowan, Carleton University Press, Ottawa, 1982, pp. 56-63.
"Ultimate Respectability: Fur-Trade Children in the 'Civilized World.' " [Pt. 1.] *The Beaver*, Outfit 308, No.3 (Winter 1977), pp. 4-10. Winnipeg.
"Ultimate Respectability: Fur-Trade Children in the 'Civilized World.' " [Pt. 2.] *The Beaver*, Outfit 308, No. 4 (Spring 1978), pp. 48-55. Winnipeg.

Budd, Henry
The Diary of the Reverend Henry Budd, 1870-1875. Ed. Katherine Pettipas. Manitoba Record Society, Winnipeg, 1974. Manitoba Record Society Publications, 4.

Burnett, John
A History of the Cost of Living. Penguin, Harmondsworth, Eng., 1969.
A Social History of Housing, 1815-1970. David and Charles, Newton Abbot, Eng., 1978.
Plenty and Want: A Social History of Diet in England from 1815 to the Present Day. Thomas Nelson, London, 1966.

Burnham, Dorothy K.
Cut My Cote. Royal Ontario Museum, Toronto, 1973.

Campbell, Marjorie Elliott (Wilkins)
The North West Company. Macmillan, Toronto, 1957.

Canada. National Archives. Manuscript Division.
MG17, B1, Society for the Propagation of the Gospel in Foreign Parts.
MG17, B2, Church Missionary Society.
MG19, A21, Hargrave Family.
MG19, A46, Henry Hulse Berens Journal.
MG19, D23, York Factory, "Unfinished Journal of a Clerk [James Hargrave] at York Factory, Hudson's Bay Company, 1828-1829."
MG19, El, Thomas Douglas, fifth earl of Selkirk.
MG20, Hudson's Bay Company Archives (microfilm).
Section A: Headquarters Records
A.5/4, London Correspondence Books Outwards, General Series, 1796-1808.
A.5/15, London Correspondence Books Outwards, General Series, 1845-48.
A.6, London Correspondence Outwards, Hudson's Bay Company — Official, 1787-1871.
A.11, London Inward Correspondence from Hudson's Bay Company Posts, 1787-1870.
A.30, Lists of Servants, 1788-1831.
A.63/10, Fur Trade Miscellanea, Watch Repair Book, 1804-26.
A.64, Miscellaneous Books, 1791-1918.
Section B: Post Records
B.42/a/32, Churchill Fort, Post Journals, 1748-49.
B.42/a/50, Churchill Fort, Post Journals, 1757-58.
B.235/c/1, Winnipeg, Correspondence Inward, 1820-70.
B.239/a, York Factory, Post Journals, 1788-1852.
B.239/b, York Factory, Correspondence Books, 1787-1878.
B.239/c, York Factory, Correspondence Inward, 1807-52.
B.239/d, York Factory, Account Books, 1789-1870.
B.239/e, York Factory, Reports on Districts, 1815-68.
B.239/g, York Factory, Abstracts of Servants' Accounts, 1821-70.
B.239/k, York Factory, Minutes of Council and Council Resolves, 1821-70, 1822-41.
B.239/1, York Factory, District Statements, 1823-70.
B.239/x, Servants' Ledgers, 1821-76.
B.239/z, York Factory, Miscellaneous Items, 1808-78.
B.239/aa, York Factory, Inventories, 1821-55.
Section G: Maps, Plans, Charts, etc.
G.2/26, Prince of Wales's Fort.

The Canadian Encyclopedia
Hurtig Publishers, Edmonton, 1985. 3 vols.

Chalmers, John W.
"Education and the Honourable Company." *Alberta Historical Review*, Vol.
13, No. 3 (Summer 1965), pp. 25-58. Calgary.

Chappell, Edward
*Narrative of a Voyage to Hudson's Bay in His Majesty's Ship Rosamond
Containing Some Account of the North-Eastern Coast of America and of the
Tribes Inhabiting that Remote Region.* Reprint of 1817 ed. Coles Publishing,
Toronto, 1970.

Dictionary of Canadian Biography
University of Toronto Press, Toronto, 1966-.

A Dictionary of Canadianisms on Historical Principles
W.J. Gage, Toronto, 1967.

Dobbs, Arthur
*An Account of the Countries adjoining to Hudson's Bay in the North-West
Part of America.* Reprint of 1744 ed. Johnson Reprint Corporation, New
York, 1967.

Donaldson, Bruce F.
"York Factory: A Land-Use History." Manuscript Report Series, No. 444,
Parks Canada, Ottawa, 1981.

Douville, Raymond, and Jacques Casanova
Daily Life in Early Canada from Champlain to Montcalm. Trans. Carola
Congreve. Allen and Unwin, London, 1968.

[Drage, Theodore Swain]
*An Account of a Voyage for the Discovery of a North-West Passage by
Hudson's Streights, to the Western and Southern Ocean of America. Per-
formed in the Year 1746 and 1747, in the Ship California, Captain Francis
Smith, Commander. By The Clerk of the California. Adorned with Cuts and
Maps.* Printed and sold by Mr. Jolliffe et al., London, 1748-49. 2 vols.
Vol. 1.

Eccles, William John
The Canadian Frontier, 1534-1760. Holt, Rinehart and Winston, New York,
1969.

Ellis, Henry
A Voyage to Hudson's Bay, by the Dobbs Galley and California, in the Years 1746 and 1747. Reprint of 1748 ed. Johnson Reprint Corporation, New York, 1967.

Ewart, William B., MD
"Causes of Mortality in a Subarctic Settlement (York Factory, Man.), 1714-1946." *Canadian Medical Association Journal,* Vol. 129, No. 6 (15 Sept. 1983), pp. 571-74. Ottawa.

Foster, John E.
"Paulet Paul: Métis or 'House Indian' Folk Hero?" *Manitoba History,* No. 9 (Spring 1985), pp. 2-7. Winnipeg.

Francis, Daniel, and Toby Morantz
Partners in Furs: A History of the Fur Trade in Eastern James Bay, 1600-1870. McGill-Queen's University Press, Montreal and Kingston, 1983.

Friesen, Gerald
The Canadian Prairies: A History. University of Toronto Press, Toronto, 1984.

Galbraith, John S.
The Little Emperor: Governor Simpson of the Hudson's Bay Company. Macmillan, Toronto, 1976.

Glass, David Victor
"Population and Population Movements in England and Wales, 1700 to 1850." In D.V. Glass and D.E.C. Eversley, eds., *Population in History: Essays in Historical Demography,* Edward Arnold, London, 1965, pp. 221-46.

Glover, Richard Gilchrist
"The Difficulties of the Hudson's Bay Company's Penetration of the West." *Canadian Historical Review,* Vol. 29, No. 3 (Sept. 1948), pp. 240-54. Toronto.

Gluek, Alvin Charles
Minnesota and the Manifest Destiny of the Canadian Northwest; A Study in Canadian-American Relations. University of Toronto Press, Toronto, 1965.

Goldring, Philip
"Lewis and the Hudson's Bay Company in the Nineteenth Century." *Scottish Studies*, Vol. 24 (1980), pp. 23-42. Edinburgh.
"Papers on the Labour System of the Hudson's Bay Company, 1821-1900: Volume I." Manuscript Report Series, No. 362, Parks Canada, Ottawa, 1979.
"Papers on the Labour System of the Hudson's Bay Company, 1821-1900: Volume II." Manuscript Report Series, No. 412, Parks Canada, Ottawa, 1980.

Goosen, Norma Jaye
"The Relationship of the Church Missionary Society and the Hudson's Bay Company in Rupert's Land, 1821 to 1861, with a Case Study of Stanley Mission under the Direction of the Rev. Robert Hunt." MA thesis, University of Manitoba, Winnipeg, 1975.

Graham, Andrew
Observations on Hudson's Bay, 1767-91. Ed. Glyndwr Williams, intro. Richard G. Glover. Hudson's Bay Record Society, London, 1969. Hudson's Bay Record Society Publication, Vol. 27.

Greer, Allan
"Fur Trade Labour and Lower Canadian Agrarian Structures." [Canadian Historical Association] *Historical Papers/Communications historiques* (1981), pp. 197-214. Ottawa.

Gustafson, Robert Walter
"The Education of Canada's Indian Peoples: An Experience in Colonialism." MEd thesis, University of Manitoba, Winnipeg, 1978.

Hargrave, James
The Hargrave Correspondence, 1821-1843. Ed. and intro. G.P. de T. Glazebrook. Champlain Society, Toronto, 1938. Publications of the Champlain Society, Vol. 24.

Hargrave, Letitia (Mactavish)
The Letters of Letitia Hargrave. Ed. and intro. Margaret Arnett MacLeod. Champlain Society, Toronto, 1947. Publications of the Champlain Society, Vol. 28.

Hearne, Samuel
A Journey from Prince of Wales's Fort in Hudson's Bay to the Northern Ocean, 1769, 1770, 1771, 1772. Ed. and intro. Richard G. Glover. Macmillan, Toronto, 1958.

Helmcken, Dr. John Sebastian
The Reminiscences of Doctor John Sebastian Helmcken. Ed. Dorothy Blakey Smith, intro. W. Kaye Lamb. University of British Columbia Press in cooperation with the Provincial Archives of British Columbia, Vancouver, 1975.

Hobsbawm, Eric J.
Labouring Men; Studies in the History of Labour. Weidenfeld and Nicolson, London, 1964.

Hudson's Bay Company
Saskatchewan Journals and Correspondence: Edmonton House, 1795-1800; Chesterfield House, 1800-1802. Ed. and intro. Alice M. Johnson. Hudson's Bay Record Society, London, 1967. Publications of the Hudson's Bay Record Society, Vol. 26.

Hussey, John A.
" 'Unpretending' But Not 'Indecent': Living Quarters at Mid-19th Century HBC Posts." *The Beaver*, Outfit 305, No. 4 (Spring 1975), pp. 12-17. Winnipeg.

Innis, Harold Adams
The Fur Trade in Canada: An Introduction to Canadian Economic History. Rev. ed. University of Toronto Press, Toronto, 1956.

Isham, James
Observations on Hudson's Bay, 1743.... Ed. and intro. E.E. Rich, with A.M. Johnson. Champlain Society, Toronto, 1949. Publications of the Champlain Society, Hudson's Bay Company Series, Vol. 12.

Judd, Carol M.
" 'Mixt Bands of Many Nations': 1821-70." In Carol M. Judd and Arthur J. Ray, eds., *Old Trails and New Directions*: *Papers of the Third North American Fur Trade Conference*, University of Toronto Press, Toronto, 1980, pp. 127-46.

L'Ami, C.E.
"Priceless Books from Old Fur Trade Libraries." *The Beaver*, Outfit 266, No. 3 (Dec. 1935), pp. 26-29, 66. Winnipeq.

Laslett, Peter
The World We Have Lost: England before the Industrial Age. Charles Scribner's Sons, New York, 1971.

Lefroy, Sir John Henry
In Search of the Magnetic North; A Soldier-Surveyor's Letters from the North-West, 1843-1844. Ed. George F. Stanley. Macmillan, Toronto, 1955.

Lloyd, Wyndham E.B.
A Hundred Years of Medicine. 2nd ed. Gerald Duckworth, London, 1968.

Lytwyn, Victor P.
"York Factory Native Ethnohistory: A Literature Review and An Assessment of Source Material." Microfiche Report Series, No. 162, Parks Canada, Ottawa, 1984.

McDougall, John
Forest, Lake, and Prairie. Twenty Years of Frontier Life in Western Canada, 1842-62. William Briggs, Toronto, 1895.

MacKay, Douglas
The Honourable Company: A History of the Hudson's Bay Company. McClelland and Stewart, Toronto, 1966.

McLean, John
John McLean's Notes of a Twenty-Five Years' Service in the Hudson's Bay Territory. Ed. W.S. Wallace. Champlain Society, Toronto, 1932. Publications of the Champlain Society, Vol. 19.

McNeill, William H.
The Great Frontier: Freedom and Hierarchy in Modern Times. Princeton University Press, Princeton, 1938.

McTavish, George Simpson
Behind the Palisades; An Autobiography. E. Gurd/Gray's Publishing, Sidney, B.C., [1963].

Malcolmson, R.W.
Popular Recreations in English Society, 1700-1850. Cambridge University Press, Cambridge, 1973.

Manitoba. Provincial Archives.
MG1, D5, John MacLeod Diary.
MG1, D11, William Lane Correspondence.
MG1, D16, Roderick Macfarlane Papers.
MGI, D20, Donald Ross Correspondence.

Marrus, Michael Robert, comp.
The Emergence of Leisure. Harper and Row, New York, 1974.

Mason, Tony
Association Football and English Society, 1863-1915. Harvester Press, Brighton, 1980.

Mercer, John
Hebridean Islands: Colonsay, Gigha, Jura. Blackie, Glasgow, 1974.

Moat, Gordon R.
"Canada Stoves in Rupert's Land." *The Beaver*, Outfit 310, No. 3 (Winter 1979), pp. 54-57. Winnipeg.

Moodie, D.W., and Barry Kaye
"Taming and Domesticating the Native Animals of Rupert's Land." *The Beaver*, Outfit 307, No. 3 (Winter 1976), pp. 10-19. Winnipeg.

Morton, Arthur Silver
A History of the Canadian West to 1870-71, being a History of Rupert's Land (the Hudson's Bay Company's Territory) and of the North-West Territory (including the Pacific Slope). 2nd ed. Ed. Lewis G. Thomas. University of Toronto Press, Toronto, 1973.

Morton, William Lewis
Manitoba, A History. University of Toronto Press, Toronto. 1961.

Mott, Morris Kenneth
"Manly Sports and Manitobans, Settlement Days to World War One." PhD thesis, Queen's University, Kingston, 1980.

Newman, Peter C.
Company of Adventurers. Viking-Penguin Books, Markham, Ont., 1985.

Nicks, John
"Orkneymen in the HBC, 1780-1821." In Carol M. Judd and Arthur J. Ray, eds., *Old Trails and New Directions: Papers of the Third North American Fur Trade Conference*, University of Toronto Press, Toronto, 1980, pp. 102-26.

Nicolson, James R.
Traditional Life in Shetland. Robert Hale, London, 1978.

Oliver, Edmund Henry, ed.
The Canadian North-West; Its Early Development and Legislative Records; Minutes of the Councils of the Red River Colony and the Northern Department of Rupert's Land.... Government Printing Bureau, Ottawa, 1914-15. 2 vols. Vol. 2.

Ouellet, Fernand
Le Bas-Canada, 1791-1840: changements structuraux et crise. Éditions de l'université d'Ottawa, Ottawa, 1976. Université d'Ottawa, Cahiers d'histoire, No. 6.

Pannekoek, Frits
" 'Corruption' at Moose." *The Beaver*, Outfit 309, No. 4 (Spring 1979), pp. 4-11. Winnipeg.
"The Rev. James Evans and the Social Antagonisms of Fur Trade Society, 1840-1846." In *Religion and Society in the Prairie West,* ed. Richard Allen, Canadian Plains Research Center, University of Regina, Regina, 1974, pp. 1-16. Canadian Plains Studies, No. 3.

Parker, Stanley
The Sociology of Leisure. Allen and Unwin, London, 1976.

Parsons, Ralph
"Catalogue of the Fur Trade Library." Manuscript on file, Hudson's Bay House, Winnipeg, 1932.

Pascoe, Charles Frederick, comp.
Classified Digest of the Records of the Society for the Propagation of the Gospel in Foreign Parts, 1701-1892. 6th ed. Society for the Gospel in Foreign Parts, London, 1898.

Payne, Michael
"Prince of Wales' Fort: A Social History, 1717-1782." Manuscript Report Series, No. 371, Parks Canada, Ottawa, 1979.
"A Social History of York Factory, 1788-1870." Microfiche Report Series, No. 110, Parks Canada, Ottawa, 1984.

Payne, Michael, and Gregory Thomas
"Literacy, Literature and Libraries in the Fur Trade." *The Beaver*, Outfit 313, No. 4 (Spring 1983), pp. 44-53. Winnipeg.

Plumb, J.H.
"The New World of Children in Eighteenth-Century England." *Past and Present: A Journal of Historical Studies,* No. 67 (1975), pp. 64-95. Oxford.

Porter, Roy
English Society in the Eighteenth Century. Penguin Books, Harmondsworth, Eng., 1982.

Ray, Arthur J.
Indians in the Fur Trade: Their Role as Trappers, Hunters and Middlemen in the Lands Southwest of Hudson Bay, 1660-1870. University of Toronto Press, Toronto, 1974.
"Smallpox: The Epidemic of 1837-38." *The Beaver*, Outfit 306, No. 2 (Autumn 1975), pp. 8-13. Winnipeg.
"York Factory: The Crises of Transition, 1870-1880." *The Beaver*, Outfit 313, No. 2 (Autumn 1982), pp. 26-31. Winnipeg.

Ray, Arthur J., and Donald B. Freeman
"Give Us Good Measure": An Economic Analysis of Relations between the Indians and the Hudson's Bay Company before 1763. University of Toronto Press, Toronto, 1978.

Rich, Edwin Ernest
The Fur Trade and the Northwest to 1857. McClelland and Stewart, Toronto, 1976.
The History of the Hudson's Bay Company, 1670-1870. Hudson's Bay Record Society, London, 1958-59. 2 vols. Vol. 1: 1670-1763; Vol. 2: 1763-1870. Hudson's Bay Record Society Publications, Vols. 21 and 22.

Robinson, Henry M.
The Great Fur Land; or, Sketches of Life in the Hudson's Bay Territory. Reprint of 1879 ed. Coles Publishing, Toronto, 1972.

Robson, Joseph
An Account of Six Years Residence in Hudson's Bay, from 1733 to 1736 and 1744 to 1747. Reprint of 1752 ed. Johnson Reprint Corporation, New York, 1965.

Ross, Eric
Beyond the River and the Bay; Some Observations on the State of the Canadian Northwest in 1811 with a View to Providing the Intending Settler with an Intimate Knowledge of that Country. University of Toronto Press, Toronto, 1970.

Rudé, George F.
Paris and London in the 18th Century; Studies in Popular Protest. Fontana/Collins, London, 1974.

Sealey, D. Bruce
"Education of the Manitoba Métis: An Historical Sketch." Paper presented at the Métis Historical Conference, Brandon University, Brandon, Manitoba, 6 and 7 May 1977.

Séguin, Robert-Lionel
La civilisation traditionelle de l' "habitant" and 17e et 18e siècles; fonds matériel. Fides, Montreal, 1967.

[Smellie, William]
The Sea; Sketches of a Voyage to Hudson's Bay; and Other Poems. By The Scald [pseud.] Hope and Co., London, 1855.

Stefansson, Vilhjalmur
Arctic Manual. Macmillan, New York, 1944.

Stock, Eugene
The History of the Church Missionary Society, Its Environment, Its Men and Its Work. Church Missionary Society, London, 1899. 3 vols.

Strutt, Joseph
The Sports and Pastimes of the People of England; including the Rural and Domestic Recreations, May Games, Mummeries, Shows, Processions, Pageants, and Pompous Spectacles from the Earliest Period to the Present Time. New ed. by William Hone. William Reeves, London, 1830.

Tanner, Adrian
"The End of Fur Trade History." *Queen's Quarterly*, Vol. 90, No. 1 (Spring 1983), pp. 176-91. Kingston.

Thistle, Paul Clifford
Indian-European Trade Relations in the Lower Saskatchewan River Region to 1840. University of Manitoba Press, Winnipeg, 1986.

Thomas, Gregory
"The Smithsonian and the Hudson's Bay Company." *Prairie Forum: The Journal of the Canadian Plains Research Center,* Vol. 10, No. 2 (Fall 1985), pp. 283-305. Regina.

Thompson, David
Narrative, 1784-1812. Ed. and intro. Richard G. Glover. Champlain Society, Toronto, 1962. Publications of the Champlain Society, Vol. 40.

Thompson, Edward Palmer
The Making of the English Working Class. Penguin, Harmondsworth, Eng., 1968.
"Time, Work-Discipline, and Industrial Capitalism." In M.W. Flinn and T.C. Smout, eds., *Essays in Social History,* Clarendon Press, Oxford, 1974, pp. 39-77.

Trevelyan, George Macaulay
Illustrated English Social History. Longman's, Green and Company for Readers' Union, London, 1958. Vol. 4: The Nineteenth Century.

Tyrrell, Joseph Burr, ed.
Documents Relating to the Early History of Hudson Bay. The Champlain Society, Toronto, 1931. Publications of the Champlain Society, Vol. 18.

Umfreville, Edward
The Present State of Hudson's Bay, Containing a Full Description of That Settlement, and the Adjacent Country; and Likewise of the Fur Trade, with Hints for its Improvement, &c. &c.... Ed. and intro. W. Stewart Wallace. Ryerson Press, Toronto, 1954. Canadian Historical Studies, Vol. 5.

Van Kirk, Sylvia
"Fur Trade Social History: Some Recent Trends." In Carol Judd and Arthur J. Ray, eds., *Old Trails and New Directions: Papers of the Third North American Fur Trade Conference,* University of Toronto Press, Toronto, 1980, pp. 160-73.
"Many Tender Ties": Women in Fur-Trade Society in Western Canada, 1670-1870. Watson and Dwyer, Winnipeg, 1980.

Wallace, William Stewart, ed.
Documents Relating to the North West Company. The Champlain Society, Toronto, 1934. Publications of the Champlain Society, Vol. 22.

West, John
The Substance of a Journal during a Residence at the Red River Colony, British North America; and Frequent Excursions among the North West American Indians in the Years 1820, 1821, 1822, 1823. Reprint of 1824 ed. Johnson Reprint Corporation, New York, 1966.

Williams, Glyndwr
"Highlights in the History of the First Two Hundred Years of the Hudson's Bay Company." *The Beaver*, Outfit 301, No. 2 (Autumn 1970), pp. 4-63. Winnipeg.

Wilson, Keith
"The Development of Education in Manitoba." PhD thesis, Michigan State University, East Lansing, 1967.